Gender and Psychology

Series editor: Sue Wilkinson

This international series provides a forum for the growing body of disti[...]
tively psychological research focused on gender issues. While work on [...]
psychology of women, particularly that adopting a feminist perspecti[...]
will be central, the series will also reflect other emergent trends in the fi[...]
of gender. It will encourage contributions which are critical of t[...]
mainstream of androcentric or 'gender-neutral' psychology and al[...]
innovative in their suggested alternatives.

The books will explore topics where gender is central, such as social a[...]
sexual relationships, employment, health and illness, and the developme[...]
of gender identity. Issues of theory and methodology raised by the stu[...]
of gender in psychology will also be addressed.

The objective is to present research on gender in the context of its broad[...]
implications for psychology. These implications include the need [...]
develop theories and methods appropriate to studying the experience [...]
women as well as men, and working towards a psychology which reflect[...]
the experiences and concerns of both sexes.

The series will appeal to students of psychology, women's studies an[...]
gender studies and to professionals concerned with gender issues in thei[...]
practice, as well as to the general reader with an interest in gender an[...]
psychology.

Sue Wilkinson is principal lecturer and head of the psychology section a[...]
Coventry Polytechnic.

Also in this series

Subjectivity and Method in Psychology
Wendy Hollway

Feminists and Psychological Practice
edited by Erica Burman

Feminist Groupwork
Sandra Butler and Claire Wintram

Motherhood

Motherhood

Meanings, Practices and Ideologies

edited by

Ann Phoenix, Anne Woollett and Eva Lloyd

SAGE Publications
London • Newbury Park • New Delhi

SAGE Publications Ltd
6 Bonhill Street
London EC2A 4PU

SAGE Publications Inc
2455 Teller Road
Newbury Park, California 91320

SAGE Publications India Pvt Ltd
32, M-Block Market
Greater Kailash – I
New Delhi 110 048

British Library Cataloguing in Publication data

Motherhood: Meanings, practices and ideologies. — (Gender
and psychology)
  I. Lloyd, Eva   II. Phoenix, Ann
  III. Woollett, Anne   IV. Series
  306.874

  ISBN 0-8039-8313-1
  ISBN 0-8039-8314-X pbk

Library of Congress catalog card number 91-53092

Typeset by Mayhew Typesetting, Rhayader, Powys
Printed in Great Britain by Biddles Ltd, Guildford, Surrey

For Aisha, Kate and Owen, Angèle Reichling,
Margaret Lewis and Esme Hercules

Contents

Part 5 The Question of Employment

Notes on the Contributors

Julia C. Berryman is Lecturer in Psychology in the Department of Adult Education at Leicester University. Prior to her present post she worked as a Research Fellow in the Department of Psychology, also at Leicester University, researching parental and social behaviour in non-human animals. She has published widely in this area and her other publications include research on sex and gender, human/animal relationships and psychology in adult education. Her interest in research on motherhood arose out of her work on non-human animals, her teaching on the psychology of women, and her own experience of becoming a mother at 40-plus. She is currently engaged in a prospective study of experiences of pregnancy, birth and motherhood in women of all ages.

Susan Gregory is a developmental psychologist and is currently a Senior Lecturer in Psychology at the Open University where she is responsible for developing courses on deafness. Her research interests include patterns of interaction between deaf and hearing children and their deaf or hearing parents, the school experience of deaf children and, more recently, a longitudinal study of deaf young people and their families.

Suzan Lewis lectures in psychology at Manchester Polytechnic where she also runs workshops and short courses for industry and other organizations. Her consultancy work includes advising companies on the implementation of 'family-friendly' policies. Her research interests include dual-earner families and occupational stress, and she is the co-author with C.L. Cooper of *Career Couples: Contemporary Lifestyles and How to Manage Them* (Unwin Hyman, 1989) and co-editor of *Dual-Earner Families: International Perspectives* (Sage, forthcoming). She is the mother of three sons.

Eva Lloyd works as a Research Officer in the Policy and Research Unit at Save the Children UK. Previously she was part of research teams looking at daycare and pre-school provision at the Thomas Coram Research Unit, Institute of Education, University of London. Before taking up psychology, she taught Dutch at Bedford College, University of London. She is co-author, together with Máire Messenger-Davies and Andreas Scheffler, of *Baby Language* (Unwin, 1987).

Jacqueline McGuire studied the impact of children's gender on family relationships as part of a PhD at the Institute of Education, University of London. Her research interests include behavioural and emotional problems of young children, the effects of group day-care on behaviour and identifying patterns of maladaptive parenting. She is currently conducting research at Harvard Medical School, the Developmental Epidemiology

Unit, Judge Baker's Children's Center, Massachusetts. The project is investigating the development of conduct problems, delinquency and criminality.

Harriette Marshall is a Senior Lecturer in social psychology in the Psychology Department, Polytechnic of East London. She has previously carried out research in areas including social identity and the social construction of 'race' and gender using discourse analysis and Q methodology. Her current work includes health carers' accounts of maternity care; this is part of a larger research project investigating parenthood and parenting practices in a multi-ethnic context. She is also carrying out research into the media and its audience, examining both the production of ideologies in television drama documentaries and the inter-pretational processes engaged in by various audience groups.

Penny Munn is Research Fellow at the Department of Psychology, University of Strathclyde, where she is currently researching daycare environments for pre-school children, and the influence that these have on emergent literacy and numeracy skills. Her previous work has focused on young children's socio-cognitive development in the context of their family relationships.

Ann Phoenix is a researcher at the Thomas Coram Research Unit, Institute of Education, University of London, where she is currently working on a study of the social identities of young people living in the Greater London area. She is the author of *Young Mothers?*, published by Polity Press (1991).

Barbara Tizard was, until recently, director of the Thomas Coram Research Unit, Institute of Education, University of London. Her previous work includes research on residential nurseries, a longitudinal study of adoption and research on nursery and infant schools. Her two most recent books are *Young Children Learning* with Martin Hughes (Fontana, 1984) and *Young Children at School in the Inner City* (Lawrence Erlbaum, 1988). She is currently Emeritus Professor at the Institute of Education and is researching social identities in adolescence.

Anne Woollett is Deputy Head of the Department of Psychology and lectures in developmental psychology at the Polytechnic of East London. Her research interests include child development, reproduction (including fertility) and motherhood. With Naomi Pfeffer she wrote *The Experience of Infertility* (Virago, 1983). Currently she is engaged in a study of the attitudes and experiences of Asian women in East London to pregnancy, childbirth and childcare, funded by the Economic and Social Research Council. With David White she has just completed a book about families and children's development (*Families; a Context for Development*), to be published by Falmer in 1992.

Acknowledgements

This book started life as a symposium which Eva Lloyd organized at Brunel University in 1987, entitled 'Motherhood and Psychology'. Our planning for that symposium started our discussions about motherhood. We would like to thank Paula Nicolson for her help and support at that stage and Sue Wilkinson for encouraging us to turn our ideas into a book proposal. The book and its underlying themes came from our long discussions about the nature of motherhood and the scarcity of psychological material on the place of motherhood in women's lives and their experience of it.

Our thanks are due to the women psychologists who have contributed to this book. Although all were studying motherhood and mothering, some have studied mothers indirectly, as part of their work on children's development. Yet all were prepared to reflect on their work from the viewpoint of the mothers they studied. We would particularly like to thank them for their enthusiasm, willingness to restructure their material and to keep to deadlines. They made editing this book a pleasant task.

In the long months spent turning our ideas into chapters many people have helped in many different ways – by telling us we were on the right track, reading chapters, suggesting articles to read, being tolerant of our own preoccupations and providing childcare. Some of them come from the institutions in which the three of us work – the Polytechnic of East London, Save the Children Fund (UK) and the Thomas Coram Research Unit – while others work in a range of mainly British, but also Australian and US institutions. They are: Mel Bartley, Bill Bell, Chris Griffin, Paul Hodge, Jan Mason, Paula Nicolson, Charlie Owen, Naomi Pfeffer, Phil Salmon, Jan Savage, Barbara Tizard, Mariamne Whatley, David White and Nancy Worcester. Sue Wilkinson and Sue Jones have given active and useful editorial comments and support. We owe the title to Sue Jones. Maria Harrison and Susamma Pius made our task lighter by helping with the typing. Our thanks go to them all. Finally, we would like to thank all those mothers and children who took part in the studies discussed in the chapters that follow. Without them this book would not have been possible.

1

Introduction

Ann Phoenix and Anne Woollett

Motherhood is a popular subject of conversation and of study. Most people have been mothered at some time, and whether that experience has been good or bad, relationships with mothers usually generate strong feelings for much of the life course. There have been substantial changes in women's lives over the past fifty years. Women now have fewer children and participate in the employment market more than they did. Yet, most women still become mothers, and motherhood continues to occupy a large proportion of their lives, to be a major part of their responsibilities and to be central to their perceptions of themselves (whether or not they are mothers). It is not surprising, therefore, that motherhood has provided a popular focus for a variety of writers and researchers.

Over the past two decades a wealth of material on motherhood has been published. Five particular (and sometimes overlapping) types of writings on motherhood can be identified:

1 Developmental psychology texts which present theories of mothering based on empirical research on mothers' attitudes to childrearing and how they interact with their infants (see chapter 2). The ideas they discuss frequently influence more popular accounts, and the attitudes and practices of health professionals.
2 Childcare manuals, often written by medical practitioners but sometimes by psychologists, which are basically 'cookbooks', telling women how to mother properly (see chapter 4).
3 Research studies which have concentrated on the transition to motherhood and the early months or first few years in children's lives (Birksted-Breen, 1986; Boulton, 1983; Moss et al., 1987; Newson and Newson, 1968; Oakley, 1981).
4 Autobiographical writings which deal with the experience of being mothered and/or of mothering (Dowrick and Grundberg, 1980; Gieve, 1989; Heron, 1985; Steedman, 1986).
5 Feminist texts which have theorized motherhood as a crucial part of women's lives, affecting women's position in the social structure and the ways in which the next generation's gendered

identities develop. Much of these writings have focused particularly on the psychodynamics of the mother–daughter relationship (Apter, 1990; Chodorow, 1978; Eichenbaum and Orbach, 1985; Gordon, 1990; Rowbotham, 1989).

Why this book?

The literature described above is extensive and comes from a variety of disciplines. But it neglects many important issues and leaves many questions unanswered. As women working within developmental psychology we were particularly interested in the implications of the ways in which psychology addresses or fails to address issues concerning motherhood. The impetus for this book came from a symposium organized by Eva Lloyd at the Women and Psychology conference held at Brunel University in 1987. The discussions generated by that symposium helped us to articulate our concerns about the limitations of literature on motherhood and mothering in developmental psychology. It encouraged us to re-examine and rethink research in developmental psychology in an attempt to make it more salient to the issues which are of concern to women and affect mothers' lives. Two issues were of particular interest.

Firstly, we were struck by the contrast between the attention given to children in developmental psychology and the lack of attention given to their mothers. For while 'normal' mothers have been well researched in developmental psychology, they are generally only discussed as people who are the most important influences on their children. Women's experiences of motherhood and feelings about being mothers are rarely directly explored but can sometimes be found tucked away in studies about children. Similarly, the varieties of situations in which women mother are generally not considered. The phrases 'the mother' and 'the child' reflect the tendency to view motherhood and childhood as homogeneously universal categories. Knowledge about motherhood tends, therefore, to be assumed rather than examined.

Secondly, we noted that there was more direct interest in mothers who are constructed as deviant than in mothers who are taken for granted as 'normal'. Thus there are psychological studies of depressed mothers, lone mothers, employed mothers, working class mothers, and mothers in their teenage years. This interest in mothers considered marginal rather than those considered mainstream made us think about the ways in which 'good mothers' and hence 'deviant mothers' are socially constructed. This book is an attempt to explore those social constructions and to begin to document the reality of motherhood for women. It, therefore, discusses the real-life situations many mothers are faced with but that are frequently omitted from psychological texts. These include mothering more than one child, mothering girls or boys, mothering children who, because deaf, are not included in the category 'normal' and combining employment and mothering.

Why a focus on psychology?

This book is particularly concerned with psychological work which has a bearing on motherhood. Psychology has had a marked impact on theoretical knowledge about both motherhood and mothering and because psychological concepts have filtered through to popular texts, it has also had an important effect on the ways in which many parents and professionals concerned with children see motherhood. Psychology has, for instance, influenced the ways in which the types of writing mentioned above describe motherhood. Even where texts are not directly prescriptive, much of what is said emphasizes the responsibility of mothers to ensure that their children 'turn out right', together with the difficulty of doing that task well (see chapter 4).

Yet much that psychology has contributed to this thinking is implicit rather than explicit, for psychologists rarely focus on mothers themselves, but consider them mainly as 'influences' on children's development. Mothers, therefore, often appear in psychological texts only as principal caregivers. By concentrating on the mother–child dyad as the primary unit in which children develop, developmental psychology construes mothers as critical influences on children's intellectual and emotional well-being. At the same time it lends support to the notion that the ideal childrearing environment for young children is at home, spending all day with their mothers. With this narrow focus, psychology has little to say about the meanings of motherhood for women, what motherhood entails on a day-to-day basis, how mothers feel about motherhood and how motherhood interrelates with other careers women may pursue.

Why mothers, not fathers?

Early studies of child development assumed either explicitly or implicitly that mothers, not fathers, nannies or others, should and did do the 'mothering' of children. The psychoanalyst Winnicott (1964), for example, considered that after birth, fathers' main task was to ensure that mothers were protected from anxieties, for example about money, and could, therefore, spend as much time with their infants as possible. Bowlby, similarly, considered the mother–infant relationship to be the crucial one for child development (see chapters 8–11).

In the 1960s and 1970s, however, there were a number of shifts in ideas about parenting. Feminist writings pointed out how little most fathers did for and with their children. There was a shift on the part of some researchers to observations in family homes rather than laboratories. Some psychologists began to recognize that some children were deeply attached to their fathers (Schaffer and Emerson, 1964) leading to a greater interest in fathers' part in childrearing (see, for example, Lamb, 1981). More recently, with the supposed advent of the 'New Man' (who is considered to share childcare equally with mothers) and the arguments of feminists and others that women should not take sole responsibility for childcare tasks, some writers assume that mothers and fathers are now interchangeable. This assumption of interchangeability is demonstrated in accounts that discuss 'parenthood' rather than 'motherhood'. Such assumptions – that parenting is gender-free – are questionable (Busfield, 1987).

Although fathers are now seen to be taking a greater interest in their children than they did in previous decades, their involvement is to be found only in a limited number of areas. Unfortunately, there is no evidence that the New Man is much more than a figment of media imagination. The *majority* of fathers who live with their children do not take responsibility for childcare nor are they involved with their children as much as mothers are (Backett, 1982; Boulton, 1983; Brannen and Moss, 1988; Lewis and O'Brien, 1987; Phoenix, 1991).

Evidence about the experience of fathering suggests that, in significant ways, fatherhood is experienced in different ways from motherhood. Being a parent is a less all-embracing definition of a man than of a woman. To know that a man is a father is generally less informative about how he spends his time and energies than to know that a woman is a mother. It is still possible for men to be seen and to see themselves as 'good fathers' without being closely involved in childcare or spending much time with their children. Men are more able to opt in or to remain removed from childcare and to justify it on the grounds that good fathers need only provide material resources. Although concern is expressed in the literature about 'father absence', relatively little concern is expressed about the development of those children whose fathers frequently go away on business or, as Hardyment argues, whose jobs keep them out of their homes during most of their children's waking hours.

> The family income can be halved at a stroke when mother gives up work, and father is likely to work overtime in response. One man in four works more than 50 hours a week; three-quarters of all male workers work more than 40 hours a week. Most mothers are, in effect, single parents. (Hardyment, 1990, p. 8)

This discussion is not meant to suggest that fathers, when available, are not important and should not be studied. We recognize that a minority of fathers do genuinely share or have major responsibility for childcare. Since, however, mothers are still the people who do most childrearing and have most responsibility for children, any examination of parenting has to take seriously this gender differentiation and the ways in which it is underpinned by power relations. The focus on motherhood in this book attempts to do this.

The title of the book

The title, 'Motherhood: Meanings, Practices and Ideologies', makes conceptual distinctions between:

1 The meanings that motherhood has for women (whether or not they are mothers).
2 The ways in which women actually mother within the circumstances in which they live, i.e. the *mothering* they provide.
3 The ideologies that underpin 'commonsense' ideas about motherhood and produce much of the theoretical work and discourses on motherhood. Those ideologies then help construct what motherhood is considered to be and hence circumscribe the range of practices that mothers seek to employ with their children.

Meanings, practices and ideologies are, of course, interlinked and the choice of the three terms indicates the book's treatment of the ways in which motherhood is socially constructed in the 1990s and how this intersects with the reality of mothering as the day-to-day management of childrearing. This book, therefore, seeks to ground theory in practice and reality. It does this by considering the implications of current social constructions of motherhood for mothers and by examining the ways in which motherhood is ideologically and structurally situated. This is not generally done within psychological work.

Although there is a lot of psychological interest in individual differences, psychology has not generally explored the different ways in which mothers think about, and experience, their lives as mothers. It has, furthermore, studied mothers in isolation from their more general life experiences (Birns and Hay, 1988). In a similar way, sociological work has emphasized structural factors in motherhood, but has not, for example, generally related women's structural positions to their life histories, living circumstances, health and ideas about mothering. This book is concerned with women's subjective experiences of motherhood as well as how these intersect with social, political and psychological ideologies.

The word 'motherhood' emerged as a concept in Victorian times when it was reified as being motherliness, of mothering (Dally, 1982). Motherhood is now usually considered to be an essential task or stage of women's development as well as a crucial part of their identity, often from childhood (Birksted-Breen, 1986; Rich, 1977). In addition to establishing women's credentials as women, it also provides women with an occupational and structural identity because it takes a great deal of women's time and energy and can be a substitute for involvement in other activities such as employment (Trebilcot, 1984). Analysis of the situations in which motherhood is not considered appropriate throws light on ideas which, because they are seen as normal and natural, are rarely articulated. How motherhood is understood and hence how women view themselves as mothers is very much part of the historical period and ideological circumstances in which ideas develop. It is, for example, now relatively commonplace for young women to express dissatisfaction with the institution of marriage (which is socially constructed as a precursor of motherhood). Yet most young women envisage that they will marry in the future because there is an absence of realistic and satisfying alternatives for most women (Griffin, 1985; Lees, 1986, Phoenix, 1991).

'Mothering' refers to the daily management of children's lives and the daily care provided for them. Incorporated within the term 'mothering' is the intensity and emotional closeness of the idealized mother–child relationship as well as notions of mothers being responsible for the fostering of good child development. The use of the word 'motherhood' in the title does not preclude an examination of 'mothering'. The institution of motherhood, explored here through meanings and ideologies, is inextricably linked with the experiences of mothering, which is explored here through practices.

The main themes

The chapters in this volume contribute to an understanding of the commonalities and differences in motherhood for women. Chapters address women's experiences of mothering but they do this in different ways and a number of interrelated themes emerge. These are:

1. That women continue to be defined in terms of their biological functions. Motherhood, and particularly childbearing, continues to be defined as the supreme route to physical and emotional fulfilment and as essential for all women (Ussher, 1990). This view encourages an inappropriate romanticization of motherhood and of mother–child relationships. Childless women are also defined in relation to childbearing, either as *potential* bearers of children (which can affect their employment prospects), as failed childbearers or selfish individualists who have chosen to remain childless.

2. That while motherhood is socially constructed as valued and important, the circumstances and age at which women are supposed to become mothers proscribe motherhood for women who are, for example, considered too young or too old. Mothers in the 'wrong' age group are, therefore, in the contradictory position of being devalued although they have entered a status that is, in theory, valued.

3. That motherhood has been professionalized. The childcare manuals available demonstrate how motherhood has been claimed as an area of expertise by 'experts' who are frequently men and often doctors.

4. That there are contradictions between prescriptions about what mothers should do and assertions that there are no hard and fast rules about mothering and that childrearing should be an individual, private affair.

5. That advice to parents about how to interact with their children comes from observations of white, middle class mothers with able bodied children and often assumes that 'the child' is male (Walkerdine, 1984). Ideas gathered from this limited constituency produce narrow normative assumptions and are generalized to all parents, in spite of the lack of evidence that particular types of interaction with children have developmental significance or educational benefits (Schaffer, 1986; Tizard, 1977; Urwin 1985). Advice to parents of disabled children to interact with their children in these ways can be damaging rather than helpful (see chapter 7). Such issues illustrate the potential contradictions between 'outsider', expert, perspectives

of motherhood and 'insider' perspectives of women who are mothers.

6 That there are pervasive popular ideas about motherhood even where supporting evidence does not exist or is unclear. One example is the idea that mothers *should* stay at home with their children rather than participating in the employment market (Riley, 1983).

7 That differences between children affect both the ways in which they behave and their mothers' (as well as their fathers' and others') reactions to them and hence their experiences. Important differences between children include, gender, birth order, social class, colour and ethnicity (Walkerdine, 1988; see also chapters 8 and 9).

8 That mothers in different social circumstances (for example, from different social classes and living in households with varying compositions) experience motherhood differently and may have different understandings of what motherhood means. None the less there are also commonalities in the experiences of women who live in the same societies and have children of similar ages.

Structure of the book

Part 1 provides an overview of how psychology studies and constructs motherhood. Chapter 1 (by Ann Phoenix and Anne Woollett) considers how the social construction of motherhood fits with political constructions. It argues that psychological constructions of motherhood underpin and are underpinned by wider social constructions of motherhood. The second chapter (by Anne Woollett and Ann Phoenix) takes this argument further by examining the ways in which psychological concepts like 'sensitivity' have been used within psychology. It argues that they have produced a narrow definition of 'normal motherhood' which is oppressive because it requires that women stay at home full-time with their children when it has been well demonstrated that unrelieved childcare can be stressful (Boulton, 1983; Oakley, 1974; Zelkowitz, 1982).

The two chapters in part 2, entitled The Mandate for Motherhood, attempt to gain some purchase on ideological aspects of motherhood. They do this by addressing questions of what motherhood is supposed to be like and what it is reputed to mean to women. Why, for example does there continue to be a 'mandate for motherhood' despite major changes in women's status and changes in legislation designed to give women access to greater employment opportunities. Why are childless women generally construed as 'desperate' to have children? What do 'experts' tell women about motherhood? In chapter 3 Anne Woollett focuses on the symbolic value of motherhood by concentrating on the accounts of childless women and women who find it difficult to have their own biological children. Their views throw light on the reasons why motherhood is popular and why motherhood continues to be important to women's sense of identity. Harriette Marshall analyses how the tasks of mothering and the identity of motherhood are constructed within childcare manuals. In chapter 4 she uses discourse analysis to show that motherhood is portrayed as the ultimate fulfilment for women, yet, mothers are subjected to contradictory messages about how children should be brought up.

Part 3 addresses the issue of whether there is a 'right time' to have children. The two chapters in this section demonstrate the ways in which motherhood has an implicit, socially ideal age span and how motherhood is supposed to fit into adult life plans. They show how women who are considered to have children when they are 'too young' and those who have children when they are considered 'too old' both experience social disapproval and are both socially constructed in negative ways without the necessary supporting evidence. Both groups of women (although separated by several years) are contradictorily positioned because they are devalued when they enter a status that is supposedly women's supreme achievement. Chapter 5 (by Ann Phoenix) argues that when motherhood occurs in the teenage years it receives an almost universally bad press because women are studied in isolation from the structural circumstances in which they live. Women's 'insider' accounts are contrasted with official, 'outsider' views of early motherhood. Julia Berryman (chapter 6) points out that later motherhood (in women over 40) has only become rare relatively recently. Medical perspectives on later motherhood tend to stress problems, but older women take a positive view of becoming mothers after 40.

The three chapters in part 4 on mothering real children in real circumstances deal with fairly common situations which relatively few psychologists have written about or included in theoretical analyses. Together the chapters take a step towards documenting the reality of motherhood for many mothers. Chapter 7 by Sue Gregory considers the childcare advice given to mothers whose children are deaf. She argues that this is inappropriate because it comes from work on children who can hear and hence marginalizes deaf children and their mothers. Chapter 8, by Jacqueline

McGuire, considers how a child's gender has an impact on how that child is mothered. McGuire uses a study of mothers (and fathers) with either a first-born boy or a first-born girl to argue that gender affects the ways in which children are mothered. She illustrates how, very early in their lives, children are encouraged to accept gender-differentiated behaviour from their mothers and their fathers. In chapter 9 Penny Munn focuses on the mothering of two children simultaneously. Munn uses data from a study of siblings to illustrate the complexity of real-life mothering practices and how current theories in developmental psychology are relevant only to the mothering of one child. Mothers of two children have to manage children of different ages simultaneously, an important part of which is to construct relationships between the children.

The two chapters in part 5 consider motherhood and employment. Social constructions of employment and motherhood affect meanings, practices and ideologies of motherhood. Recognition is not, for example, usually given to the fact that some mothers' structural positions give them no real choice about employment. Both chapters argue that mothers' employment is not detrimental to children's development if good alternative childcare is provided. However, social constructions of employment of mothers as detrimental to children is, in reality, damaging to all women, whether or not they are mothers. Barbara Tizard uses historical and current literature and provides a careful examination of attachment theory as it applies to the employment of mothers. In chapter 10 she argues that the children of employed mothers are unlikely to suffer any ill effects if their alternative childcare is of a high quality. In chapter 11 Suzan Lewis demonstrates the commonalities shared by women with children and those who have other caring responsibilities. Lewis shows how the terms 'motherhood' and 'employee' are socially constructed as polar opposites and uses data from a study of women employees to demonstrate how the counterposing of employment and motherhood constrains the choices and identities available to women.

References

Apter, T. (1990) *Altered Loves: Mothers and Daughters during Adolescence.* Hemel Hempstead: Harvester Wheatsheaf.

Backett, K. (1982) *Mothers and Fathers.* London: Macmillan.

Birksted-Breen, D. (1986) The experience of having a baby: a developmental view. *Free Associations* 4, 22–35.

Birns, B. and Hay, D. (eds) (1988) *The Different Faces of Motherhood.* New York: Plenum.

Boulton, M.G. (1983) *On Being a Mother: a Study of Women with Preschool Children*. London: Tavistock.

Brannen, J. and Moss, P. (1988) *New Mothers at Work*. London: Unwin Paperbacks.

Busfield, J. (1987) Parenting and parenthood. In G. Cohen (ed.), *Social Change and the Life Course*. London: Tavistock.

Chodorow, N. (1978) *The Reproduction of Mothering: Psychoanalysis and the Sociology of Gender*. Berkeley, CA: University of California Press.

Dally, A. (1982) *Inventing Motherhood: the Consequences of an Ideal*. London: Burnett Books.

Dowrick, S. and Grundberg, S. (1980) *Why Children?* London: Virago.

Eichenbaum, L. and Orbach, S. (1985) *Understanding Women*. Harmondsworth: Penguin.

Gieve, K. (ed.) (1989) *Balancing Acts: on Being a Mother*. London: Virago.

Gordon, T. (1990) *Feminist Mothers*. London: Macmillan.

Griffin, C. (1985) *Typical Girls: Young Women from School to the Job Market*. London: Routledge and Kegan Paul.

Hardyment, C. (1990) Beating the parent trap. *Guardian*, 24–25 March, p. 8.

Heron, L. (1985) *Truth, Dare or Promise: Girls Growing Up in the Fifties*. London: Virago.

Lamb, M.E. (1981) *The Role of the Father in Child Development*, 2nd edn. New York: Wiley.

Lees, S. (1986) *Losing Out: Sexuality and Adolescent Girls*. London: Hutchinson.

Lewis, C. and O'Brien, M. (eds) (1987) *Reassessing Fatherhood: New Observations on Fathers and the Modern Family*. London: Sage.

Moss, P., Bolland, G., Foxman, R. and Owen, C. (1987) The division of household work during the transition to parenthood. *Journal of Reproductive and Infant Psychology* 5, 71–86.

Newson, J. and Newson, E. (1968) *Four Years Old in an Urban Community*. Harmondsworth: Penguin.

Oakley, A. (1974) *The Sociology of Housework*. Oxford: Martin Robertson.

Oakley, A. (1981) *From Here to Maternity: Becoming a Mother*. Harmondsworth: Penguin.

Phoenix, A. (1991) *Young Mothers?* Cambridge: Polity Press.

Rich, A. (1977) *Of Woman Born*. London: Virago.

Riley, D. (1983) *War in the Nursery: Theories of the Child and Mother*. London: Virago.

Rowbotham, S. (1989) To be or not to be: the dilemmas of mothering. *Feminist Review* 31, 81–93.

Schaffer, H.R. and Emerson P.E. (1964) The development of social attachments in infancy. *Monographs of Social Research in Child Development* 29, serial no. 94.

Schaffer, H.R. (1986) Child psychology: the future. *Journal of Child Psychology and Psychiatry* 27, 761–79.

Steedman, C. (1986) *Landscape for a Good Woman*. London: Virago.

Tizard, B. (1977) Play: the child's way of learning? In B. Tizard and D. Harvey (eds), *Biology of Play*. London: SIMP.

Trebilcot, J. (ed.) (1984) *Mothering: Essays in Feminist Theory*. Totowa, NJ: Rowman and Allenhead.

Urwin, C. (1985) Constructing motherhood: the persuasion of normal development.

In C. Steedman, C. Urwin and V. Walkerdine (eds), *Language, Gender and Childhood*. London: Routledge and Kegan Paul.

Ussher, J. (1990) Negative images of female sexuality and reproduction: reflecting misogyny or misinformation? *Psychology of Women Newsletter* 5, 17–29.

Walkerdine, V. (1984) Developmental psychology and the child-centred pedagogy: the insertion of Piaget into early education. In J. Henriques, W. Hollway, C. Urwin, C. Venn and V. Walkerdine, *Changing the Subject: Psychology, Social Regulation and Subjectivity*. London: Methuen.

Walkerdine, V. (1988) *The Mastery of Reason: Cognitive Development and the Production of Rationality*. London: Routledge.

Winnicott, D. (1964) *The Child, the Family and the Outside World*. Harmondsworth: Penguin.

Zelkowitz, P. (1982) Parenting philosophies and practices. In D. Belle (ed.), *Lives in Stress: Women and Depression*. London: Sage.

1

Motherhood: Social Construction, Politics and Psychology

Ann Phoenix and Anne Woollett

Regardless of whether women become mothers, motherhood is central to the ways in which they are defined by others and to their perceptions of themselves. Motherhood is romanticized and idealized as the supreme physical and emotional achievement in women's lives (Ussher, 1990), but when women become mothers (as most do) they find that the everyday tasks of mothering are socially devalued and relegated to individual households (Antonis, 1981). Furthermore, the tasks of mothering are socially prescribed so that many mothers learn that it is extremely difficult to mother well (see chapter 4).

This chapter argues that psychology has been instrumental in constructing the ways in which motherhood is seen and in maintaining mothers in their current social position. It examines the ways in which psychology is implicated in social constructions of motherhood and then considers how those social constructions fit with political ideologies about 'the family' and with psychological ideas of good mothering. It argues that the social and the psychological constructions of 'normal' mothers (with 'normal' being synonymous with 'good' and with 'ideal') run counter to the reality of motherhood for many mothers. As a consequence, many mothers are socially constructed as pathological and differences between mothers are not adequately studied or written about. The chapter concludes by discussing some of the gaps in our knowledge of what motherhood is really like for many women.

Social constructions of 'good/normal' mothering

Social construction is concerned with the ways in which ideas, and hence our experiences of the world are dynamic, multiple and highly complex. Furthermore they are specific to the period of history and the society in which they are produced. Ideas are not, therefore, static, unitary entities (Gergen, 1985; Henriques et al., 1984; Kitzinger, 1987). For example, it is possible to identify many (sometimes competing) ideas about motherhood in modern Western societies. These are produced in different contexts and serve varied functions. Considerations of the language and discourses used about motherhood allow analyses of current social constructions of it. According to social constructionists, interpretations of discourses will vary according to who is doing the interpreting and their political perspective (Potter and Wetherell, 1987).

Manning (1987) argues, for example, that both the Left and the Right have used social constructionist views of social problems to serve different ends. Such analyses of the ways in which discourses are socially constructed allows recognition that knowledge is not value-free and objective (Henriques et al., 1984), that people occupy different positions of power within society and that their experiences are structured by their differing relationships to power and hence their different political interests (Potter and Wetherell, 1987). These analyses allow the deconstruction of both existing knowledge about people and about society and the production of radically different forms of political knowledge (Kitzinger, 1987).

Normative social constructions of 'good/normal' mothers are usually implicit rather than explicit. It is, however, possible to make assumptions about families explicit by examining the circumstances in which public censure of, or concern about mothers is expressed. An examination of welfare policy suggests that traditional assumptions about families are still dominant (Henwood et al., 1987). An important element of such traditional constructions is that mothers should ensure that independent provision is made for their children in such a way that neither the children nor the mothers themselves come to public attention (Wicks, 1987).

It is mothers who are seen to have the responsibility of ensuring that their children 'turn out right' (Hardyment, 1990). This is seen in current emphases on the importance of bringing children up in the 'right circumstances'. The correct circumstances in which to rear children are, however, rather limited. For example, in discussions of the implementation of clause 28 of the 1988 Local Government Act (which made it illegal to 'promote' homosexuality) politicians and others from the New Right explicitly stated that children should be reared in 'real' families (heterosexual couples) rather than 'pretended' families (gay or lesbian couples). Lone parent families similarly fail to qualify as 'real families'. Such is the importance of the family to welfare policy (Loney, 1987; Smart, 1987) that it seems likely that in the 1990s attempts will be made to use the legal system in order to delay divorce where separated couples have children.

Not only are the circumstances in which women should give birth prescribed, but the age at which they should give birth and how they should live after birth are also the subjects of political statements. Women who give birth in their teenage years, mothers who are employed outside the home and women bringing up children on their own after divorce are, for example, all censured because their children are considered likely to create problems for society or to come to public attention because they are in need of public provision of benefits (see chapters 5, 10 and 11).

According to current ideologies, then, the ideal circumstances in which to have and rear children are with mother and father being over 20 years of age (but not too old, that is, not above 40), married before birth and for the duration of childhood. After birth a gendered division of labour should pertain with mothers staying at home with their children while fathers are employed outside the home earning enough money to make adequate economic provision for their wives and children. The fact that cohabitation is becoming increasingly common has not led to a comparable accommodation in dominant ideologies of motherhood which still require mothers to be married when they give birth (Busfield, 1987).

There is an apparent contradiction between social constructions of childrearing and parenting as belonging to the private sphere (and hence beyond the range of public concern and control) and the concern expressed about some women's perceived failure or refusal to conform to the elements of that construction (for example, those who become lone mothers). Statutory interventions in cases of child abuse or neglect also appear to counter notions that childrearing is an entirely private function.

This contradiction is, however, illusory rather than real. State institutions in their attempt to oversee how children are reared, intervene in the privacy of families, making mothers the targets of that surveillance (Mason, 1989a; Mayall and Foster, 1989; Rose, 1986). Also, as New and David suggest:

> The belief that childcare is purely a private business has definite political effects. It makes it less likely that working people will get together and make demands on behalf of their children . . . It fits in with the official view that family problems and family failures can be put down to the inadequacy of particular individual parents. (New and David, 1985, p. 77)

The relegation of childcare to the private sphere has political implications for motherhood itself and serves political functions in all societies (Walkerdine and Lucey, 1989; Yuval-Davis and Anthias, 1989) and it is for this reason that high emotions and concerns are generated when the 'wrong women' give birth in the 'wrong' circumstances (Bland, 1982; Mort, 1987).

The politics of motherhood

'The family' is a civil institution which is important for the passing on of state ideologies. It is arguably when 'the family' changes in ways that conflict with a state's political aims that concerns about motherhood and 'the family' are expressed because state practices contain prevalent cultural constructions about women. 'The state' is not unitary or monolithic either ideologically or in its practices. Yet, there are obviously state institutions (such as medical, welfare and educational agencies) which are designed to enforce government edicts, and hence which seek to control citizens. Modern liberal-democratic states (such as those in the West) are dependent on the appearance of consensus in the implementation of their laws. They do not, therefore, rely only on the processes of law and on state education but also depend on other institutions like the media as well as on families for passing on and producing ideologies which serve the state's political ends (Brittan and Maynard, 1984).

For parents, these political ends include economic support and provision of care for their children as well as the teaching of behaviours appropriate and acceptable to the society in which their children are growing up. If parents do not provide for their children so that they are supported, cared for and taught in ways deemed adequate by the state, the state (at least in liberal democracies) incurs a responsibility to intervene in the (private) family sphere to ensure, for example, that children do not starve and are not beaten to death. Many lone parents (who are predominantly mothers) are dependent on the provision of state benefits. It is not, therefore, surprising that as rates of divorce and of births to single women rise, politicians are less able to maintain a laissez-faire, non-interventionist approach to family life and attempt to discourage lone parenthood (albeit through statements rather than through legislation).

Yuval-Davis and Anthias (1989) demonstrate how national states regulate women's lives and the ways in which women participate in ethnic and national processes. Although their analyses are of women in general, their categories are relevant to a consideration of mothers in particular. Mothers are biological reproducers of ethnic collectivities and reproducers of the boundaries between ethnic/national groups. Women are divided by 'race' and ethnicity and different states can and do encourage or discourage various groups of women from having 'too many' children. With expressed fears in the UK, for example, that the nation is in danger of being 'swamped' by alien cultures, it is not surprising that more health education leaflets on contraception have been translated into Asian languages, than on any other health issue (Brent Community Health Council, 1981). Given the concerns about rates of birth to black women in the USA, it is also not surprising that black women are more likely than white women to have been sterilized without their knowledge and against their will (Davis, 1981). Similarly French pronatalist policies, which provide financial benefits to women who have children as an inducement to increase the French birth rate, are not denied to black French women, but are really aimed at white women (Phoenix, 1990).

Governments, state institutions and individuals who practise within those institutions clearly differentiate between different 'racial' and ethnic groups with regard to motherhood. Some groups of mothers (particularly those from minority ethnic groups) are less valued than others in Western societies and, in consequence, women are important in maintaining the distinctiveness of ethnic/national groups (Yuval-Davis and Anthias, 1989). It is obvious in an extremist state, like South Africa, that the state has a dread of the valued 'race' mixing with the devalued one. Until the late 1980s sexual relations between black and white people were legally proscribed in South Africa. In Western societies such legal proscriptions do not exist, yet moral proscriptions, albeit increasingly ineffective ones, do. These are often couched in terms of benevolent concern for the marginal position occupied by the children produced by such liaisons (for example those with one black and one white parent) (Wilson, 1987), but they function to deter.

Yuval-Davis and Anthias (1989) also suggest that women participate in the ideological reproduction of the state collectivity and are transmitters of its culture. This is the form of women's involvement in state practices that receives most attention in this book. By virtue of the fact that mothers generally bear the major responsibility for their children's upbringing and usually spend more time with them in their early years than does anyone else, women are often seen as reproducers of culture. The responsibility vested in them to ensure that their children develop into responsible and mature citizens necessarily requires that they instil dominant ideological notions of what it is to be a mature and responsible adult.

Walkerdine and Lucey (1989) demonstrate how mothers in the UK are expected to be guardians of the liberal democracy by bringing their children up to be self-regulating. In this way the citizens produced believe that they are free but, in reality, have been produced to accept, and hence to maintain, the political status quo. This expectation places women in a double bind. In order to ensure that their children become self-regulating, they have to control them while not imposing overt restrictions on them. The onus is on mothers to be constantly working to educate their children and to teach them self-regulation without appearing to do so (see chapter 2).

A major problem with prescriptions for mothering is that they take no account of structural differences between mothers. Working class mothers usually have less disposable income and material resources than their middle class counterparts. The ways in which they mother their children are, therefore, likely to be different in some respects from those of middle class mothers because they are more likely to have to deny their children the goods they want and to have to try to minimize difficulties associated with a lack of material resources and less social power (Newson and Newson, 1968; Walkerdine and Lucey, 1989; Zelkowitz, 1982). By failing to recognize such issues, current social constructions of normal motherhood do not reflect the realities of working class mothers' and children's lives, and this results in any differences between them and middle class mothers and children being seen as pathological or deviant. In a similar way black mothers and those from minority ethnic groups are socially constructed as 'other' and hence are viewed as deviating from 'good/normal' mothering. Ironically, then, differences between mothers are glossed over where they have social significance and commonalities that do exist are obscured by the construction of the 'normal/deviant' couplet.

The surveillance of mothers and children

Western societies generally have a range of institutions geared to ensuring the welfare of children. At first sight these seem to have only philanthropic aims, but historically and currently they have barely veiled political aims:

> Historical analysis of child protection policies in New South Wales, informed by political economy and feminist perspectives, highlights the extent to which these policies have functioned as a mechanism for social control of poor persons, in particular mothers, in the interests of maintaining established economic interests and values which

emphasise the responsibility of women for the reproduction of a compliant labour force. (Mason, 1989b, p. 1)

The aim of child welfare policies is surveillance, with the threat of removal of children as the ultimate sanction of the state and thus the greatest inducement to parents to reform their behaviour. In the past removal of children has been used as a way of Americanizing immigrant children, of ensuring that Aboriginal children did not grow up to be like their parents and as a means of producing industrious workers in Britain (Mason, 1990; Rose, 1986). Currently such surveillance is used to ensure that children are brought up in ways acceptable to professionals in state institutions (such as social workers and educational psychologists) and to attempt to prevent children from growing up to be criminals or dependent on welfare agencies.

The major impact of child welfare policies is on poor mothers who are often made more powerless through such interventions. The process by which this happens is one in which professionals responsible for guaranteeing child welfare operate on the basis of stereotypic constructions of what good mothers are like (Mayall and Foster, 1989). Sometimes the link between poverty and being socially constructed as inadequate parents is more obvious. In New South Wales, for example, it is not possible for parents to claim emergency welfare unless their children are registered as being 'at risk'. Similarly, in Sweden benefits are provided by social work departments and hence to be poor is synonymous with being an inadequate parent.

New and David (1985) point out that 'inadequate people' are not considered to be fully entitled to family privacy. Intervention into families tries to force parents into adequacy by making them conform to the elements of the social constructions described above. Some groups of parents, however, are more likely to be considered inadequate than others.

> Of course, children are only taken into care reluctantly . . . This reluctance is far more readily overcome when the 'inadequate' families are poor or black or are headed by a lone mother. The supporters of the family are less than enthusiastic about such families. Their 'cure' is doubly punitive: it confirms the parents in their status as unfit, and the alternative offered the children – local authority care, usually in a series of foster homes – confirms them too in their marginal status. (New and David, 1985, p. 78)

Professionals in statutory agencies, who have either been born or been educated into the middle classes, are more likely to share dominant definitions of family life. They are, therefore, likely to perceive mothers who are poor, working class, single and black as more problematic than they are white, middle class ones. 'Dominant definitions are those of the "ruling" classes' (Oakley, 1986, p. 127).

These dominant definitions can be seen in access to daycare for the under-5s. Council day nurseries are the only childcare provision provided by local authorities in the UK. They constitute a scarce resource and access to them is strictly limited. As a result council day nurseries are now almost entirely filled with children deemed by social workers or health visitors to have 'special needs', that is, children whose mothers are working class and/or single and/or black (McGuire and Richman, 1987). So while provision of council day nursery places seems benevolent, and is indeed essential to some women and children who live in poverty, they also allow easy surveillance of children placed in them. Mothers with children in publicly provided daycare do not have as much privacy as mothers who stay at home with their children or mothers who are able to employ nannies or *au pairs* to care for their children.

The above argument is not intended to imply that childrearing should be left to parents to do exactly as they wish with their children. With increasing recognition of the prevalence of child abuse, there clearly need to be checks on the exercise of parental power. What is being suggested is that the privatization of 'the family' together with social constructions of 'good parents' which omit many mothers, particularly those who are black, working class and single, makes some mothers liable to state intervention based on their structural position rather than because they are inadequate (New and David, 1985).

Psychological constructions of motherhood

Just as social constructions of ideal motherhood articulate well with state policies on families, so too they fit with psychological constructions of motherhood. Psychology, particularly developmental psychology, has provided support for ideas on motherhood that are held by many politicians, paediatricians, obstetricians and popular writers. It has done so because many psychologists keep their own experiences isolated from their research in the name of scientific objectivity. Yet although they consider themselves to be using objective measures, they take 'commonsense' ideas about motherhood for granted without recognizing that these have specific ideological underpinnings (Billig, 1990; Lawrence, 1982). With regard to motherhood, psychology tends to provide support for ideas about the circumstances in which motherhood should occur and how mothers should interact with their young children. In this it demonstrates how constructions of knowledge articulate with established power relationships (Burman, 1990; Henriques et al., 1984).

By confining many studies of mothers and infants to mother–infant pairs where mothers are married and are observed when they spend their days alone at home with their children (while the children's fathers are employed outside the home), psychologists reify popularly accepted notions about the circumstances in which motherhood should occur (see Antonis (1981) and Busfield (1987) for discussion of the constituents of reproductive ideologies about 'normal mothers').

Psychology also confirms dominant views about suitable mothers by informing and providing support for policy discussions on childcare and on family legislation. Most studies of 'normal development', designed to provide better understandings of the processes involved in mothering, tend not to use black mothers and working class mothers as respondents. This omission has been partly deliberate because it is considered that the marginal, devalued status of black people and sections of the working classes makes it unlikely that they will illuminate the processes of *normal* development. In addition, differences in culture or in working class mothering styles are considered likely to muddy results by introducing a surplus of dependent variables into studies. *Nice to know I'm doing a good job as a single w/c mum then!*

The omission of black and working class mothers from studies of normal processes has, however, also been because psychologists often use samples of opportunity. For example, they tend to study mothers who live in comfortable housing, relatively close to academic institutions, and who are happy to have researchers in their homes at pre-arranged times for long periods, preferably during the day. This constellation of factors often results in an over-representation of white, middle class mothers and children in studies (Phoenix, 1986/1990).

The converse of this omission from psychological studies when 'the normal' is being studied is an over-representation of black and working class families when the pathological is being studied. There are two notable effects of this 'normalized absence/pathological presence'. Firstly, it lends support to ideas that black women and white working class women are pathological mothers. These negative social constructions are common in society and although psychology has not created them, it does provide them with implicit support (Lawrence 1982; McAdoo, 1988; New and David, 1985; Phoenix, 1986/1990, 1988; Walkerdine and Lucey, 1989).

The second effect of the 'normalized absence/pathologized presence' is that it masks the fact that there are huge gaps in our understanding of motherhood. Acceptance that particular groups of people make poor parents does not encourage imaginative attempts to understand how motherhood fits into the lives of, for example, black women or working class women. An early attempt to ground theory in the reality of mothers' lives is provided by Newson and Newson (1968). They recognized that attitudes to everyday tasks of mothering such as toilet training could not be separated from the resources available to women, and hence from social class. Women who do not have washing machines are more concerned to have their infants toilet trained because nappy washing imposes a burden from which they are anxious to free themselves as soon as possible. For women who have washing machines, however, nappy changing and hence toilet training is less of an issue. More recently Walkerdine and Lucey's *Democracy in the Kitchen* (1989) presents an analysis of how the experiences of mothers at home with 4-year-old daughters differs with their social class. Some detailed work has also been done on black families (see, for example, Heath, 1983; Stack, 1974), but most work on black families does not focus on the impact of racism and ethnicity on motherhood.

Within Europe the experiences and practices of motherhood may differ for white mothers of the same social class who live in different societies. It seems, for example, that children's worlds are not as separated from adult worlds in Italy as they are in the UK or in the USA. There is more involvement of children in family activities and less concern with strict bedtimes and with 'child-centred' activities. Children are encouraged to play with one another and are given plenty of adult attention but little that would be considered 'sensitive' or 'responsive' in the developmental psychology of the UK and the USA (New, 1988).

Psychological research on differences between mothers

Psychological constructions of motherhood are based on a limited constituency of mothers and allow for only a limited range of acceptable maternal behaviours. Yet women come to motherhood from a variety of backgrounds and bring with them a variety of life experiences. Thus mothers can be black or white, of different ethnicities, from a range of social classes and income brackets. They can be lesbian or heterosexual and a range of ages (from teenage to middle age), having a first or subsequent child, single, married or divorced. They can engage in full-time mothering or combine full-time or part-time employment (at home and else-where) with motherhood. The route by which women become mothers also varies. In vitro fertilization, artificial insemination by donor, adoption and step-parenting as a result of remarriage all provide alternative routes to motherhood from the more usual sexual reproduction and birth. The types of relationships mothers have with their children, the numbers of children they have, the sex of those children, how they feel about motherhood and the social support available to them as mothers also differ.

Although the social constructions of motherhood used in psychology are often very restricted and do not reflect the reality of most mothers' lives, some psychological research has examined differences between mothers. For example, some psychologists have attempted to find out how mothers' personalities or their psychological state (with depression being the usual focus) affect their style of mothering: see, for example, Puckering (1989) and Longfellow et al. (1982).

Issues such as women's social positions, employment situations and financial circumstances are, of course, likely to influence the ways in which they mother and how they interpret and understand what they are doing as mothers. For example, a mother who has space at home or has child-free time in which to do housework at her leisure is likely to find it easier to comply with childcare advice which emphasizes the benefits of water play or painting or suggests that children should be encouraged to feed themselves from an early age. Cleaning up the resulting mess is less likely to be an extra, exhausting task for them. Women who live in bed and breakfast accommodation are likely to find such advice impossible to follow, and hence may feel less confident of themselves as mothers. Thus, structural factors like social class are relevant not only to how mothers are socially constructed, but also to their experiences of motherhood.

Negative constructions of 'young mothers', 'employed mothers' and 'lone mothers' all question the competence of particular groups of mothers (see chapters 5 and 6). It is sometimes argued, for example, that the children of lone mothers do badly educa-tionally and are more likely than children raised with two parents to become delinquent because they have less opportunity to observe appropriate models of male behaviour (Pilling and Pringle, 1978). Working class mothers and 'teenage mothers' are argued to provide less educative, stimulating and linguistically rich environments for their children than do middle class mothers (Hess and Shipman, 1965).

Such analyses tend to employ oversimplistic models to explain the links between structural factors and children's development: for example, it is unsatisfactory to impute poor educational achievement to mothers' age when many children born to young women either live with or spend a lot of time with other members of their families as well as their mothers (Phoenix, 1991) and when children spend a great deal of time at school. It is similarly unsatisfactory to blame lone mothers for children's developmental problems when, for most children, living alone with one parent is a temporary phase and when fathers are equally responsible for the creation of one-parent families. Newson and Newson suggest that some middle class mothers provide rational explanations long before their children are capable of understanding such explanations because 'this line of action is rooted in attitudes and ideals about life to which they are deeply committed' (1968, p. 461). It is not, therefore, because they are genuinely more 'child-centred' than working class mothers, but because they value these particular aspects of their behaviour and life style.

Walkerdine and Lucey (1989) powerfully criticize the notion that working class mothers' childrearing practices are necessarily pathological. They argue that since working class mothers face more economic pressures and constraints than middle class mothers, social class necessarily affects the ways in which they mother. Low-income mothers who experience stress or are anxious or depressed are more likely than those who are not to 'make greater maturity demands on their children', to be less tolerant of bids for attention, to be more concerned with socially appropriate behaviour and to expect immediate compliance with their requests (Zelkowitz, 1982). Zelkowitz argues that it is only possible to account for this constellation of attitudes by examining women's life circumstances. Emphasis on obedience, for example, 'may well be related to very real concerns about the safety of the neighbourhood . . . Similarly, the assignment of household responsibilities to her children may also serve to alleviate a part of the burden shouldered by the low-income mother under stress' (p. 161).

The fact that the mothers Zelkowitz is discussing are working class is not, she suggests, an explanation of their childrearing styles.

> The use of social class as an explanatory variable is somewhat simplistic since it is not one variable but many. It can encompass differences in income, education, housing, the quality of schools, and the safety of the environment, among others. (Zelkowitz, 1982, p. 155)

In discussions of structural factors such as social class and 'race', it is often assumed that working class women and black women constitute a unitary group. However, they are not homogeneous or necessarily different from middle class or white women in any essential ways. There is clearly a great deal of variability between women within the same 'race' or social class. Indeed, the very fact that everyone simultaneously has a social class, 'race' and gender position makes it impossible for there to be essential social class or 'race' qualities (Phoenix, 1988). None the less, social class and 'race' do have important effects on people's lives. These effects, and the differences that result from them must be recognized if we are to get a clearer understanding of the reality of people's (in this instance, mothers') lives.

Conclusion

This chapter has argued that what is widely accepted as 'good mothering' by 'good mothers' is socially constructed and has political implications and consequences. It is because there are connections between 'the family' and maintenance of the political status quo that official concern is expressed about 'the family' at times when there are changes in family structures. Thus, currently, increases in rates of birth to single women and increases in parental rates of divorce are identified as cause for concern.

Since psychology and psychologists are part of society, it is not surprising that psychological constructions of motherhood have both echoed and bolstered the general social constructions of motherhood. As a consequence, much psychological work on child development and mothering has not reflected the reality of mothering for many women.

The narrow focus of such work has helped to maintain negative social constructions of groups such as black and working class mothers. It has also done little to further understanding of mothers in everyday circumstances such as employment, with more than one child and mothering girls as well as mothering boys. The chapters that follow begin to rectify that situation.

References

Antonis, B. (1981) Motherhood and mothering. In Cambridge University Women's Studies Group (eds), *Women in Society: Interdisciplinary Essays*. London: Virago.

Billig, M. (1990) Stacking the cards of ideology: the history of the 'Sun Souvenir Royal Album'. *Discourse and Society* 1, 17–38.

Bland, L. (1982) 'Guardians of the Race' or 'Vampires upon the Nation's Health'? Female sexuality and its regulation in early twentieth-century Britain. In

E. Whitelegg, M. Arnot, E. Bartels, V. Beechey, L. Birke, S. Himmelweit, D. Leonard, S. Ruehl and M.A. Speakman (eds), *The Changing Experience of Women*. Oxford: Basil Blackwell.

Brent Community Health Council (1981) *Black People and the Health Service*. London: Brent Community Health Council.

Brittan, A. and Maynard, M. (1984) *Sexism, Racism and Oppression*. Oxford: Basil Blackwell.

Burman, E. (ed.) (1990) *Feminists and Psychological Practice*. London: Sage.

Busfield, J. (1987) Parenting and parenthood. In G. Cohen (ed.), *Social Change and the Life Course*. London: Tavistock.

Davis, A. (1981) *Women, Race and Class*. London: Women's Press.

Gergen, K. (1985) The social constructionist movement in modern psychology. *American Psychologist* 40, 266–73.

Hardyment, C. (1990) Mum's the word no more. *Guardian*, 3–5 November, p. 8.

Heath, S.B. (1983) *Ways with Words: Language, Life, and Work in Communities and Classrooms*. Cambridge: Cambridge University Press.

Henriques, J., Hollway, W., Urwin, C., Venn C. and Walkerdine, V. (1984) *Changing the Subject: Psychology, Social Regulation and Subjectivity*. London: Methuen.

Henwood, M., Rimmer, L. and Wicks, M. (1987) *Inside the Family: Changing Roles of Men and Women*. London: Family Policy Studies Centre, Occasional Paper no. 6.

Hess, R. and Shipman, M. (1965) Early experience and the socialisation of cognitive modes in children. *Child Development* 36, 869–86.

Kitzinger, C. (1987) *The Social Construction of Lesbianism*. London: Sage.

Lawrence, E. (1982) In the abundance of water the fool is thirsty: sociology and black 'pathology'. In Centre for Contemporary Cultural Studies, *The Empire Strikes Back: Race and Racism in 70s Britain*. University of Birmingham: Centre for Contemporary Cultural Studies.

Loney, M. (1987) Public policy and the family. In M. Loney (ed.), *The State or the Market: Politics and Welfare in Contemporary Britain*. London: Sage.

Longfellow, C., Zelkowitz, P. and Saunders, E. (1982) The quality of mother–child relationships. In D. Belle (ed.), *Lives in Stress: Women and Depression*. London: Sage.

McAdoo, H.P. (1988) *Black Families*, 2nd edn. London: Sage.

McGuire, J. and Richman, N. (1987) *Management of Behaviour Problems in Day Nurseries*. Report from the Academic Department of Child Psychiatry, Institute of Child Health, University of London, to the Department of Health and Social Security.

Manning, N. (1987) What is a social problem? In M. Loney (ed.), *The State or the Market: Politics and Welfare in Contemporary Britain*. London: Sage.

Mason, J. (1989a) In whose best interests? Some mothers' experiences of child welfare interventions. *Australian Child and Family Welfare* 4, 4–6.

Mason, J. (1989b) Families and Child Welfare Interventions. Presented at the Third Australian Institute of Family Studies Conference, Melbourne, November 1989.

Mason, J. (1990) Child Welfare Policy in Australia. Seminar at the Thomas Coram Research Unit, University of London, Institute of Education.

Mayall, B. and Foster, M-C. (1989) *Child Health Care: Living with Children, Working for Children*. Oxford: Heinemann Nursing.

Mort, F. (1987) *Dangerous Sexualities: Medico-Moral Politics in England since 1830*. London: Routledge and Kegan Paul.

New, R. (1988) Parental goals and Italian infant care. In R.A. Levine, P.M. Miller and M.M. West (eds), *Parental Behaviour in Diverse Societies*. London: Jossy-Bass.

New, C. and David, M. (1985) *For the Children's Sake: Making Childcare More than Women's Business*. Harmondsworth: Penguin.

Newson, J. and Newson, E. (1968) *Four Years Old in an Urban Community*. Harmondsworth: Penguin.

Oakley, A. (1986) Feminism, motherhood and medicine – who cares? In J. Mitchell and A. Oakley (eds), *What is Feminism?* Oxford: Basil Blackwell.

Phoenix, A. (1986) Theories of gender and black families. In M. Arnot and G. Weiner (eds), *Gender Under Scrutiny*. London: Hutchinson. Reprinted (1990) in T. Lovell (ed.), *British Feminist Thought*. Oxford: Basil Blackwell.

Phoenix, A. (1988) Narrow definitions of culture: the case of early motherhood. In S. Westwood and P. Bhachu (eds), *Enterprising Women: Home, Work and Culture among Minorities in Britain*. London: Routledge.

Phoenix, A. (1990) Black women and the maternity services. In J. Garcia, R. Kilpatrick and M. Richards (eds), *The Politics of Maternity Care: Services for Childbearing Women in Twentieth-Century Britain*. Oxford: Clarendon Paperbacks.

Phoenix, A. (1991) *Young Mothers?* Cambridge: Polity Press.

Pilling, D. and Pringle, M.K. (1978) *Controversial Issues in Child Development*. London: Elek.

Potter, J. and Wetherell, M. (1987) *Discourse and Social Psychology: Beyond Attitudes and Behaviour*. London: Sage.

Puckering, C. (1989) Maternal depression. *Journal of Child Psychology and Psychiatry* 30, 807–18.

Rose, N. (1986) *The Psychological Complex*. London: Routledge and Kegan Paul.

Smart, C. (1987) Securing the family? Rhetoric and policy in the field of social security. In M. Loney (ed.), *The State or the Market: Politics and Welfare in Contemporary Britain*. London: Sage.

Stack, C. (1974) *All our Kin: Strategies for Survival in a Black Community*. New York: Harper Row.

Ussher, J. (1990) Negative images of female sexuality and reproduction: reflecting misogyny or misinformation? *Psychology of Women Newsletter* 5, 17–29.

Walkerdine, V. and Lucey, H. (1989) *Democracy in the Kitchen: Regulating Mothers and Socialising Daughters*. London: Virago.

Wicks, M. (1987) Family matters and public policy. In M. Loney (ed.), *The State or the Market: Politics and Welfare in Contemporary Britain*. London: Sage.

Wilson, A. (1987) *Mixed Race Children: a Study of Identity*. London: Allen and Unwin.

Yuval-Davis, N. and Anthias, F. (eds) (1989) *Woman–Nation–State*. London: Macmillan.

Zelkowitz, P. (1982) Parenting philosophies and practices. In D. Belle (ed.), *Lives in Stress: Women and Depression*. London: Sage.

2

Psychological Views of Mothering

Anne Woollett and Ann Phoenix

The previous chapter has discussed ways in which psychology reproduces dominant ideologies and legitimates current views about motherhood as well as producing new orthodoxies about the nature of good mothering. But psychology's treatment of motherhood is not monolithic: psychologists have differing and sometimes contradictory, theoretical perspectives and address different questions around motherhood. This chapter considers two disparate psychological approaches to motherhood. The first, stemming from developmental psychology, is predominantly concerned with the environment mothers provide for children and the ways in which this may influence children's development. Although psychologists generally argue that mothers are the central figures in their children's lives, as carers, 'socializers' and providers of stimulating and sensitive environments, they are rarely considered as having an existence of their own or a perspective on what they do as mothers. Rather they appear as shadowy figures, managing from behind the scenes. This results in definitions of 'good' mothering which are concerned with children's 'needs' often to the exclusion of mothers' views of themselves, their own needs or the family context in which they bring up children.

A second general approach to motherhood, having its roots in social psychological and psychoanalytic theories, focuses more directly on women's identity and experiences as mothers. In this approach motherhood is generally seen as an essential stage in women's adult development and as providing them with a central identity as women and as adults. This approach places women's experiences centre stage and concentrates on the ways in which mothers manage the disjunctures between models of motherhood and the realities of their lives. However, it tends to concentrate on the transition to motherhood and mothering in the early months. It has, therefore, less to say about how motherhood intersects with women's other identities, about structural factors, and the circumstances in which women bring up children or how constructions of motherhood have an impact on women's interactions and relationships with their children.

This chapter attempts to bring together some aspects of these two approaches, which tend to remain isolated and hence contribute little to one another. This is done by examining some attempts by psychologists to isolate key aspects of mothers' attitudes and behaviour which are considered to be associated with children's development, especially those labelled as 'sensitive' or 'child-centred'. These ideas are criticized because of the narrow view they take of the contexts in which women have children and bring them up. A wider context is examined, looking in particular at the wider family and at some different approaches to motherhood, women's identity as mothers and their understandings of their positions and functions as women.

Maternal styles: control and child-centredness

For the past four decades the influence on children's development of the environment in which they grow up has been a major concern. It has been frequently argued that mothers' attitudes towards childrearing are major determinants of their children's development and as a result there has been a long history of studies of parenting styles or attitudes. Mothers are generally considered to be the most crucial figures in their children's environment and hence mothers (rather than fathers or others) are the usual focus of studies. Even when psychologists use the term 'parent' they generally study only mothers. It is assumed that the key elements of mothering can be identified and isolated from the context in which mothers bring up their children. These aspects of mothers' behaviours are seen as the key elements determining children's development, in spite of the limited success of such an approach:

> That parents do have an effect on children may seem obvious, yet in practice it has often proved extraordinarily difficult to demonstrate such an effect. It is ironic that in spite of the enormous amount of research in this area we still face the challenge of specifying as to what really goes on between parent and child that has such an impact on the child's development. (Schaffer, 1986, p. 769)

Early studies differentiated mothers' attitudes to childrearing along a number of dimensions, including warmth and nurturance, permissiveness and restrictiveness, use of physical or psychological forms of control, child-centredness, democracy and demands for mature behaviour. In these studies it was assumed that mothers could be readily assigned to one category or point on a single dimension and that terms such as 'warm' or 'permissive' could be used to summarize the complexity of mothers' behaviours and feelings towards their children. A number of psychologists recognized the inadequacy of such an approach and tried to construct more complex models of mothering and of the ways in which different styles of mothering can be differentiated.

One attempt was that of Baldwin (1948), who considered that mothering was best described by considering two aspects of mothers' attitudes in combination. He named these dimensions 'control' and 'democracy'. By control he meant the extent to which mothers thought it important to restrict their children's behaviour and ensure their compliance. A democratic maternal style was seen as one in which there was open communication between parent and child. Democratic parents were seen as committed to giving explanations for disciplinary action and obtaining children's consent. Mothers were thereby assigned to one of four categories. These could be, for example, controlling and democratic or democratic but not controlling. Children reared by mothers who were labelled as democratic were considered to be more active and assertive and also more aggressive, curious and disobedient. Parental control was related to conformity; children whose parents used a controlling style were more obedient, unassertive and lacking in tenacity. 'Good mothering', according to this approach, combines a democratic and controlling style. Children who were socially and intellectually competent were more likely than their less competent contemporaries to have mothers who employed firm control *and* were prepared to discuss things with children.

In this context, the use of terms such as 'democratic' does more than describe one pattern of childrearing style or one set of attitudes. The use of such terms does not merely assign mothers to one category rather than another, it involves an evaluation of maternal behaviour, although the criteria on which such evaluations are made are rarely made explicit.

Baumrind (1967, 1973) took a wider and more complex view of motherhood. She argued that an account of mothering required consideration of four dimensions in combination: control, clarity of communication, nurturance and demands for mature behaviour. Her concept of control is similar to that of Baldwin and what Baldwin called 'democracy' she refers to as 'clarity of communication'. By 'nurturance' she meant the amount of warmth and parental involvement in caretaking. 'Demands for mature behaviour' refers to parental pressures or encouragement for children to perform well. She considered that these characteristics of mothering are not independent of one another but cluster into three patterns: permissive, authoritarian and authoritative. Mothers who are permissive are high in clarity of communication, moderately high in nurturance and low in maturity demands and control. Mothers who are authoritarian are high in control and maturity demands, low in clarity of communication and somewhat low in nurturance. And mothers who are authoritative are high in control, clarity of communication, nurturance and maturity demands. Baumrind saw authoritative mothers as the most effective. Even though her work is more than twenty years old, the mix of firm control and high demands for competence with warmth and a willingness of parents to communicate with children, listening to their point of view and expressing their own, which she labelled as 'authoritative' parenting, matches current ideologies about the nature of 'good' parent–child relationships and hence is seen as desirable (for example, NSPCC, 1989).

Authoritative parenting was also considered to be better than other parental styles because it seemed to be more effective in terms of children's social and intellectual development. Baumrind argued that children brought up by mothers employing the other two styles – authoritarian or permissive – tended to be less competent. Children whose mothers were authoritarian were considered to be overprotected and hence to have fewer opportunities for using their initiative and developing assertiveness and self-reliance. As a result they tended to be withdrawn and this was thought to restrict their development. Permissiveness was also viewed as less than optimal because permissive parents do not encourage children to confront and deal with the consequences of their actions (Maccoby and Martin, 1983). These accounts see the context mothers provide for children as having a considerable impact on their development but there is little analysis of why some women mother in one way rather than another, or of mothers' perceptions or understandings of what they do as mothers. Mothers' style is probably associated with a range of factors such as personality, current ideologies and fashions in parenting and structural factors such as the support mothers receive from fathers or their financial and housing positions.

Mothers' understandings of what they do as they bring up their children and the impact of their structural position were given more consideration by Newson and Newson (1968, 1976) in their interviews with mothers about bringing up young children. Two themes emerged consistently from mothers' accounts. These were, firstly, controlling children and ensuring their compliance and, secondly, child-centredness. Controlling children featured strongly in mothers' accounts:

In any discussion of child-upbringing, the question of discipline must be at once the central and the most controversial issue. It is central because it arises in some form at every turn of the child's daily life; it is controversial because human beings, whether parents or not, tend to have views on how parents ought to behave towards their children. (Newson and Newson, 1968, p. 411)

In a chapter entitled 'Patterns of persuasion and compulsion', Newson and Newson (1968) indicated that mothers felt strongly about their children's compliance because having children who behave well and do not 'show them up' in public is important for mothers' self-esteem. But at the same time, many mothers recognized that they needed to concede some autonomy to children. Some mothers conceded autonomy more readily than others and were more prepared to take their children's perspectives into account. Newson and Newson (1976) called this 'child-centredness' and defined it as follows: 'the keynote to this attitude is the parents' recognition of the child's status as an individual with rights and feelings that are worthy of respect' (p. 312). One way in which mothers were rated as child-centred when their children were 4 years old was to what extent mothers were prepared to accept children's claims that they were busy. Mothers rated as child-centred answered questions about this in terms such as 'I'd like him to wait until I'd finished doing something. So I think it's only fair for me to wait until he's finished', whereas mothers rated as less child-centred replied in terms such as 'Well, then I would say, "Now get up and do it"; because I think that's the age when they start to tell you what to do, I mean Carolyn would' (Newson and Newson, 1968, p. 420). When children were 7 years old, Newson and Newson (1976) reported social class differences in mothers' attitudes to child-centredness, with middle class mothers more likely to be rated as 'child-centred' than working class mothers, and working class mothers more likely to be rated 'child-centred' towards girls than boys. This research takes more of an 'insider' position than previous research by identifying issues which matter to mothers and considering ways in which general dimensions of maternal style such as 'control' or 'child-centredness' are translated into practice. They also provide important information about the ways in which mothers' behaviour and attitudes are influenced by structural factors such as social class and financial position.

These studies which have examined parental style and mothers' reports of how they behave towards their children provide powerful information about how mothers think and feel about mothering and motherhood. Mothers' reports may or may not be accurate accounts of their mothering practices. They do, however, supply us with useful information about the cultural and ideological context in which children act and mothers interpret and respond to their children's actions. Studies of parenting attitudes and styles are now less popular, but many of their assumptions and ideas about good parenting are to be found in more recent studies, in more or less modified forms.

Responsiveness and sensitivity

In the 1970s and 1980s it became fashionable to explore mothers' influence on their children's development by observing mother-child interactions directly. Such studies examined in great detail mothers' behaviour and how it is synchronized with that of their children. This enables psychologists to examine what mothers and children do as distinct from what mothers say they do, reassuring them that they are dealing with 'objective reality'. In addition, observational techniques have allowed very young children to be studied and have increased psychological knowledge about early competence. In many studies mothers and children were observed on their own in a laboratory setting rather than in their homes. This, and the concentration on very young children, has meant that conflicts between mothers and children were infrequently observed. As a result, children's compliance – a major focus of mothers' accounts of bringing up older children – has been superseded by a major concern with mothers' child-centredness which in observational studies is more frequently labelled as 'responsiveness' or 'sensitivity'.

Stern (1977) filmed the face to face interactions between three-month-old infants and their mothers. Rather than a disorganized pattern, the play behaviour is a highly orchestrated interchange, with both mother and infant adjusting their behaviour throughout the play period. Both mothers and infants show a pattern of mutual approach and withdrawal that permits the mutual regulation of stimulation. . . . Mothers constantly shift their behaviour in order to elicit and maintain the baby's attention . . . When the amount of stimulation is too much, the infant turns away. In turn the mother reduces her input . . . Stern has characterized the mutual regulatory actions of both partners who are constantly making readjustments in their behaviour during play as a 'waltz'. (Hetherington and Parke, 1986, p. 251)

We can see here how sensitivity is considered the key element of mothers' behaviour as they encourage a 'highly orchestrated interchange' and 'mutual regulation'. Such dialogues are seen to be important for mothers as well as children:

> Through this interaction, adults are learning to more sensitively and accurately 'read' their baby's early social signals and adjust their behaviour to maintain the baby's attention and interest. It is out of these early dialogues that adults become increasingly more attached to their infants, as well as their infants' developing an attachment to their caregivers. (Hetherington and Parke, 1986, p. 251)

By interacting with their infants, it is argued that good mothers learn to be sensitive and through their sensitivity they become attached to and assist their children's development. The benefits of maternal sensitivity for mothers are seen in terms of enhancing their attachment to their children. There is no consideration of what implications such sensitivity might have for mothers, nor the impact it may have on their relationships with partners or other children (chapter 9).

This construction of good mothering is also reflected in accounts of children's emotional development by Bowlby (1969) and Ainsworth and others (1974, 1978). They view a warm, intimate and continuous relationship with mothers as a necessary condition for children's normal functioning and the establishment of secure attachments. The mother who responds in sensitive and contingent ways and who works 'with the grain of her baby's social repertoire' (Ainsworth et al., 1974, p. 107) is more likely to have children who are securely attached (and more compliant). Children who do not receive such mothering, but are subjected to 'maternal deprivation', are at risk and likely to develop a range of psychiatric and psychological problems (Rutter, 1981) (see also chapter 10).

We have tried to show that there is a consensus in developmental psychology about the value of child-centredness or sensitivity, which is discussed almost to the exclusion of other aspects of mothers' behaviour.

> In brief, it is sensitive mothering, evidencing appropriate responsiveness to infant cues, that appears to foster optimal development . . . These findings strengthen the argument that sensitivity is THE influential dimension of mothering in infancy: it not only fosters healthy psychological functioning during this developmental epoch, but it also lays the foundation on which future experience will build. (Belsky, 1981, p. 8)

This preoccupation with maternal sensitivity and its supposed benefits for children has meant that the implications of sensitivity for mothers and children are taken as granted. As far as mothers are concerned, there is little consideration of mothers' feelings about and experiences of behaving in ways which psychologists would classify as 'sensitive'. Nor are the difficulties and costs of remaining constantly 'in tune' with a baby or young child assessed. From the infants' point of view there is little overwhelming evidence on which to base the confident claims made for sensitivity, such as those quoted above (Schaffer, 1986; Urwin, 1985).

Being a sensitive mother

The picture of good mothering which emerges from observational studies is of the mother who provides a stimulating and sensitive environment. Sensitivity takes many forms but involves an awareness of children's behaviour, a reasonably accurate interpretation of their behaviour, as well as prompt and appropriate responses. Sensitive mothering is done explicitly, through activities such as reading to children or engaging them in conversations and 'incidentally' as part of the everyday business of shopping, food preparation and housework (Tizard and Hughes, 1984; Walkerdine and Lucey, 1989). Mothers' sensitivity is seen to be of value for a number of reasons. It provides feedback and encourages children to use adults as a resource, it teaches children about social interactions and conversations, and reinforces children's sense of themselves as people who may legitimately demand and reasonably be the centre of attention (Belsky, 1981; Feiring and Lewis, 1984).

While 'parenthood' is the term often used, in practice sensitivity is perceived as a key element of mothering rather than fathering. This is because sensitivity is thought to require the intimate knowledge of a child which comes only through being closely involved in their day-to-day activities. Lack of sensitivity is considered to have different consequences depending on whether it is part of mothering or fathering. Insensitivity in mothers would be viewed as pathological and as having a negative impact on children's development. In fathers, however, the same behaviour is often seen as beneficial, providing children with a context in which they can learn about unpredictability and how to express themselves explicitly (White and Woollett, 1992). The overwhelming emphasis on the value of maternal sensitivity and the domestic conditions under which it can be achieved constitute 'scientific' justification for mothers, but not fathers, to stay at home when their children are young and demonstrates the ways in which psychological and 'commonsense' notions interrelate. Prescriptions about children 'needing' their mothers and hence mothers 'needing' to stay at home with children and about mothers 'needing' to behave sensitively arise within psychology because many psychologists accept dominant ideologies about ideal families and reproduce them in their work.

Work on maternal sensitivity rarely considers individual differences in mothers' sensitivity, and even less what the costs of sensitivity might be for mothers. Belsky et al. (1984) list the qualities which they consider essential if mothers are to behave sensitively. These include the patience to listen and to hold their own feelings in check, endurance, energy and good health to cope with the physically exhausting demands of parenting, and commitment which ensures that they become involved with their children. They do not, however, offer any analysis of situational or family factors which enable mothers to hold their feelings in check or to invest themselves so heavily in their children. To behave sensitively mothers must be prepared to submerge their own needs and interests in those of their children, a degree of self-effacement which in relationships other than the mother–child one would be judged pathological. In addition, such child-focused attention from mothers presents children with unrealistic and unhelpful models of appropriate ways of relating to others.

There is little direct evidence about mothers' views on sensitivity or how they are incorporated into their understandings of motherhood and themselves as mothers. Urwin (1985), for example, suggests that many mothers are concerned with ensuring 'normal' development and view activities such as engaging in joint play as ones that promote their children's development. However, these views are not shared by all mothers. Urwin (1985) notes that mothers whose children were at school were less certain about the extent to which they could influence their children's development. They recognized they had little control over many of the powerful forces influencing their children's lives. This kind of evidence suggests that being responsive to their children is only one childcare objective for mothers; they are equally committed to ensuring that their children behave in appropriate and 'mature' ways and are reasonably compliant and obedient (Tizard and Hughes, 1984). Childcare is only one task among many. Mothers' accounts emphasize the demands of housework and activities outside the home which often require that they sometimes behave in ways in which developmental psychologists would not consider sensitive or child-centred (Boulton, 1983). Furthermore, factors such as social class, financial constraints, mothers' employment outside the home or the number of children in a family may also influence mothers' priorities and the extent to which they are able to engage in child-centred activities (for example, Walkerdine and Lucey, 1989).

Limits to sensitivity

Sensitivity and responsiveness are often considered to be beneficial because they give control and autonomy to children. But in fact mothers have to retain much power and are committed to ensuring that their goals and objectives are achieved. These goals relate to general principles such as wanting children to be obedient or sociable and day-to-day goals such as ensuring that housework is completed. Children's compliance is achieved directly through mothers' instructions to children or more indirectly making use of children's interests, explaining the need to get toys put away or the benefits for mother and child of having free time together. Indirect strategies are often thought to be more child-centred than direct control, although the underlying message is often the same. Attempts to involve children in decisions by questions such as 'Shall we put the toys away?' or explanations such as 'Granny will be here soon and we want the place to look tidy for her, don't we?' by making reference to children, appear to be sensitive to their needs. But analysis of mothers' control indicates the limited range of choices for both children and mothers. Society demands that mothers be in control, blames them when they are not, and has the power to remove children from their care if they consider that mothers' control is insufficient (see chapter 1).

The contrast between 'control' and 'sensitivity' should not be over drawn. As Stern (1977) suggests, mothers need to be sensitive if they are to control effectively. The forms and explicitness of mothers' control may differ, with implications for what children learn about control. 'Sensitive' mothers, as Walkerdine and Lucey (1989) argue persuasively, regulate their children not by overt commands but through an illusion of autonomy. Children do what their mothers want but the illusion is maintained that children make an autonomous choice. How this is done can be seen in mothers' use of language which includes questions to which mothers know the answer, such as 'What colour is that?' or 'How many people are coming to tea?' The purpose of such questions is to encourage children to talk and to be indirectly educative rather than seeking information (the usual reason for asking a question). Mothers also tend to use instructions or imperatives phrased as questions, such as the one quoted earlier: 'Shall we put the toys away?' To understand this sentence and act appropriately, the child has to recognize that this is not a question to which an answer of 'No' is acceptable. Many exchanges between mothers and children run smoothly because there is a consensus about the real meaning of mothers' questions. The nature and extent of mothers' control may be apparent only when children do not comply and mothers exert greater pressure or switch to 'less sensitive' and more directly controlling strategies such as 'I told you to put those toys away' or 'Do it now' (Dunn, 1988).

A consideration of the ways in which mothers' sensitivity is moderated by their other childrearing objectives, including how caring for children fits into other activities, elaborates the psychological model of sensitivity and suggests limits to it. In addition it points to the complex nature of mothering and the problems inherent in advocating, whether implicitly or explicitly, simplistic models of good mothering. The limitations of the model are further clarified by examination of the conflicting demands of childcare and housework on mothers' time and energy, and by the demands of family life, that is by the totality of relationships within families.

Beyond the dyad: mothering in context

Mothers frequently appear in psychological texts as, and only as, principal caregivers. By concentrating on the mother–child pair (or dyad), developmental psychology assumes that mothers are the critical influences in children's lives. Fathers and other important people are viewed as only marginally significant and the impact of factors such as social class, lone mothering and divorce are rarely considered. Conceptually this is a limited view but it is also one which ignores the reality of mothers' and children's lives (Bronfenbrenner, 1979; White and Woollett, 1992).

Analysis of family interaction patterns points to the significance of other family members and other dyads within families. Fathers influence mothers' behaviour in a number of ways. For example, mothers play less with children and are less responsive when fathers are present (Clarke-Stewart, 1978). In addition, interactions between mothers and fathers which occur in the presence of children but in which children do not participate may provide them with information about how adults interact and about gendered behaviour. Fathers also influence their children through the quality of the marital relationship. Mothers are more sensitive to children when marital quality is good, but when parents are divorcing they find it difficult to give children their attention or interest (Hetherington et al., 1982).

Siblings (brothers and sisters) also have an impact on mother–child relations. Siblings increase the number of family interactions and thereby reduce the opportunities for sensitive dyadic mother–

child relations. In large families (which may include families with step-siblings) mothers and fathers ask fewer questions and are less positive to children and, in turn, children make fewer demands of parents (Feiring and Lewis, 1984). The birth of a sibling increases conflict between mothers and older children and their conversations tend to focus on the new baby rather than older children as mothers and children discuss the activities, motives and intentions of younger children. This is considered to encourage children's perspective-taking (Dunn and Kendrick, 1982). Younger children's language development may also be assisted by overhearing conversations between mothers and older siblings (Woollett, 1986).

Using a family-based approach encourages psychologists to acknowledge how children create and modify the environment in which they are brought up. In spite of work looking at the impact of factors such as children's gender, birth order and age, psychologists still tend to study mother–child interactions as if 'influence' was unidirectional, coming only from mothers to children. In addition, families do not operate in a vacuum; children are exposed to television, other children, other families, doctors and clinics, welfare services, schools and other institutions which set agendas that may or may not coincide with those of mothers (New and David, 1985).

Motherhood from the perspective of mothers

Observational studies provide information as to some of the things mothers do around children, but little about their feelings, ideas and beliefs concerning children, childcare and themselves as mothers. Mothers hold a variety of views about children and parenting which, as we have shown, are not necessarily in agreement with those of formal psychology and these may influence how they interact with their children (Goodnow, 1988; Urwin, 1985). Some mothers find that being 'sensitive' does not come easily. This may be because they cannot relate easily to their children, because they are depressed or isolated, or because they do not believe that sensitivity is an important part of their relationship with the child. For some mothers there may be a mismatch between their behaviour and feelings and those prescribed by psychological theories; and there may be conflict between their own needs and those of their children. All these factors may influence how women feel about themselves as mothers but they are rarely examined in studies of mother–child interaction. One study that does consider the implications of childcare and parenting styles for mothers is that of Newson and Newson (1968). They suggest that mothers' self-esteem may be influenced, for example, by how effectively they manage to ensure their children's compliance, and they point to the variety of reasons mothers might have for wanting to ensure compliance. These range from wanting to enhance their own self-esteem to concerns for their children's safety and respect for obedience as a quality in its own right.

The explanatory power of many studies in developmental psychology is lessened because they do not recognize mothers' experience and do not address the issues women encounter around motherhood. These issues include their identity as mothers, their feelings towards their children, how they translate their attitudes and understandings into action and their ways of coping with the discrepancies between the ideal of motherhood and the realities of their lives. The invisibility of mothers in much psychological work is probably linked with the lack of a conceptual framework for analysing mothers' feelings and experiences as different from those of their children. It is not surprising, then, that conceptualizations of motherhood and of good mothering merely reflect ideas about children. What children are thought to need for development is generalized to define good mothering. As children are considered to need sensitivity and responsiveness, this is perceived as the key feature of mothering.

Elsewhere in psychology and in sociology there is greater interest in motherhood from women's perspectives, with a variety of studies and approaches to women's experiences of mothering. Common to all these is a view of motherhood as an important identity, as an essential stage of development and as ultimate fulfilment for all women (Antonis, 1981; Busfield, 1987; Oakley, 1981). The traditional psychoanalytic approach sees motherhood as based on innate instinctual drives and hence as a normal characteristic of women's female identity. Problems around motherhood (including infertility or depression) are seen as evidence of women's poor adjustment to their adult female identity. This approach concentrates on the inner conflicts for women. In motherhood women achieve a new stage of ego development as they identify with their children and also with themselves as people who have been children, reactivating earlier conflicts around their own experiences of being mothered. Women's experiences are seen as rooted within the context of their own development and their establishment of an adult identity. The traditional psychoanalytic approach has little to say about women's perceptions and understandings of motherhood on a day-to-day basis nor mothers' interactions and relations with their children. In addition, it takes little account of the wider social, structural and economic contexts in which women become mothers and bring up their children (Birns and Hay, 1988; Gordon, 1990).

Developing from psychoanalytic theories, attachment theories also emphasize the emotional experience of motherhood and the development of attachment relationships. Using an ethological approach to mother–child relations, attachment and bonding are seen as key concepts for explaining how children's needs are met and how mothers come to love and feel responsible for their children's care and to behave sensitively. Because motherhood is seen almost entirely as instinctual, it is considered natural for mothers to love and 'bond' with their infants and such emotions are viewed as the central core of women's experiences of motherhood. This approach underplays the variety of women's experiences. Feelings of anger or hostility towards their children and depression or boredom with the tasks of childcare are viewed as indicating some individual pathology rather than as a consequence of the contexts in which many women mother (Boulton, 1983) (see also chapter 10).

Feminist, sociological and social psychological theories tend to be more concerned with social constructions of motherhood, the functions motherhood serves for society and its impact on women's social position. They argue that the desire to be a mother is not so much a part of women's 'natural' biological inheritance but is learned, along with the skills of motherhood, as women grow up. Women learn that being a mother is a normal and proper part of being adult for women and that, for those in heterosexual relationships, motherhood is an integral part of their relationships, even though becoming a mother may trigger developmental crises. Studies point to the emotional rewards of motherhood but also to the frustrations, which are explained in terms of the structural context, such as women's isolation in individual households or conflicts with employment outside the home, rather than in terms of the emotional or psychological state of individual women (see chapter 11) (Antonis, 1981; Busfield, 1987; Segal, 1987).

Conflicts between the meanings and practices of motherhood are examined by Boulton (1983). In a study of mothers with pre-school children she examined women's experiences and distinguished between their feelings about looking after children and the meaning and purpose motherhood provides. Roughly half of the women enjoyed childcare while half found it stressful or a threat to their individuality. Well over half found that motherhood gave them a sense of purpose but a large minority did not. While the two aspects of motherhood went together for many women, for others there was a mismatch which Boulton labelled as 'in conflict' or 'alienated'. She found that working class women were more likely to say they enjoyed the tasks of childcare than middle class women and were less likely to experience a conflict between the meaning motherhood provided for them and their enjoyment of childcare.

Social constructionist views of motherhood articulate a model of 'normal motherhood', against which to compare the experiences of deviant mothers, such as single mothers or young mothers. Dominant constructions of motherhood are viewed as existing within the wider society and are recognized by individual women who use them as standards against which to evaluate their own experiences and construct their own ideas. Studies in this tradition compare women's experiences with their own constructions of motherhood and with more idealized and public versions, and consider how women deal with inconsistencies and make sense of their experiences (Boulton, 1983). Gordon (1990), for example, examined the experiences of mothers with an ideological commitment to feminism. She found that in many ways the experiences of feminist mothers reflected those of other women, for example in terms of the pleasure they obtained from their children and motherhood as a valued social position. But feminist mothers also found it more difficult to find a comfortable balance between their identities as mothers and other important identities, and they articulated more problems around raising sons.

Motherhood is a social position actively sought by women and is often seen as an essential stage of development. In part this is because of the scarcity of acceptable alternatives (see chapter 3). Motherhood is defined in a number of ways, as identity, feelings (emotional commitment and romantic attachment), social position and practices (what women do on a day-to-day basis). It is often viewed as essentially similar for all women but some approaches point more clearly to variability in women's experiences – as related to their individual characteristics, close relationships, structural factors and to other social positions and relationships, including employment outside the home (Boulton, 1983; Gordon, 1990).

The professionalization of motherhood

Psychology is becoming increasingly involved in the creation of a body of specialist knowledge about mothers and children which mothers are encouraged to use as their model of good practice. Psychological research suggests, on the one hand, that motherhood is natural and that mothers' knowledge and their skills in childcare emerge easily and instinctually. But on the other hand, research also emphasizes the highly skilled and serious nature of motherhood and the need for women to acquaint themselves with formal knowledge (New and David, 1985). For example, women are expected to ensure that they are healthy and 'ready' for motherhood, that their children are planned rather than conceived accidentally and are born into a nuclear family with both a mother and a father. Mothers are expected to learn about pregnancy and childbirth and to attend antenatal classes so they are initiated by the medical 'experts' into the necessary rites and knowledge. Once their children are born, mothers are expected to give them good diets, to take them for regular medical check-ups and to devote themselves exclusively to their care and upbringing (Antonis, 1981; Busfield, 1987).

Much of the creation of the body of specialist knowledge about motherhood relates to the medicalization of childbirth and childcare. The largely negative impact of medical supervision on women's experience of pregnancy and childbirth has been well documented (for example, Oakley, 1981). More recent medical innovations include the use of fetal monitoring in pregnancy and reproductive technologies such as IVF (in vitro fertilization)[1] which involve medical manipulation of conception (Stanworth, 1987). These influence the experience of motherhood for the women involved but also have an impact on the attitudes of the wider society. This may be seen, for example, in assumptions that reproductive problems should have medical solutions, in the debate about whether mothers can 'bond' with children they have adopted and, by raising expectations that medical technology can ensure a perfect baby, in attitudes towards handicap (Richards, 1989).

The expertise claimed by the medical profession in pregnancy and childbirth has been extended to childcare. Many popular childcare manuals are written by doctors who consider that they are competent to advise not only on feeding, immunization and child health but also on childcare, child development and women's reactions to motherhood. One result of this may be the medicalization of problems associated with motherhood, for example, post-natal depression is seen as an illness rather than a reaction to isolation or lack of support (Nicolson, 1986).

Books offer advice to women about many aspects of childcare (see chapter 4). They explicitly encourage women to distrust their own expertise or that of their family and friends (sometimes referred to as old wives' tales) and to seek instead advice and expertise from the medical professionals (old doctors' tales). The mismatch between women's expectations and the reality of motherhood may encourage women to seek such 'expert' advice. The strongly expressed ideas of such experts about bonding or the instant attachment of mother and baby have influenced ideology and public policy around childcare, even though there is very little scientific evidence for such ideas (Rutter, 1981). Not surprisingly the advice does not, by and large, consider the perspectives of mothers nor does it have much to offer mothers who have taken the advice of the 'professionals' to stay at home with their children and then experience isolation, lack of fulfilment and identity problems (Gordon, 1990).

Conclusion

Psychological approaches to motherhood are disparate. While some theories consider women's identities as mothers, the major body of theory in developmental psychology and investigations around mother–child relations has concentrated on children and their development. From this, psychologists make judgements about how women should conduct themselves as mothers. Concepts like 'maternal deprivation', 'sensitive mothering', 'bonding' indicate clear norms for mothers. These include strong feelings of attachment, taking major responsibility for their children's care, staying at home while their children are young and being sensitively responsive to their behaviour and individuality. Many of these assumptions about how women should mother have passed into general use and are included in professional advice to mothers. The applicability of much advice, however, is limited because psychologists insufficiently analyse the experiences of women and the impact of the contexts in which they mother.

Note

1 In vitro fertilization (IVF) involves the fertilization of a woman's egg and her partner's sperm outside the body. The fertilized egg is then placed in the woman's uterus.

References

Ainsworth, M.D.S., Bell, S.M. and Stayton, D.J. (1974) Infant–mother attachment and social development: 'socialisation' as a product of reciprocal responsiveness to signals. In M.P.M. Richards (ed.), *The Integration of the Child into a Social World*. London: Cambridge University Press.

Ainsworth, M.D.S., Blehar, M.C., Waters, E. and Wall, S.L. (1978) *Patterns of Attachment*. Hillsdale, NJ: Erlbaum.

Antonis, B. (1981) Motherhood and mothering. In Cambridge University Women's Studies Group (eds), *Women in Society: Interdisciplinary Essays*. London: Virago.

Baldwin, A. (1948) Socialization and the parent–child relationship. *Child Development* 19, 127–36.

Baumrind, D. (1967) Child care practices anteceding three patterns of preschool behaviour. *Genetic Psychology Monographs* 75, 43–88.

Baumrind, D. (1973) The development of instrumental competence through socialisation. In A.E. Pick (ed.), *Minnesota Symposium on Child Development*. Minneapolis: University of Minnesota Press.

Belsky, J. (1981) Early human experience: a family perspective. *Developmental Psychology* 17, 3–23.

Belsky, J., Robins, E. and Gamble, W. (1984) The determinants of parental competence: towards a contextual theory. In M. Lewis (ed.), *Beyond the Dyad*. New York: Plenum Press.

Birns, B. and Hay, D.F. (eds) (1988) *The Different Faces of Motherhood*. New York: Plenum.

Boulton, M.G. (1983) *On Being a Mother: a Study of Women with Preschool Children*. London: Tavistock.

Bowlby, J. (1969) *Attachment and Loss*, vol. 1: *Attachment*. Harmondsworth: Penguin.

Bronfenbrenner, U. (1979) *The Ecology of Human Development: Experiments by Nature and Design*. London: Harvard University Press.

Busfield, J. (1987) Parenting and parenthood. In G. Cohen (ed.), *Social Change and the Life Course*. London: Tavistock.

Clarke-Stewart, K.A. (1978) And daddy makes three: the mother–father–infant interaction. *Child Development* 49, 466–78.

Dunn, J. (1988) *The Beginnings of Social Understanding*. Oxford: Basil Blackwell.

Dunn, J. and Kendrick, C. (1982) *Siblings: Love, Envy and Understanding*. London: Grant McIntyre.

Feiring, C. and Lewis, M. (1984) Changing characteristics of the US family: implications for family networks, relationships, and child development. In M. Lewis (ed.), *Beyond the Dyad*. New York: Plenum.

Goodnow, J.J. (1988) Parents' ideas, actions, and feelings: models and methods from developmental and social psychology. *Child Development* 59, 286–320.

Gordon, T. (1990) *Feminist Mothers*. London: Macmillan.

Hetherington, E.M., Cox, M. and Cox, R. (1982) Effects of divorce on parents and children. In M. Lamb (ed.), *Non-Traditional Families*. Hillsdale, NJ: Erlbaum.

Hetherington, E.M. and Parke, R.D. (1986) *Child Psychology: a Contemporary Viewpoint*, 3rd edn. New York: McGraw Hill.

Maccoby, E.E. and Martin, J.A. (1983) Socialisation in the context of the family. In E.M. Hetherington (ed.), *Handbook of Child Psychology*, vol. IV: *Socialisation, Personality and Social Development*, 4th edn. New York: Wiley.

New, C. and David, M. (1985) *For the Children's Sake: Making Childcare More than Women's Business*. Harmondsworth: Penguin.

Newson, J. and Newson, E. (1968) *Four Years Old in an Urban Community*. Harmondsworth: Penguin.

Newson, J. and Newson, E. (1976) *Seven Years Old in the Home Environment*. Harmondsworth: Penguin.

Nicolson, P. (1986) Developing a feminist approach to depression following childbirth. In S. Wilkinson (ed.), *Feminist Social Psychology*. Milton Keynes: Open University.

NSPCC (1989) *Putting Children First: an NSPCC Guide*. London: NSPCC.

Oakley, A. (1981) *From Here to Maternity: Becoming a Mother*. Harmondsworth: Penguin.

Richards, M.P.M. (1989) Social and ethical problems of fetal diagnosis and screening. *Journal of Reproductive and Infant Psychology* 7, 171–86.

Rutter, M. (1981) *Maternal Deprivation Reassessed*, 2nd edn. Harmondsworth: Penguin.

Schaffer, H.R. (1986) Child psychology: the future. *Journal of Child Psychology and Psychiatry* 27, 761–79.

Segal, L. (1987) *Is the Future Female? Troubled Thoughts on Contemporary Feminism*. London: Virago.

Stanworth, M. (ed.) (1987) *Reproductive Technologies: Gender, Motherhood and Medicine*. Cambridge: Polity Press.

Stern, D. (1977) *The First Relationship: Infant and Mother*. London: Fontana.

Tizard, B. and Hughes, M. (1984) *Young Children Learning: Talking and Thinking at Home and School*. London: Fontana.

Urwin, C. (1985) Constructing motherhood: the persuasion of normal development. In C. Steedman, C. Urwin and V. Walkerdine (eds), *Language, Gender and Childhood*. London: Routledge and Kegan Paul.

Walkerdine, V. and Lucey, H. (1989) *Democracy in the Kitchen: Regulating Mothers and Socialising Daughters*. London: Virago.

White, D. and Woollett, A. (1992) *Families: a Context for Development*. Basingstoke: Falmer.

Woollett, A. (1986) The influence of older siblings on the language environment of young children. *British Journal of Developmental Psychology* 4, 235–45.

3

Having Children: Accounts of Childless Women and Women with Reproductive Problems

Anne Woollett

This chapter considers the ideas about motherhood of childless women and those who have difficulties in becoming mothers. Women who remain childless do not follow the usual pattern of development in adult life. Because they do not become mothers, or do so only after a delay, through medical treatment or adoption, such women are often asked to explain their non-conformity to reproductive norms and, as part of their medical treatment or adoption procedures, have to reflect on why they want children and what motherhood means for them. This chapter considers the reasons such women give for wanting to be mothers. These include the symbolic value of motherhood, as evidence of their achievement of full adult identity, the opportunities motherhood provides for establishing close intimate relationships and overcoming the negative identity associated with infertility and childlessness. Women's accounts are discussed within the framework of studies of the value of children to parents and the meaning of motherhood.

What does motherhood mean?

Studies that assess the value of children to parents point to a variety of symbolic and concrete values associated with having children and becoming parents (Antonucci and Mikus, 1988; Busfield, 1974; Fawcett, 1988; Hoffman, 1975; Michaels, 1988; Newson and Newson, 1976). These values include:

1 primary group ties – children provide parents with opportunities for expressing and receiving affection and establishing close

relationships with other people: some parents also point to the value of children in promoting and strengthening mother–father relationships and those with the wider family;

2 enjoyment and fun – children are seen to bring interest and variety to their parents' lives;

3 expansion of self – parenting is seen as growth, as adding to the meaning of life and ensuring continuity for parents;

4 validation of adult status and identity – parenthood is valued as an integral part of one's self-definition, allowing people to be accepted as responsible and mature members of their community;

5 achievement and creativity from helping children grow – the power and influence parents have over their children and the prestige they gain from their children's accomplishments are often seen as valuable;

6 contribution to personal development – parenthood is sometimes seen as helping parents to become less selfish and to contribute to society.

These values are balanced against the actual and potential costs of having children. These include, in Western societies, financial costs of bringing up children and reduction of employment opportunities for mothers. These costs are often discussed in models of contraception behaviour, but not by parents. In contrast, parents' discussion of the costs of parenting focus more upon their anxieties about their children's health, development and social activities and the ways in which children may limit their freedom and activities.

These values are derived from studies with people who are parents but they are also articulated by people interviewed before they marry or become parents (Michaels, 1988). This suggests that such values do not develop only or even predominantly through being a parent but that they provide a powerful framework for young people's decisions and aspirations in adult life. Having children and becoming mothers are frequently referred to when girls talk about their expectations and ideas of their future lives as women (Griffin, 1985; Lees, 1986). Most young women see their life plans as including work, marriage and motherhood. While their ideas tend to be vague, most girls expect to have one or two children and a life plan similar to their mothers' even though they may express dissatisfaction with the quality of their mothers' lives (Beckett, 1986; Sharpe, 1976).

Analysis of the value of children for parents points to the variety of satisfactions children provide and the ways in which having children is seen to influence people's lives, relationships and identities. For women a major reason for having children is the identity and status which motherhood provides. Women's experiences as mothers and the value and meaning of motherhood is increasingly being studied, as the chapters in this volume testify. Surprisingly perhaps, given the constraints children impose on mothers' activities, and the low status of women's domestic roles, motherhood is perceived in largely positive terms (for example, Antonis, 1981; Oakley, 1980; Sharpe, 1984). It is seen as providing a means by which women achieve full adult status and demonstrate their feminine identity (Busfield, 1987; Notman and Nadelson, 1982; Salmon, 1985).

Although most women expect to become mothers, there is considerable variation in their adjustments and, one would predict, in how salient are particular reasons for having children. Achieving adult status and identity may be more salient, for example, for childless women than for women who have a child already. For mothers with one child, the value of having a second child might lie in conforming to norms about 'proper' families having two children. Having children is central to most women's adult identity, whether or not they have strong employment or career orientations. Motherhood as an occupation and a means of acquiring adult identity is often compared favourably with other outlets and the jobs available to most women (Baker, 1989). Motherhood is seen as providing women with more control and autonomy over their lives than many of the jobs available to them (Sharpe, 1984). There is, however, little research evidence about how women's attitudes towards children and motherhood relate to other aspects of their value systems or about the family, cultural and historical context in which values are translated into individual practice and experience.

Infertility and childlessness

A factor sometimes thought to influence women's adjustments to motherhood, although one not frequently studied, is their reproductive history (Antonucci and Mikus, 1988; Bromham et al., 1989; Pfeffer and Woollett, 1983). While many women conceive easily and give birth to live, healthy children, others experience difficulties. Infertility is usually defined as an inability to conceive after a year or so of trying to do so. Infertile women include those who take a long time to conceive and also those who are childless or have fewer children than they would like because of miscarriage or problems of conception. Women may experience problems conceiving first or subsequent children. Some childless women adopt children and others are involved in bringing up step-children. Infertility is, therefore, a complex concept which results in childlessness, in fewer children, or in women having children only after a delay, after medical investigations or adoption (Steinberg, 1989). Because they do not conform to common reproductive patterns, infertile women are often asked to articulate their ideas about motherhood and indeed are often required to so as part of their infertility investigations or adoption procedures (Callan, 1985; Mahlstedt, 1985; Pfeffer and Woollett, 1983). As a result, childless and infertile women may be more conscious than women with children of implicit normative ideas about motherhood. In addition, they bring their own perspectives, feelings and concerns to their analyses of motherhood. This may be the perspective of childless women or, because infertility, like choosing not to have children, is not necessarily a permanent state, it may be the perspective of women who become mothers only after a delay.

Those who have chosen not to have children constitute another group of childless women. They may not be in a social position to have children or they may have decided (for the time being at least) to remain childless. These women may be subject to the same disapproval and stigma as infertile women but their attitudes to children and motherhood may be different (Campbell, 1985; Veevers, 1980).

The data presented in this chapter come from interviews conducted by Naomi Pfeffer and myself as part of a study of women's experiences of infertility (Pfeffer and Woollett, 1983; Woollett, 1985). Infertile women's accounts are compared with autobiographical accounts of childless women and women with infertility problems, especially those in a collection edited by Dowrick and Grundberg (1980), and with findings reported in four studies of mothers and women who have chosen to remain childless. These are (i) Oakley's (1981) study of sixty white, London-based women having their first babies (aged between 19 and 32 years); (ii) Boulton's (1983) study of mothers with two or more pre-school children, all married, not in full-time employment, living in London and probably white; (iii) Sharpe's (1984) study of working mothers, largely white, working class women, living in different parts of the UK; and (iv) Campbell's (1985) study of forty-four married women who chose not to have children, living in a Scottish city.

In our study of women's experiences of infertility, we asked forty women who were childless or had experienced problems in having children about motherhood and their reasons for wanting children. Their experiences were very varied. Most had sought medical help and so had experience of the medical treatment of infertility or miscarriage. The majority had been given some explanation for their infertility. These explanations included problems to do with the women themselves (for example, lack of ovulation) or with their partners (for example, low sperm count). Some women were experiencing problems with a first pregnancy, whereas others had a child already and were experiencing problems conceiving a second or subsequent child. Some women had remained childless whereas others had become mothers. These included women who had conceived and carried through a pregnancy to term as well as women who had adopted children and those who were step-mothers. Women were aged between 24 and 41 years (mean age 31.4 years). Women's current concerns about motherhood varied considerably: some women wanted to talk at length about motherhood, but others were more pre-occupied with different aspects of their experiences. Because infertility is a dynamic state, the views they express are not necessarily representative of their views at different stages.

Two general themes emerged from women's accounts. The first is a positive view of motherhood based on a variety of social, interpersonal and psychological criteria. The second is the negative portrayal of childlessness which makes it, for many, an uncomfortable and unacceptable alternative to motherhood.

Positive aspects of motherhood

Not surprisingly, given the efforts many had put into becoming mothers, childless women and those with reproductive problems saw motherhood in positive terms, and from their accounts three closely related themes can be identified. These are motherhood as mandatory, motherhood as adult female identity and the establishment of intimate relationships.

Motherhood as mandatory

Many writers have pointed to the normative or mandatory quality of motherhood: all women who are married or in stable hetero-sexual relationships are expected to become mothers and it is considered 'normal' for them to want to do so. In this ideological context, women's decisions are not so much about whether or not to become mothers but about when to have children, how many to have or in which social context to have them. Whatever else they do with their lives, women are supposed to be mothers, with the result that variability in women's feelings and experiences are rarely taken seriously (Antonis, 1981; Busfield, 1974; Franklin, 1989; Pfeffer and Woollett, 1983).

The taken-for-granted quality of motherhood is a common theme in the accounts of childless women and those with reproductive problems, as the following quotations indicate. In contrast, it is not a theme commonly articulated in studies that discuss the reasons parents give for wanting children (Campbell, 1985; Monarch, 1991; Payne, 1978).

> I've spoken to lots of newly married wives – friends – and say 'Are you going to have children?' And they say, 'I'm on the pill just now, I've thought about it, I don't really want them but . . .', and you say, 'Why but?' And they say, 'Everybody has children'. (A woman who has chosen to remain childless: Campbell, 1985, p. 95)

> I always assumed there would be a baby in our lives. (Woman undergoing treatment for primary infertility)

> I've always wanted children. When I was a child I always played with younger children. I never played with children my own age. I used to cart loads of little kids around. As I got older I didn't want to get married. I wanted to have children. (Woman undergoing treatment for primary infertility)

> We had been married four years and I thought it would be quite nice to have a baby. It wasn't very practical, we were more or less living in one room. But I didn't think about that, I thought it would be quite nice to have a baby. (Woman who adopted two children after unsuccessful infertility treatment)

A consequence of living in a pronatalist climate is that childless women and those with reproductive problems are often asked to explain themselves, in contrast to parents, who are rarely asked to justify their conformity to reproductive 'normality' (Woollett, 1985). The necessity and difficulty of explaining occur commonly in women's accounts. Wileman (1980) compares her experience of adoption and hospital investigations:

> In fact the contrast between the two baby-producing establishments never ceased to amaze me. Whereas the adoption people left no stone unturned in their desire to make sure that we would make conscientious and loving parents, the hospital did not give a single thought to how fit we were to care for the babies they were trying to give us. Just because the children were to emerge from our own genitals we seemed to be exonerated from all responsibilities. (p. 217)

And another woman describes the difficulties of answering the questions asked by adoption agencies:

> They ask you all sorts of things. One of her questions was 'Why did

you marry your husband?' I wanted to ask her why she married her husband. And 'Why do you want a baby?' You always have to put that on the form. You try to think of a reason why. It's difficult isn't it? (Woman who adopted two children)

Sometimes when women do become pregnant, they say they feel unusual or out of step, indicating not merely the normative quality of motherhood but also that there are rules about when to have children and how many children to have. Breaching these rules can make women feel very uncomfortable.

Being elderly didn't help. There was a young woman in the next bed who said 'Do you realise you are old enough to be my mother?' (Woman who conceived some years after giving up infertility investigations and adopting two children)

A family to me is two adults and two children. (Woman having treatment for secondary infertility)

Adult female identity

Motherhood also bestows positive identity on women. Motherhood is highly valued symbolically as the key to adulthood: having a child makes a women a mother *and* an adult. Women who do not have children may experience difficulties in being recognized as fully adult and grown-up people (Salmon, 1985). Women's maturation and achievement are often viewed as dependent on their becoming mothers (Antonucci and Mikus, 1988; Busfield, 1974; Rapoport et al., 1977). This approach is endorsed by psychological theories of adult development which provide 'scientific validation' for motherhood as a major growth point in women's lives (Antonis, 1981; Notman and Nadelson, 1982). Growing up and acquiring adult identity is a point taken up by a woman who adopted a child after unsuccessful infertility investigations:

I think there are two things which make you grow up, you either have a child or one of your parents dies. I think my father died before I had Emma and that made me grow. That changed me. I became an adult at that point.

Motherhood is symbolically important, too, because it confirms women's female identity and is in this respect central to their sense of themselves. It demonstrates women's physical and psychological adequacy and, as the producers of the next generation, gives them identifiable social functions (Busfield, 1987; Rapoport et al., 1977).

Women's plans for their future lives are often tied up with their expectations of becoming mothers (Baker, 1989; Beckett, 1986). The idea that only women with children are 'proper' women is pervasive in spite of public commitment to sexual equality and is experienced by women whether or not they hold traditional sex role attitudes (Gerson, 1980).

Childless women are very aware of this value of children and recognize that by failing to comply with one of the most salient features of female identity, they open themselves up to charges of being unfeminine. Many women with reproductive problems say that infertility is failure as a mother *and* as a woman. Two women with different experiences talk in these terms:

There is the feeling of not being a proper woman, affecting your image of yourself sexually. And yet at the same time I've never wanted to be a domesticated classical woman. (Woman undergoing treatment for primary infertility)

He has been very interesting. It wasn't through any burning ambition to be a mother, although it was probably fair to say that it was nice to know that, to be trite, that I was a true woman in the sense of the word. Which had never been totally proven to me before, never having had periods regularly. It had to be there, at the back of your mind, can you have a child? (Woman who conceived after treatment for menstrual problems)

Childbirth and motherhood are talked about as achievements by childless women and women with fertility problems as well as parents. A woman who adopted a child considers childbirth a desirable achievement:

I still feel I would have liked to have given birth to her myself. I couldn't love her any more than a child I'd borne myself, but I wish she had come out of my body. . . . There is this feeling that having a baby is something to be proud of, and that you've not achieved it.

A mother of a 5-month-old baby used this idea of childbearing as achievement to describe her reactions to being a mother:

It's made me feel more fulfilled. It's given me something in life; I feel that I've achieved something now. Whereas before, I mean work and everything, maybe it was the jobs I had, but I always felt like I was in a rut and was never achieving anything. But I feel as though I've done something useful: and if I can turn her into a nice person and put her into the world I'll feel that I've really achieved something. (Oakley, 1981, p. 263)

In addition, motherhood is still considered essential if women are to be accepted as having achieved in other areas of their lives. Even in traditional female areas such as nursing or childcare, the ideology of motherhood dictates that women's success should supplement rather than replace motherhood. Many mothers who work outside the home value their work identities but do not see them as interchangeable with or as substitutes for their roles as mothers. One working woman interviewed by Sharpe (1984) sees work and family roles in the following way:

> If my kids were going to suffer, I'd give up work definitely. I think if you're going to work, you have to have your kids, your husband, your house and then your work . . . I think your work has to have its place and it should be last. . . . I put my kids before anyone or anything. (p. 220)

It is often considered that pregnancy is the time when women begin to develop their parental identity. But women's commitment to motherhood as a central aspect of their adult female identity can be seen in young women's aspirations and expectations about their lives (for example, Beckett, 1986; Lees, 1986; Sharpe, 1976). Childless women and those with reproductive problems also provide evidence that the symbolic value of motherhood and the links between motherhood and positive adult female identity often emerge prior to pregnancy. These links suggest that attitudes to having children are developed within a powerful ideological context which influences the adjustments of childless women and those with reproductive problems (Campbell, 1985; Veevers, 1980).

Having children and bringing them up grants women entry into a world of female knowledge and experience and enables them to share a common identity. Going through the same experiences (both good and bad) gives mothers a viewpoint on common concerns. The intense interactions they have with their children make women feel that their lives have purpose and meaning. Women talk about the satisfaction and frustrations they experience as mothers:

> I think I'd sooner be a mother than anything else, although I'm not very good at it and I don't 100% enjoy it. It's very responsible, very important . . . My children are an anchor for me . . . I wasn't responsible for anyone then, but now I am. . . . Now I feel I've got a purpose in life. . . . It's worth all the heartache and annoyance and trouble being a mother. (Boulton, 1983, p. 59)

> I suppose you've got a slight mystique about you once you've had a baby, which I think people had for me before I had one. And to people who HAVE got babies, you've joined the club so to speak – excuse the pun! (Oakley, 1981, p. 263)

Sometimes these shared experiences do not look so attractive:

> But I'd like to have more varied company sometimes. People with interests other than my own. Your friends tend to be leading the same kind of life as you lead, so the same daily happenings are happening to them as well. (Boulton, 1983, p. 89)

Their exclusion from the 'freemasonry of the fertile' (Monarch, 1991) is a major regret for some childless women and those with fertility problems, who sometimes wonder how they find a purpose and a structure for their lives.

> One of the things I felt is that if you have children you become part of the human race. When I started to think about doing it, one of the complex things that made me want to, was that there would be a whole lot of things that I could share, that it would give an enormous amount in common with most other people that otherwise you don't have. (Woman undergoing treatment for primary infertility)

Establishment of intimate relationships

Motherhood is often valued because of the opportunities it provides for the establishment of intimate relationships through women's relationships with their children and also through their relationships with others.

Mother–child relationship The mother–child relationship has great practical and symbolic significance for women. Psychological accounts reinforce the centrality of primary group ties and enjoyment, interest and fun as major reasons for having children, giving mothers the opportunity for caring and nurturance and the expression of love and affection. This is expressed thus by Sharpe (1984): 'Women's caring activities and their close relationships with their children mean that they have intense interaction with people they love, which can be very satisfying and meaningful' (p. 222). Children provide a context in which it is possible, and indeed is considered essential, for parents to show affection and commitment (Busfield, 1974; Newson and Newson, 1976). There may be few other opportunities for adults to express the warm, caring and selfless side of themselves (Antonucci and Mikus, 1988; Salmon, 1985). A mother makes this clear:

> The only people I can say I love with any sense of confidence are my children. I can say that because I feel more security about my feelings for, and obligations to them than I do about anyone else. (Wandor, 1980, p. 141)

This is reinforced by a woman undergoing treatment for primary infertility:

> The idea of bringing up a child is very appealing. Part of it is extremely selfish, wanting to, feeling sure that I could be a reasonably decent mother and also feeling somehow that I've got a lot of love to give.

Motherhood also provides women with long-lasting, continuous and intimate relationships. A woman who had children after infertility investigations describes this:

> I have detected in most people the need to find something fixed and long term in their lives, something that they could devote most of their energies to. It could be a job or an ideal. I suppose I have chosen people to devote my life to. (Wileman, 1980, p. 225)

Children offer a source of stimulation and fun, interest and variety in life. Mothers say that they thought their lives would be less satisfying emotionally without children and much more dull (Busfield, 1974). Fun is referred to by a woman undergoing treatment for primary infertility and being considered for adoption:

> I know all the disadvantages of children. I think it's because I have a fairly realistic view of what children are all about. I'm prepared to put up with the bad because they're a lot of fun and because we could give them a nice home and because I know that Michael is very good with children. *Want to be a part of such a relationship*

Children also allow an opportunity to view the world through the eyes of their child and to be childlike (Antonucci and Mikus, 1988). A mother can, at least temporarily, re-enter the world of childhood. Through intimate contact with their child, mothers get a glimpse into children's worlds and 'something of the freshness, the wonder, the delights of living as a child – as well as the keenness of childish griefs and troubles' (Salmon, 1985, p. 53).

The dilemma for childless women and those with reproductive problems is that the opportunities provided and the needs fulfilled by motherhood cannot readily be met elsewhere; not having a child may restrict women's opportunities to engage in close intimate and long-term relationships (Antonucci and Mikus, 1988). Sharing childcare, babysitting, being a committed aunt or friend does not involve women in the arguments, frustrations and disappointments which are as much the bases of intimate and long-lasting relationships as are affection, fun and harmony. The difficulty of replacing a relationship with an own child is one reason why infertile women show persistence in their attempts to achieve biological motherhood, in spite of the stresses and personal costs involved in medical investigations.

Relationships with partner and the wider family For married women and women in long-term relationships, the value of children for their relationships as couples is clearly articulated. The comments of childless women, women with fertility problems and parents reported by Oakley (1981) and Michaels (1988) all suggest that this is a very powerful reason for wanting children.

For some women having a child is a fairly explicit part of their plans for their life together. A woman undergoing treatment for primary infertility expressed this view:

> We both badly want children. I was certainly looking for someone who would be a father as well as a husband. He was certainly looking for a mother for his children as well as a wife. We both agreed that we badly wanted children and immediately. But I did think, just before we were married, hang on, suppose we don't have children, do I want to be with him anyway. I decided that I did.

Another woman undergoing investigations for primary infertility makes a similar point:

> Before the marriage, if he'd said he didn't want to have children, I'd have had to think very hard about it. One of the things I did think at that time was that a child was vital to the completeness of the marriage, a child was a vital glue. In a way it's been such a relief that it hasn't proved to be so at all. From my husband's point of view, a child was not an issue when we first got married.

Women's ideas reflect commonly held beliefs that children make a marriage happier and less susceptible to divorce (Busfield, 1974; Monarch, 1991).

Other women's desires for children were expressed more in terms of their relationships with their partners. A child may be seen as a public acknowledgement of a couple's commitment to one another, and a physical demonstration of the couple's love for one another or a gift from one partner to the other (Payne, 1978). A women in her second marriage makes this point:

> In a way I just wanted to give him something. Having been in a bad marriage, he has brought me so much contentment, that I wanted this for him. I think my desire to have a baby is 60% for him and 40% for me. I did feel I was failing him dreadfully. I did feel strongly it might affect the relationship later.

When AID (artificial insemination by donor) is suggested as a form of treatment or a woman approaches an adoption agency, expectations about a child resulting from the couple's relationship and the relative importance of biological and social aspects of parenthood have to be dealt with. Encountering such issues makes women with reproductive problems aware of some of the assumptions around motherhood.

> Giving birth would be an important part of my relationship with the child, but more than that, I would want my husband's child, which was something I hadn't appreciated before I got married. Now it seems of overriding importance that it's his baby I would be having. But we may change . . . (Woman undergoing investigations for primary infertility)

Dealing with such difficult issues may place considerable stress on relationships, as a woman undergoing treatment for secondary infertility makes clear:

> I think you have to look at the effect it's having on the people around you. If it's going to affect your marriage negatively, then you have to think very hard about it. My husband was always very good. Before we had our first child, because although he was very upset, he said 'I married you and that's what I want. If we have a child that will be wonderful.'

Childlessness and fertility problems also have implications for women's relationships with their wider families. Having children ensures family continuity and gives women status in their families. Women's parents often yearn for grandchildren and concerns about their feelings and reactions are sometimes voiced (Campbell, 1985). Not having a child, whether through choice or because of fertility problems, means risking parental disapproval and/or disappointment.

> To some extent one has had one's visions of having children and having a married life, and one is under certain pressures. His parents would be very uplifted by the arrival of a grandchild. There are subtle pressures there. (Woman having treatment for primary infertility)

> It is extremely difficult for me as well as painful to live with the knowledge that I willingly . . . never provided my mother with the new family and the grandchildren she was sure would appear, which she thought were her right to expect . . . Equally painful can be the excitement of parents when they inform the childless daughter of the birth of a friend's grandchild. I have heard this kind of excitement in my mother's voice, and have often resented the fact that nothing that I could achieve would elicit that tone of voice, that kind of lasting, enduring satisfaction. (Klepfisz, 1980, pp. 24–5)

The negative image of childlessness

A second theme which comes over consistently from the accounts of childless women and those with fertility problems is the negative image of childlessness. The terms for childlessness, like infertile, barren and sterile, are derogatory, implying a failure not merely in reproductive terms but as women. The lives of childless women are seen as empty, lacking the fulfilment and warmth motherhood brings. The strength of this negative image can be seen in the way in which childless people become legitimate targets for questions about their fertility as well as for disapproval of their relative affluence, as Busfield (1974) indicates:

Childless couples are liable to a variety of strictures implicitly condemning their behaviour. One argument uses the idea that children reduce a couple's freedom to suggest that married couples without children cannot cope with such restrictions and are somehow less mature and less adequate than those who can . . . Similarly, spending on consumer durables and evening entertainment, though generally regarded as pleasurable, desirable and a symbol of status, becomes reprehensible if substituted for childbearing. (p. 17)

One attraction of motherhood, therefore, is that it means a release from a negative identity, whatever the problems and difficulties involved in being a mother. This negative image of childlessness is based on a number of assumptions about childless women and those with fertility problems, including their psychological adequacy, their ability to engage in close intimate relationships and their social positions.

Psychological inadequacy

Childless women are believed to reject or to fail to reach the ultimate and proper goal for all women and hence must be mad, inadequate or somehow at odds with themselves and society. Their inadequacy is then sometimes used to explain their infertility and, indirectly, to emphasize the normality of motherhood: some women are seen to fail to conceive or to maintain a pregnancy because they are overanxious, because they reject their femininity or are not well adjusted (Callan and Hennessey, 1989; Cook et al., 1989).

This approach underlies psychological and psychoanalytic discussions of infertility, as illustrated by the following statements:

Woman have a better chance to achieve completion of their physical and emotional maturation through motherhood than they have if motherhood is denied to them. (Benedek, 1952, quoted in Notman and Nadelson, 1982)

As Harlow's disturbed monkeys could neither reproduce nor effectively nurture, that seems true for people too. It is as though to some extent one of nature's fail-safe mechanisms is infertility in those who are not psychologically healthy enough to nurture . . . Thus the potential or pre-disposition to reproduce and to parent seems a normal human development but, responsive to stress, it may not be part of the behavioural repertoire of disturbed individuals, groups or cultures. (Bardwick, 1974, p. 58)

This assumption of psychological inadequacy comes across as well in some more recent psychological studies. Predominantly studies employ measures of maladjustment or malfunctioning (such as depression, anxiety or sexual and marital problems), with the result that their subjects (usually women going through infertility investigations) are seen as more or less disturbed (for example, Connolly et al., 1987; Cook et al., 1989). There has been less interest in identifying successful strategies for coping, or in considering the extent to which evidence drawn from women undergoing infertility investigations can be generalized to childless women and those whose fertility problems are in the past.

Within such a framework it is not surprising that women are very sensitive to any negative reactions they feel and interpret any emotional ups and downs as evidence of their psychological inadequacy (Franklin, 1989; Payne, 1978).

> I said I'm spending too much of my time worrying about it to the exclusion of anything else. I'm becoming obsessed with it. I felt like a flower operating on two petals instead of five. I was so tensed up all the time. (Woman who had stopped treatment for secondary infertility)

> I was pretty desperate to have a child. I used to think about it nonstop. You can't get more desperate than that. I used to moon about. Go into dolly dreams in Mothercare. All the silly things you read about. (Woman who conceived a first child after infertility treatment)

Assumptions about psychological inadequacy also mean that women's attempts to adjust to their infertility may be negatively viewed. Persevering with infertility investigations, for example, is sometimes seen as a demonstration of women's despair or their inability to restructure their lives rather than, for example, as an indication of their commitment. Contradictorily, on other occasions deciding not to undertake in vitro fertilization (IVF) or to accept their infertility is seen as evidence of poor adjustment or lack of persistence (Franklin, 1989; Pfeffer and Woollett, 1987). Their interests and hobbies, holidays and pets are viewed as substitutes for children as they 'strive to fill an empty existence with constant and vacuous activity' (Campbell, 1985, p. 118).

The development of new reproductive technologies such as IVF has made infertility more visible but, unfortunately, has had little impact on understanding of the experience of women with fertility problems or of what motherhood means to women. Rather, the effect has been to reinforce, in both psychological and feminist analyses, the image of infertile women as psychologically inadequate, as desperate to grasp, at whatever cost, the possibilities offered by these new technologies (Franklin, 1989; Stanworth, 1987).

The stigma of infertility and the perceived inadequacy of women with reproductive problems means that women who do not have children often feel isolated. Those who try to explain their position or seek help from others may encounter anger, pity, evasion or misunderstanding (Veevers, 1980). A woman who has chosen to remain childless describes such difficulties:

> Now I don't bother saying anything unless they say something because I have had some arguments with people . . . they very condescendingly say, 'Oh when I was young I thought that. I've got three lovely boys now'. That's the most common, a patronising attitude. 'Oh you'll change your mind when you get older. I thought that but now I've got my children I wouldn't do without them and I don't know how I existed before.' (Campbell, 1985, p. 107)

One cost of disclosing infertility can be to be pitied or patronized. Here one woman expresses her regrets at telling friends and colleagues that she was going for infertility investigations:

> It's a very tricky issue talking to people about it. You feel more vulnerable. Now they know and they'll have a different image of you. You wish you hadn't betrayed yourself. But you let go in moments of weakness, when you feel defenceless and upset.

Conclusions

The meanings, practices and ideologies around motherhood are salient not only for mothers but also for childless women and those with fertility problems. Motherhood is important in all women's lives, whether or not they are or want to be mothers, because women are defined in terms of their relationship to motherhood. Women who do not become mothers are viewed negatively and have to account for their failure to achieve or their rejection of a social position to which, it is assumed, all heterosexual women in stable relationships aspire.

Having children and being a mother has meanings at a variety of levels – symbolic, psychological and interpersonal – and these meanings interrelate in complex ways. Through their marginal position and the pressures on them to explain their lack of adherence to the rules around reproduction, childless women and those with reproductive problems provide an important source of data about the reasons for wanting to be mothers, the inter-relationships between the different layers of meaning, the costs and rewards of motherhood and the constraints on women's choices.

Some meanings of motherhood are articulated by mothers and by women who are not mothers. These include the sense of achievement and identity which motherhood brings. In contrast, others are articulated more clearly by childless women and women with fertility problems. They point to some of the meanings and ideologies around motherhood which, because they form such an integral part of the context in which women become mothers and bring up children, are less often and less fully discussed. These include the ways in which motherhood links women socially and emotionally with others and provides a structure for women's lives.

Infertility investigations are the experience of a significant proportion of women with reproductive problems. Facing up to their own or their partner's infertility means that women may have to make decisions about, and therefore become more conscious of, different but closely related facets of motherhood. These include biological (conceiving, carrying a pregnancy to term, giving birth), psychological (identity and self-esteem), interpersonal (relationships with children, partner, parents, the wider family, friends and the community), and socio-cultural (their positions in society, attitudes to women, social and economic context of motherhood) aspects of motherhood. The variability in women's reactions to investigative techniques related to infertility and to adoption suggests that it is important not to allow assumptions about the normality of motherhood to mask differences in women's feelings, attitudes and reactions.

Analyses of women's reactions and adjustments to childlessness and reproductive problems indicate the structural limitations on their choices. They also point to assumptions that employment and other adult identities should be chosen in addition to rather than as replacements for motherhood. Within these limitations, a major task for childless women and women with fertility problems is one of maintaining a positive self-image of themselves as adults and as women.

Note

I would like to thank Naomi Pfeffer for all her help and support with the study of women's experiences of infertility. Special thanks are due to the many infertile and childless women who gave readily of their time to recount their experiences and who helped us to formulate our ideas and encouraged us to write about infertility and childlessness.

References

Antonis, B. (1981) Motherhood and mothering. In Cambridge University Women's Studies Group (eds), *Women in Society: Interdisciplinary Essays*. London: Virago.

Antonucci, T.C. and Mikus, K. (1988) The power of parenthood: personality and attitudinal changes during the transition to parenthood. In G.Y. Michaels and

W.A. Goldberg (eds), *Transition to Parenthood: Current Theory and Research*. London: Cambridge University Press.

Baker, D. (1989) Social identity in the transition to motherhood. In S. Skevington and D. Baker (eds), *The Social Identity of Women*. London: Sage.

Bardwick, J. (1974) Evolution and parenting. *Journal of Social Issues* 30, 39–62.

Beckett, H. (1986) Adolescent identity development. In S. Wilkinson (ed.), *Feminist Social Psychology*. Milton Keynes: Open University Press.

Boulton, M.G. (1983) *On Being a Mother: a Study of Women with Preschool Children*. London: Tavistock.

Bromham, D.R., Bryce, F.C., Balmer, B. and Wright, S. (1989) Psychometric evaluation of infertile couples (preliminary findings). *Journal of Reproductive and Infant Psychology* 7, 195–202.

Busfield, J. (1974) Ideologies and reproduction. In M.P.M. Richards (ed.), *Integration of the Child into a Social World*. Cambridge: Cambridge University Press.

Busfield, J. (1987) Parenting and parenthood. In G. Cohen (ed.), *Social Change and the Life Course*. London: Tavistock.

Callan, V.J. (1985) Perceptions of parents, the voluntarily and involuntarily childless: a multi-dimensional scaling analysis. *Journal of Marriage and Family* 47, 1045–50.

Callan, V.J. and Hennessey, J.F. (1989) Psychological adjustment to infertility: a unique comparison of two groups of infertile women, mothers and women childless by choice. *Journal of Reproductive and Infant Psychology* 7, 105–12.

Campbell, E. (1985) *The Childless Marriage: an Exploratory Study of Couples Who Do Not Want Children*. London: Tavistock.

Connolly K.J., Edelmann, R.J. and Cooke, I.D. (1987) Distress and marital problems associated with infertility. *Journal of Reproductive and Infant Psychology* 5, 49–57.

Cook, R., Parsons, J., Mason, B. and Golombok, S. (1989) Emotional, marital and sexual functioning in patients embarking upon IVF and AID treatment for infertility. *Journal of Reproductive and Infant Psychology* 7, 87–94.

Dowrick, S. and Grundberg, S. (eds) (1980) *Why Children?* London: Women's Press.

Fawcett, J.T. (1988) The value of children and the transition to parenthood. *Marriage and Family Review* 12, 12–34.

Franklin, S. (1989) Deconstructing 'desperateness': the social construction of infertility in popular representations of new reproductive technologies. In M. McNeil, I. Varcoe and S. Yearsley (eds), *The New Reproductive Technologies*. London: Macmillan.

Gerson, M.J. (1980) The lure of motherhood. *Psychology of Women Quarterly* 5, 207–18.

Griffin, C. (1985) *Typical Girls: Young Women from School to the Job Market*. London: Routledge.

Hoffman, L.W. (1975) The value of children to parents and the decrease in family size. *Proceedings of American Philosophical Society* 119, 430–8.

Klepfisz, I. (1980) In S. Dowrick and S. Grundberg (eds), *Why Children?* London: Women's Press.

Lees, S. (1986) *Losing Out: Sexuality and Adolescent Girls*. London: Hutchinson.

Mahlstedt, P.P. (1985) The psychological component of infertility. *Fertility and Sterility* 43, 335–46.

Michaels, G.Y. (1988) Motivational factors in the decision and timing of pregnancy. In G.Y. Michaels and W.A. Goldberg (eds), *Transition to Parenthood: Current Theory and Research*. London: Cambridge University Press.

Monarch, J. (1991) *Childless-no-choice*. London: Routledge.

Newson, J. and Newson, E. (1976) *Seven Years Old in the Home Environment*. Harmondsworth: Penguin.

Notman, M. and Nadelson, C. (1982) Changing views of the relationship between femininity and reproduction. In C.C. Nadelson and M.T. Notman (eds), *The Woman Patient*, vol. 2: *Concepts of Femininity and the Life Cycle*. New York: Plenum.

Oakley, A. (1980) *Women Confined: Towards a Sociology of Childbirth*. Oxford: Martin Robertson.

Oakley, A. (1981) *From Here to Maternity: Becoming a Mother*. Harmondsworth: Penguin.

Payne, J. (1978) Talking about children: an examination of accounts about reproduction and family life. *Journal of Biosocial Science* 10, 367–74.

Pfeffer, N. and Woollett, A. (1983) *The Experience of Infertility*. London: Virago.

Pfeffer, N. and Woollett, A. (1987) The presentation of infertility: how they present us. *Jewish Association of Fostering and Adoption Newsletter* 12, 5–8.

Rapoport, R., Rapoport, R.N. and Strelitz, Z. (1977) *Fathers, Mothers and Others*. London: Routledge and Kegan Paul.

Salmon, P. (1985) *Living in Time: a New Look at Personal Development*. London: Dent.

Sharpe, S. (1976) *Just Like a Girl*. Harmondsworth: Penguin.

Sharpe, S. (1984) *Double Identity: The Lives of Working Mothers*. Harmondsworth: Penguin.

Stanworth, M. (ed.) (1987) *Reproductive Technologies: Gender, Motherhood and Medicine*. Cambridge: Polity Press.

Steinberg, D.L. (1989) The depersonalisation of women through the administration of 'in vitro fertilization'. In M. McNeil, I. Varcoe and S. Yearsley (eds), *The New Reproductive Technologies*. London: Macmillan.

Veevers, J.E. (1980) *Childless by Choice*. Toronto: Butterworths.

Wandor, M. (1980) In S. Dowrick and S. Grundberg (eds), *Why Children?* London: Women's Press.

Wileman, A. (1980) In S. Dowrick and S. Grundberg (eds), *Why Children?* London: Women's Press.

Woollett, A. (1985) Childlessness: strategies for coping with infertility. *International Journal of Behavioural Development* 8, 473–82.

4

The Social Construction of Motherhood: An Analysis of Childcare and Parenting Manuals

Harriette Marshall

Current orthodoxies of good mothering have been frequently challenged by feminists, who have argued that such notions are the product of the social, historical and political context (Riley, 1983; Weedon, 1987). A number of accounts detailing the conflicting and frequently contradictory meanings of motherhood have now been produced by women writing as mothers rather than as professionals. These accounts question the prevailing assumption that motherhood is women's 'natural' biological destiny and locate it within the context of the current organization of social relations and organization of employment (Breen, 1989; Gieve, 1989).

Research has documented how the meaning of motherhood has changed through history and across cultures (Arnup et al., 1990; Fildes, 1990). Urwin (1985) examined how the categories 'mother' and 'child' have been produced historically through the circulation of discourses linked to institutionalized practices and showed how particular conceptualizations of motherhood have been constructed as 'natural' at certain times. Kitzinger (1978) argued that professionals, both doctors and psychologists, attempt to impose styles of mothering which are culture-bound and can be seen to reflect preoccupations linked to fashions in childrearing. Specific processes said to be essential to mothering have been examined, for example, the importance placed on a mother's 'bonding' with her new infant. Arney (1980) argues that although the research on bonding is methodologically flawed it is used both to maintain certain hospital practices, and at the same time serves the ideological function of keeping women as the primary caretakers in the home, thereby justifying the existing patriarchal social order. These research examples show the importance of examining notions of 'motherhood' in specific social and historical contexts and in terms of ideological functions.

When a woman becomes pregnant she is exposed to a variety

of ideas about pregnancy, childbirth and childcare. The 1960s and 1970s saw an increase in Western societies in medical intervention in childbirth, giving doctors and professionals in related areas greater confidence in their expertise around psychological aspects of development and the mother–child relationship. In line with this 'medicalization' of childbirth and childcare, increasing numbers of manuals are produced which are, for the most part, directed at first-time mothers. It is suggested that most mothers in Western countries, at some point, consult at least one of these childcare or motherhood manuals (Clarke-Stewart, 1978).

Some of these manuals focus on the antenatal period and give advice to parents up to the birth of the baby, whereas others are more ambitious and provide information and developmental guidelines for parents from conception through to the care of adolescents. This chapter examines the ways in which childcare manuals represent and discuss the experience of motherhood. Consideration is given to the way 'motherhood' is constructed by the medical and psychological 'professionals', looking in particular at the prescriptions attached to being a 'mother', how a 'good mother' should behave, the responsibilities she should fulfil and the aims she should have in mind as she brings up her children. The manuals examined in this study have been selected on the basis that they sell extensively in the UK and include some consideration of women as mothers rather than focusing purely on the child's development.

The manuals selected for the study were: Gordon Bourne, *Pregnancy* (1979); Hugh Jolly, *Book of Child Care* (1986); Penelope Leach, *Baby and Child* (1988); the National Childbirth Trust, *Pregnancy and Parenthood* (1987); Benjamin Spock, *Dr Spock's Baby and Child Care* (1988, 40th edition); Penny Stanway, *The Mothercare Guide to Child Health* (1988); and Miriam Stoppard, *Baby Care Book* (1983). With the exception of Penelope Leach, who is a psychologist, the writers are all doctors. A discourse analytic approach is used to examine the recurrent themes and constructions of motherhood in these manuals.

Discourse analysis: theory and method

Discourse analysis takes language as the site for the investigation of social phenomena. Using this approach, language is *not* taken as a straightforward description or reflection of the social world but as actively constructing versions of the social world. Given that the same phenomena could be described in a number of ways, discourse analysis examines social texts, both spoken and written, to see which linguistic constructions are selected and which are omitted. Further, consideration is given to the function of the particular linguistic constructions, both in terms of explicit functions and also broader ideological consequences.

Discourse analysis can contribute to our understanding of the ways in which motherhood is socially constructed, allowing consideration of the ideological functions of these particular constructions. This approach has received considerable attention within psychology over the past few years (Parker, 1988; Potter and Wetherell, 1987). Examples of discourse analysis can be seen in Hollway's research (1989), which examines the reproduction of gender differences in adult relations, and Marshall and Wetherell's analysis (1989) of lawyers' constructs of their work-related identity and self-image. In this chapter written accounts as produced in a number of childcare and parenting manuals are examined, looking at the recurring linguistic patterns used by medical and psychological professionals to construct 'motherhood'. Consideration is given to the clash between the simplified, unambiguous construction of the 'ideal' mother with alternative accounts which stress the ambiguous, complex meanings of motherhood. Attention is also paid to the implications for mothers of having a prescribed model against which to judge and assess their own mothering.

Motherhood as 'ultimate fulfilment'

One of the key accounts emerging from study of the manuals is the description and evaluation of motherhood as satisfying and important. The experience of childbirth, having a newborn baby and the process of childcare are all described in exalted terms. It is emphasized that this is a special experience, being essentially creative and positive. According to the manuals, women feel excitement and indeed should look forward to their new baby. Although they might also feel anxious and uncertain about how to perform their new role, the primary sensations are joyful anticipation. The end result is ultimate fulfilment for women which can be gained in no other way (see chapter 3). The Ultimate Fulfilment account can be seen clearly in the following extracts, which suggest that not only is childbearing the best way to become properly human, but that having a child *for* a man is emotionally fulfilling for a woman.

> Some women are eager to meet the challenge of motherhood which for them brings immense fulfilment and is the ultimate process whereby they become complete human beings. (Bourne, p. 421)

> As a mother holds her new baby in her arms she also experiences a
> sensation of emotional and physical fulfilment that here at last is what
> she has been waiting to see and she is also emotionally fulfilled by
> producing a child for the man she loves. (Bourne, p. 8)

Stanway, however, by her admonition to take pleasure in motherhood, suggests that ultimate fulfilment of motherhood is not as
straightforward and unproblematic as the more upbeat statements
indicate. But she implies that even women who do not take
immediately to motherhood ultimately revise their priorities and,
through engaging in an understanding of their child's development, find the rewards of motherhood.

> Remember to take pleasure in mothering . . . It's one of the most creative
> processes you will ever be involved in, and sometimes it will tax you to
> your limits. But most women say that in spite of the many difficult times,
> the high quality of the good times creates a positive and rewarding
> experience that most of them would want to repeat. (Stanway, p. 20)

Mother love as natural

This account establishes that the key ingredient of motherhood is
love between mother and child. It is characterized as 'natural',
'taken for granted' that mothers feel love for their children, not
necessarily at once, but in time. This love is said to be hard to
hold back, ready to 'burst out', it is 'total' and if it is not
immediately present this is not cause for concern because it will
inevitably grow. While the joy of *parenting* is discussed, the
manuals suggest a special relationship between mother and child,
and *maternal* love is emphasized. This is explicitly stated in some
of the manuals as resulting from feeling the baby move during
pregnancy, or as arising in the first few days following the
experience of childbirth.

> But in any case don't be surprised if you don't have the burst of
> maternal feelings towards your baby which everyone has led you to
> expect. It takes time to fall in love with your baby and many mothers
> feel unnecessarily guilty because they don't love their babies totally at
> first. Later on they seem to forget this point and fail to pass it on to
> new mothers. Presumably because their later total love for the child
> suppresses the earlier feelings. (Jolly, p. 46)

> Of course mothers do love their babies. Of course love does make
> much of the business of mothering possible and enjoyable. But interest
> in a baby and loving mothering of that baby go together. Interest in
> the processes of his development makes one look and listen closely,
> and it is by watching and listening that one sees the signs of his dawn-
> ing attachment, his love, which reinforce one's own. (Leach, p. 16)

Clearly then, this discourse presents motherhood as fulfilling, creative and characterized by loving. The way that the accounts of Ultimate Fulfilment and Mother Love as Natural work together unproblematically can be seen in the following extract.

> Of course parents don't have children because they want to be martyrs, or at least they shouldn't. They have them because they love children and want some of their very own. They also love children because they remember being loved so much by their parents in their own childhood. Taking care of their children, seeing them grow and develop into fine people, gives most parents – despite the hard work – their greatest satisfaction in life. This is creation. This is our visible immortality. Pride in other worldly accomplishments is usually weak in comparison. (Spock, p. 23)

In the first part of this extract the assumption is made that the relationship between parent and child is characterized as loving, that the parents already love children in general terms *and* that their own relationship with their parents was a loving one. In the second half the satisfaction and fulfilment derived from the experience of parenting is emphasized as being greater than any other satisfaction, but denies the variety of reasons women might have for wanting to be mothers and circumstances such as employment, financial considerations and relations with the child's father (if available) which makes such total romantic involvement difficult to sustain.

The 'unnatural mother'

Having identified the way that the Ultimate Fulfilment account constructs the experiences of the 'natural' mother unproblematically, in essentially positive terms, the manuals can be examined to see whether they allow any ambiguity or negative associations to be included in the construction of motherhood. It is clear that they only allow minor deviations from a positive account. Temporary mood swings are permissible shortly following birth but 'real' depression renders women 'unnatural mothers' and beyond the scope of the manuals.

While the meanings and prevalence of different forms of depression associated with childbirth have been examined by a number of researchers (Nicolson, 1986; Oakley, 1980), some manuals omit any mention of depression. Miriam Stoppard, for example, fails to give any consideration to post-natal depression, thereby denying that women may respond negatively to motherhood. The other manuals make a clear distinction between different types of depression, contrasting the 'blues' with 'real depression'. Depression as experienced soon after the birth (described by the belittling term the 'blues') is said to be 'natural' and experienced by most mothers. The impact of the blues is played down; they are said to be 'acute' but not long-lasting.

> 'Baby blues' or 'fourth-day blues' are not an inevitable part of the post-natal days, but they are very common. If your baby has to be in an incubator away from you, or has even the mildest problem – such as jaundice – that will be the focus for your misery. But even if you had an easy delivery, have a beautiful healthy baby and cannot think of any reason for being miserable, you can suddenly find yourself in floods of tears. Don't let those tears frighten you. And don't decide that because you are crying you must be unhappy. Tears of this sort spring partly from hormonal chaos as your body struggles to adapt to not being pregnant any more and to making milk. If you calmly let them flow – even weep luxuriously into your partner's neck – they will probably stop as suddenly as they began. (Leach, p. 43)

> After the birth the placenta is discarded and a rapid drop in the progesterone takes place. The hormonal system then lives in a temporary state of imbalance. Many women experience 'blues' in this period, with tears alternating with excitement and awe. These rapid and bewildering changes of mood may last for a few days, but with loving care, understanding and quiet confidence in your partner and attendants, you may find yourself settling down. (National Childbirth Trust, p. 262)

As the extracts suggest, the 'blues', experienced by a majority of women, are either inexplicable, irrational, 'women's troubles' or they are explained in terms of women being at the mercy of their hormones, experiencing hormonal 'imbalance' or 'chaos'. The remedies given are supposedly simple and non-medical; women should put themselves in the hands of their partner and 'settle down'. The possibility that some women may not have a partner is not admitted. The 'blues' are thus incorporated into the construction of 'natural' motherhood. The account places a different emphasis and genesis on 'real', long-lasting depression, which is described as an illness necessitating consultation with a doctor. This sets up a different kind of mother, the abnormal mother, the woman as 'faulty machine' (Dalton, 1980) who does not adapt to her baby unproblematically.

> While most women adapt very well to motherhood, a small number, through no fault of their own, suffer from post-natal depression in varying degrees of severity. Medical help should always be sought for this condition. (National Childbirth Trust, p. 242)

> Post-natal depression is not the same as the temporary mood-swings of the first days after birth. It can overwhelm you at any stage in your baby's first months and last for a long time. Depression is a real illness

> . . . So, if you should suffer from post-natal depression, you will need medical, practical and emotional help and quickly. (Leach, p. 44)

> If the depression does not lift in a few days or if it is becoming worse, you should promptly get in touch with a psychiatrist, through your regular doctor. (Spock, p. 32)

This account characterizes women who experience negative feelings as 'ill'. This effectively ignores consideration of the social context of mothering which can lead to feelings of depression. These include dissatisfaction with the treatment received in hospital, difficulties with employment prospects, financial situation and the extent to which a woman's partner (or other members of her social network) are able to offer support and get involved in childcare (Oakley, 1980).

The cumulative effect of the Ultimate Fulfilment account is to construct 'natural' motherhood in positive, rewarding terms characterized by love between mother and baby and to deny that 'natural' mothers may have negative feelings or reaction. This experience is thus constructed as unproblematically 'fulfilling' and effortlessly taking its own course.

[handwritten margin note: I expect lots of that!]

How to be a modern mother

Having outlined how motherhood is constructed as being an unquestionably positive experience, attention is now focused on how the manuals see good mothering. Here a number of contradictions are evident. While all the manuals state that flexibility in approach is perfectly satisfactory, they clearly set out the nuclear family as being the best context for childrearing and lay down prescriptions for how mothers should behave towards their babies and their partners within the family. Three accounts, Flexibility, Happy Families and Sharing the Caring, are now examined in turn, with regard to both the implicit and explicit functions of the accounts and the inherent contradictions between them.

Anything goes: the flexible approach

The Flexibility account states that women can mother in many varied and satisfactory ways and that there is no *one* right way within the context of a loving and caring relationship. It suggests that almost 'anything goes' in terms of childrearing and that a limitless range of individual differences in childcare beliefs and practices will not be detrimental to the child.

> Do whatever suits you: so long as your baby is loved, fed and washed he will be alright. (Jolly, p. 127)

We know for a fact that the natural loving care that kindly parents give their children is a hundred times more valuable than their knowing how to pin a diaper on just right or how to eat at sensible hours and later learn good table manners. (Spock, p. 1)

Mothering and fathering are a matter of common sense and individual taste. There are few right or wrong ways to do things, just as there is no standard way of being a daughter, wife, son or husband. (National Childbirth Trust, p. 203)

So even though this book is not designed to tell mothers how to rear their babies, but how their babies develop, and therefore what they need, I hope it will help mothers to find ways of doing the job so that life is as satisfactory as possible for the infant and therefore as easy as possible for themselves. (Leach, p. 18)

However, while the Flexibility account 'plays down' the advice given in the manuals, it is clear that there are certain 'rules' that a good mother should follow. The first rule made explicit in some manuals is that mothers should look to the experts for guidelines and that the experience passed on by other mothers is not sufficient. Commonsense, contrary to what the NCT says, is not enough.

The modern mother takes for granted that she will have the advice of experts and will not have to rely on the advice of her mother. The previous generation of mothers may not necessarily be the best advisers of the present generation. (Jolly, p. 1)

At present there are so many gaps in the average woman's knowledge of pregnancy that she is extremely vulnerable to the many old wives' tales, horror stories and unfounded advice which continues to surround motherhood, and there is no comprehensive work to which she can turn to relieve her anxiety and answer her questions. This book is a genuine attempt to fulfil this need. (Bourne, p. vii)

Here it is quite clearly stated that the expert advice from both doctors and psychologists concerning pregnancy and motherhood which is based on observation rather than experience, is more valid than women's experience. The derogatory use of the phrase 'old wives' tales' in the extract from Gordon Bourne illustrates total dismissal of advice given by women speaking as mothers. Here the version of motherhood presented by the experts is constructed as being more valid than any other accounts of motherhood. The implication is that women should not turn to other women but to the experts to tell them what motherhood is all about. Further, a contradiction can be seen in that while, as shown in the Ultimate Fulfilment account, it is said to be 'natural' for mothers to grow to love their children, this is not enough to be a good mother. Mothers need to turn to the experts to find out about 'normal' child development and how to care for children. The 'modern' mother, by implication an informed and concerned mother, is one who listens to the experts and then acts in accordance with their prescriptions.

> Modern antenatal care is designed to ensure that you will have a normal baby and that you yourself will be fit and healthy afterwards, and if you obey these principles you can rest assured that nothing will harm your baby. (Bourne, p. 25)

> Today's doctors no longer sit on a pedestal doling out orders to their patients. They must have your partnership as parents if they are to get your child well as quickly as possible, and then help you to keep him well. (Jolly, p. 3)

So, the 'experts' writing the manuals might initially appear to 'play themselves down', but on closer examination they consider that they *do* know better than the 'old wives'. Today's mothers should turn in the first instance to the medical experts, the doctors, obstetricians and health visitors and then later to psychological advisers. If a mother is efficient and obeys their advice, then her child's well-being is apparently assured. This constructs the medical experts as possessing almost god-like powers when, as the rates of handicap, perinatal death and obstetric complications indicate, doctors cannot guarantee, even to 'good mothers', a perfect baby.

Happy families: mother, child and father

A second contradiction to the notion of flexibility can be seen in the approach which views mothers as operating most effectively within the structure of the 'family'. This can be called the Happy Families account. The happy family, supposedly a nuclear family, is presented as both unequivocally desirable and enduringly stable.

> The basic family unit as we know it today has been found in every race or tribe since people first inhabited the earth. The family has been, and still is, the cornerstone of society and its main function is to create a secure environment in which children can be raised. There is no-one to whom the family is more important than a baby; it forms his or her entire universe. (Stoppard, p. 9)

> It's my belief that children need the interest, the help, the support, the teaching, the counselling and the love of fathers. Certainly in matters of discipline, both parents are needed because families should make important decisions as a unit, and children should see both their parents taking an interest in and making decisions about the important times in their lives. (Stoppard, p. 14)

History is drawn on to establish stability and the enduring nature of the family as the best site for childrearing. This is despite statistics suggesting that at any one time about one in seven children are being brought up in a household with only one parent (NCOPF, 1990). The emphasis on the desirability of mothers operating within the nuclear family is seen particularly clearly as alternative household arrangements are not mentioned, or are 'put down' as aberrations or inherently problematic. Single parents have to perform their job as childrearers doubly well and take it even more seriously than parents in nuclear families because they are setting up obstacles to the 'normal' development of their children. Spock expresses particular concern about the problems for young boys growing up without fathers.

> Let's take the first example of the boy who has no father . . . If the job is handled well, the child, either boy or girl, can continue to grow up well adjusted . . . The mother can help by being extra hospitable to male relatives, sending her son or daughter to a camp that has some male counsellors, picking a school, if she has the choice, that has some male teachers, encouraging a child to join clubs and other organisations that have male leaders . . . The temptation of the mother . . . is to make him her closest spiritual companion, getting him interested in her particular preoccupations, hobbies, and tastes. If she succeeds in making her world more appealing to him, easier to get along in than the world of boys . . . then he may grow up precocious with predominantly adult interests (Spock, p. 672)
>
> A parent bringing up children alone has to avoid becoming over possessive and yet, to some extent, has to assume the dual role of mother and father. (Jolly, p. 32)

Hugh Jolly's section on 'the one parent family' is left to the end of the book, just before a section on bereavement. The notion of 'single' here assumes that women were once married and that divorce or death of a parent ended the relationship; the conceptualization is limited by not including women who have children outside the context of any permanent relationship. The section is devoted to negative consequences, and the difficulties for children and parents of living in structures other than the nuclear family are stressed. The implication is thus that 'singleness' is fraught with problems and is an 'abnormal' state. Other manuals make no explicit statement on the family but the language used throughout assumes that parents are a heterosexual couple. The implication is that children 'need' this family base of two parents, and will be lacking in certain ways if they do not have it, hence making marginal or problematic the experiences of a considerable number of women.

Within the family structure the mother's responsibilities for children are presented as clearly primary. The father's role might be stated as important, but it is not crucial to the provision of daily care, being rather that of provider of financial support for mothers' and children's material needs. The prescriptions go further in constructing the 'modern' mother. It is not sufficient simply to live within the nuclear family; mothers must act both as mother and as wife. No longer an independent woman, her responsibility is first to her baby.

> You may never actually enjoy your baby except when he is asleep. You can feel physically unattractive, uninterested in sex, and mentally blank. It is natural to feel like this to some extent at this stage, since with a new baby to care for, you must act primarily, if only temporarily, as a mother rather than a wife. You have to be a maternal rather than a sexual figure or an intellectual force, because this is the role nature means you to play for the benefit of your child. (Jolly, p. 129)

Relations between women and their partners are transformed, although there are definite warnings for women to ensure that these changes do not get out of hand and women do not forget their wifely roles.

> When birth is this big event in your life, a number of changes take place: the baby is born, you become a mother, your partner is transformed from lover to father, and a new family begins. (National Childbirth Trust, p. 261)

> So taking the baby's point of view does not mean neglecting yours, the parents', viewpoint. Your interests and his are identical. (Leach, p. 8)

Women are told to put aside their intellectual and sexual identity, in fact to lay aside identities other than mother and wife. Further, a mother's interests are said to be identical to her child's; the two merge in a role for which she is supposedly biologically pre-adapted. Leach's assertion of the identity between the interests of babies and those of their mothers is ingenious because it functions to encourage mothers to give up aspects of their lives without resentment. The manuals then set out the responsibility of the 'good mother' to relate to her child and her husband in specific ways. She must attend to him, ensure that she does not ask too much of him, give him enough time and encouragement to check that he plays his role of father adequately.

> At one end of the scale you may have a woman with a gentle doting partner who is so self indulgent about her vulnerability as a mother that she tricks him into doing everything for her: what starts as constant requests for help can turn, over the months into a full-blown matriarchy and exploitation of the man's good nature. Heavy-handed patriarchs, at the other end of the scale, are not common nowadays,

but if your partner shows this tendency in a way which you feel is damaging to the marriage or to the baby, use your skill and patience to divert him from this role. (National Childbirth Trust, p. 267)

The mother (as if she didn't have enough to do already!) has to remember to pay some attention to her husband. And she should encourage him to share in the care of the baby. (Spock, p. 33)

It should be remembered that men are sometimes neglected when their wives are pregnant and therefore require just as much attention as the new arrival. Every woman should make sure that the new member of the family does not mean that her husband has less of her love, time and affection. (Bourne, p. 143)

Here it can be seen that mothers are responsible for monitoring fathers' behaviour, and ensuring that they behave in certain ways towards the baby. The account gives no consideration to the structural backing given to male authority within the family. Instead the unqualified statement is made that 'heavy-handed patriarchs' are now virtually extinct and that it is up to the individual woman to divert her husband from any behaviour that is destructive to either the marriage or the baby.

Sharing the caring: a family contract
Within the family structure the prescription of Sharing the Caring is stated by all the manuals.

In looking at the needs of the parents the needs of BOTH must be taken into consideration. In this day and age parents can be nothing but equal, and parenting and childrearing must be equally shared. It should be viewed as a contract: you're equally responsible for your child's conception so you should take equal responsibility for rearing him or her. (Stoppard, p. 13)

The National Childbirth Trust take this further. In their emphasis on the mother not monopolizing the baby, much of what is said about the special, intense and natural relationship between mother and baby is undermined.

Some people think that babycare is 'woman's work' and this can cause problems. It may be that the new mother gets pleasure from feeling indispensable, or that she has old fashioned ideas about gender roles. By monopolizing the baby she can frustrate her partner's desire to be a tender and caring father, and can hurt him very much. (National Childbirth Trust, p. 269)

A contradiction can be seen here in that while the manuals state that they are not laying down rules, clearly a moral order is being laid out. Not only must mothers be married, they must also play a sharing role with their partners. This is the ideal, the married couple engaging in shared childcare with mothers taking responsibility for involving fathers, ensuring that fathers are not excluded or allowed to behave unreasonably.

Having outlined sharing as desirable, it can be seen that the notion of sharing does not entail equal time spent with the child, nor equal allocation of childcare tasks. The father's part is to 'be there' at certain salient times, for example at antenatal classes, and at the birth. By implication mothers are to carry out all the 'maintenance' work, the cooking, the shopping, the washing, 'being there' for the baby throughout the day, changing the nappies. Having paid lip service to the value of fathers the account appears to outline the reality of limited childcare from fathers and even to turn it into a virtue. The manuals state that the 'reality' is that most fathers cannot be as involved as mothers, because of the existing social structure. Restricted notions of 'egalitarian' and 'sharing' are being used here.

> Unless your husband is able to take over shopping and cooking or you have someone to help you, stock up with food for easily made meals to see you through the first days at home with your baby. (Jolly, p. 20)

> Even today few fathers are in a position to receive their baby's very first attachment because mundane matters like jobs prevent them from being ever-present, always responsive people. But a father who can accept, support and encourage the unique relationship between his partner and his child will find that there is a unique relationship waiting for him too. (Leach, p. 122)

Spock takes a similar line but does at least recognize that mothers may have commitments outside the family.

> When I said that I thought fathers and mothers had an equal responsibility in child care I didn't mean that they must necessarily put in the same number of hours at it. That decision would depend on several considerations, e.g. family finances, flexibility of each parent's work schedule, as well as the mother's and father's preferences. (Spock, p. 42)

> Some parents may decide on a more radical division of childcare or feel that in their case it is more appropriate that the mother goes to work and the father looks after the child(ren). It can prove difficult to break the traditional role-pattern established in one's own childhood, not only domestically but also in relation to the world outside. A man may feel ill at ease using facilities for children where their attending adults are usually women (for example play groups); when taking a child out the poor provision of social facilities can become all too evident as the need to change a nappy develops into a major problem . . . (National Childbirth Trust, p. 271)

Here then, the good mother is one who unselfishly shares the baby with the father although the meaning of sharing is limited to the most positive aspects of childcare. The social world is presented as conventional, static, resistant to change, inadequate to meet the needs of 'radical' social relationships, thus resulting in the manuals' tacit encouragement of maintaining the status quo. The reasons given for the undesirability of alternative work-sharing are framed in terms of individual fathers' discomfort but mothers' comfort is not discussed. While the traditional division of labour is represented as unproblematic (unless overindulged in by mothers), other 'radical' alternatives are characterized as fraught with consequent difficulties and tensions. So then, while the manuals might refer to 'parents' we are to accept that the 'parent' engaging in everyday childrearing tasks is most likely and indeed *ought* to be the mother, whatever her situation, even when she goes out to work (see chapter 11).

The Happy Families and Sharing the Caring accounts work together to lay down prescriptions which situate mothers in the traditional position of wives and mothers. These accounts work against the notion of flexibility proposed in the manuals, under-cutting any alternative childcare structures by constructing them as problematic.

The active mother monitoring normality

In the Happy Families account the mother is seen in relation to others, to the father, to her new baby and less frequently to her other children. All the manuals discuss the crucial contribution of mothers to their child's 'normal' development. The importance of early maternal care is juxtaposed with the Ultimate Fulfilment account. The ideal mother has to match up to many different criteria. As outlined in the Sharing the Caring account, she is the person who spends considerable amounts of time with her child, but further, this contact needs to be of a certain nature. The mother needs to be stimulating and to facilitate her child's development by providing a safe and secure emotional environ-ment, looking out for any abnormalities and monitoring 'normal progress' against certain behavioural yardsticks. In this respect the mother is told to act as the 'naive scientist', as ally to the psychologists. The emphasis is placed on the 'active' mother.

> In fact it is both natural and necessary for parents to feel partially responsible for their baby's development rather than to wait passively while 'nature takes its course'. It is natural because it prepares you for your total responsibility for your baby once he is born. (Jolly, p. 7)

The importance of the mother's active intervention in her child's development is emphasized because it is assumed that early childhood experiences have a long-lasting effect. The model presented by the parent lays down a pattern for the way children behave as adults. This direct influence of early experience and 'cycles of deprivation' is taken for granted, although both have been questioned within developmental psychology (Clarke and Clarke, 1976; Rutter, 1981).

> Fortunately, most of us bring to this task [bringing up children] the in-built expertise given by our parents in the way they handled us as children. If we were mothered well by our parents we have at least a head start on those whose intellect is the same but whose childhood experiences were less happy. The early years of life are the most vital in laying down an individual's future pattern, . . . as regards whether he is sufficiently secure and well rounded as a personality. (Jolly, p. 1)

Here a clear-cut set of prescriptions is laid out, with all the manuals describing, down to the fine details, how the mother ought to behave to change the 'natural' to the 'normal'. These prescriptions start before the birth of the baby and set out all the ways in which the mother should intervene in her baby's development. The responsibility of the mother for monitoring her child's progress is emphasized because it is said to affect the child's future physical, intellectual, emotional and moral development.

> Children learn to relate to other people by what they experience in their own family. Your relationship with your partner will affect how your child will relate to his or her partner in the future. (Stanway, p. 21)

> One of the most important aspects of parenting is being a model for your developing child . . . As they grow older they will determine their own moral values and their standards from those which are displayed by their parents. (Stoppard, p. 13)

> Whereas a baby, let's say it is a girl, who's cared for by loving, enthusiastic parents (perhaps with the help of others) surges ahead. Some of the things they give her are their visible love, their pride and joy in her tiny accomplishments, thoughtful playthings, answers to her questions and willingness to let her play freely as long as she does no damage. They read to her, show her pictures. These are the attitudes and activities that foster emotional depth and keen intelligence. (Spock, p. 44)

> If you're not sure what you believe or have no spiritual beliefs, it's still worth encouraging your child to consider other people's ideas. You could also try to find a way of developing a broader perspective on life, something that goes on beyond you. You might, for instance, be aware of a sense of wonder at the beauty, majesty and power of nature, or you could entrust yourself to a creative and loving power

even though you don't understand what you're doing. (Stanway, p. 43)

Part of your role will be to teach your child to respect other people's rights and property, and this will be enforced through discipline . . . Very often a child's delinquent act is directed at a neglectful parent with whom he cannot communicate. (Stoppard, p. 13)

Good childrearing is a considerable responsibility. The mother is to be a good role model, presenting a good relationship with her husband, showing high standards, ideals and moral values and developing a 'spiritual awareness' even if she does not know 'what she is doing'. The suggestion is that if the child grows up 'abnormally' in any respect, or has not attained certain goals at the right time then the responsibility lies with the mother. She has obviously not given enough attention to facilitating the 'surging ahead' that *could* take place. As Urwin (1985) points out, the idea is that bad parenting results in amoral, undisciplined, maladjusted delinquents, which in the final count, is to the detriment of society. Social ills can thus be blamed on the individual mother.

The following extract from Gordon Bourne illustrates the ease with which the Active Mother Monitoring Normality account and the Ultimate Fulfilment account can be combined.

The creation of life and the growth of a baby within a uterus is indeed an incredible, wonderful and extraordinary event. Anyone who has actually seen a baby delivered will never cease to marvel at the myriad factors which must have taken place at exactly the correct time to produce this fabulous new-born creature. That this chain of events can proceed normally, naturally and to its final culmination with the natural delivery of a normal infant is by far the greatest wonder of the world, and it is right that a woman should always have a twinge of anxiety concerning not only the welfare of her unborn or newly born child but also his normality. This is natural motherhood. (Bourne, p. 9)

This extract starts off with the Ultimate Fulfilment account, using a liberal splattering of adjectives – 'wonderful', 'incredible', 'fabulous' – to emphasize the 'specialness' of childbirth. It then moves on, unproblematically, to the notion of the 'naturalness' of this process, the 'wonder of nature', the set pattern of development which results in the 'natural' delivery. Finally the mother is positioned in relation to this process as 'naturally' worrying, and concerned that her baby is 'normal'. This sets in train the mother's concern throughout the child's subsequent development that everything is going 'normally'. Two accounts are combined here: first, the wonder of childbirth, with the naturalized construct of 'motherhood', leading to the clear prescription that the mother monitors normality.

How motherhood is constructed in the childcare manuals

The various accounts work together to construct motherhood as a wholly positive experience. The Ultimate Fulfilment account shrouds any negative or ambivalent feelings women may experience by characterizing them as unnatural. The fact that mothering and childrearing do not carry with them any financial recognition or institutionalized backing is omitted from the manuals or undermined by the emphasis on how 'special' it is to be a mother, almost as though a price could and should not be placed on this work. An important element of this account is 'love', which is said to grow inevitably between mother and child. Here then we see the 'myth of motherhood' veiling alternative evaluations and the contradictory nature of the experience of mothering for many women.

This can be seen clearly in relation to the treatment of depression associated with childbirth. The 'blues' is subsumed into the notion of 'natural' motherhood, but any more severe feelings are said to be indicative of 'mental illness' or 'real' sickness. The discourse missing here is one that gives consideration to depression associated with the social environment and changes in women's lives as a consequence of having children, including their financial situation, dissatisfaction with medical intervention or giving up employment outside home. Similarly no mention is made of depression as a result of adjusting to loss of independent identity, being defined in relation to others and the segregation of roles when they become mothers. These omissions from the discourse need consideration if manuals are to provide the down-to-earth advice they claim to offer.

The 'experts' writing these manuals all make the point of talking about the individuality of each baby and state an explicit 'flexibility' in modern mothering. However, when this account is examined in conjunction with the advice offered, it is clear that this notion of flexibility falls within narrow, fixed parameters. Intense and unswerving love for the child and a reasonable healthy child are assumed. The mother is constructed in a heterosexual marriage. Difficulties associated with the nuclear family are minimized and difficulties are emphasized only when alternative structures are being discussed. In this respect the manuals give support to the nuclear family as 'obviously' the best childrearing environment. While 'modern' marriages are constructed as 'egalitarian' and up-to-date mothers are expected to engage in a 'sharing' contract with their husbands, the concept of sharing is clearly limited. So then, not only is the desirability of the nuclear family stated, but the sexual division of labour is constructed as inevitable. Once again, the consequence is maintenance of the status quo.

Finally, consideration was given to the way mothers should behave towards their children and their concomitant responsibilities. Here the emphasis is placed on the notion of the 'active', 'interventionist' mother. While the occasional presence of the father is 'essential', the mother must be present and engage in 'active' childcare. She must both facilitate and monitor her child's 'normal' development. A direct model of influence is widely accepted here. If children are 'well mothered' it is assumed that they will grow up to be good parents to their children. The child who has been exposed to good parental moral behaviour will display good adult moral behaviour. A totally individualistic model of development is assumed here, with the childrearing practices of individual mothers being seen as the main if not only determinants of the values and behaviour of later generations. The entire responsibility is placed on mothers; external influences to which children are exposed, such as schools, television and other children, are ignored. This constructs infancy as the prime site for intervention in childrearing because only then are mothers so much in contact with their children.

Conclusion

The childcare manuals construct the nature of motherhood for women as crucial. The responsibility falls on to mothers for the 'normal development' of a well-adjusted individual. To mother adequately a woman needs to be present with her child 24 hours each day and to be continually and actively engaged, providing stimulating and attentive company. If her child's development is not normal, the blame falls on the mother. The guilt induced in a mother whose child does not meet the relevant yardstick at the right time would seem to be one obvious consequence of following the word of the manuals. Another implicit consequence is to level the responsibility for the next generation's moral welfare on individual women's shoulders and to locate any social problems in faulty mothering. Again, society and structural influences are omitted from the equation.

The cumulative effect of these accounts is to construct an essentially consistent medical/psychological discourse which presents one version of the meaning of motherhood. Alternative ways of viewing motherhood or contradictory meanings of motherhood are either omitted or discounted. The discourse ensures that women turn to the 'experts' – both medical and psychological professionals – for the definition and understanding of motherhood.

References

Arney, W. (1980) Maternal–infant bonding: the politics of falling in love with your child. *Feminist Studies* 6 (3), 547–71.

Arnup, K., Levesque, A. and Roach Pierson, R. (eds) (1990) *Delivering Motherhood: Maternal Ideologies and Practices in the 19th and 20th Centuries.* London: Routledge.

Bourne, G. (1979) *Pregnancy.* London: Pan.

Breen, D. (1989) *Talking with Mothers,* 2nd edn. London: Free Association Books.

Clarke, A.M. and Clarke, A.D.B. (1976) *Early Experience: Myth and Evidence.* London: Open Books.

Clarke-Stewart, K.A. (1978) Popular primers for parents. *American Psychologist* April, 359–69.

Dalton, K. (1980) *Depression After Childbirth.* Oxford: Oxford University Press.

Fildes, V. (ed.) (1990) *Women as Mothers in Pre-Industrial England.* London: Routledge.

Gieve, K. (ed.) (1989) *Balancing Acts: on Being a Mother.* London: Virago.

Hollway, W. (1989) *Subjectivity and Method in Psychology.* London: Sage.

Jolly, H. (1986) *Hugh Jolly Book of Child Care. The Complete Guide for Today's Parents.* London: Unwin.

Kitzinger, S. (1978) *Women as Mothers.* Glasgow: Fontana.

Leach, P. (1988) *Baby and Child: From Birth to Age Five.* Harmondsworth: Penguin.

Marshall, H. and Wetherell, M. (1989) Talking about career and gender identities: a discourse analysis perspective. In S. Skevington and D. Baker (eds), *The Social Identity of Women.* London: Sage.

National Childbirth Trust (1987) *Pregnancy and Parenthood.* Oxford: Oxford University Press.

NCOPF (National Council for One Parent Families) (1990) *One Parent Families: Information Manual,* 2nd edn. London: National Council for One Parent Families.

Nicolson, P. (1986) Developing a feminist approach to depression following childbirth. In S. Wilkinson (ed.), *Feminist Social Psychology.* Milton Keynes: Open University.

Oakley, A. (1980) *Women Confined: Towards a Sociology of Childbirth.* Oxford: Martin Robertson.

Parker, I. (1988) Deconstructing Accounts. In C. Antaki (ed.), *Analysing Everyday Explanation.* London: Sage.

Potter, J. and Wetherell, M. (1987) *Discourse and Social Psychology: Beyond Attitudes and Behaviour.* London: Sage.

Riley, D. (1983) *War in the Nursery.* London: Virago.

Rutter, M. (1981) *Maternal Deprivation Reassessed,* 2nd edn. Harmondsworth: Penguin.

Spock, B. (1988) *Dr Spock's Baby and Child Care*, 40th Anniversary edn. London: Allen.

Stanway, P. (1988) *The Mothercare Guide to Child Health*. London: Conran Octopus.

Stoppard, M. (1983) *Dr Miriam Stoppard's Baby Care Book*. London: Dorling Kindersey.

Urwin, C. (1985) Constructing motherhood: the persuasion of normal development. In C. Steedman, C. Urwin and V. Walkerdine (eds), *Language, Gender and Childhood*. London: Routledge and Kegan Paul.

Weedon, C. (1987) *Feminist Practice and Poststructuralist Theory*. Oxford: Basil Blackwell.

PART 3

THE 'RIGHT TIME' TO HAVE CHILDREN

5

Mothers under Twenty: Outsider and Insider Views

Ann Phoenix

When motherhood occurs in the teenage years it is generally considered to be problematic. It has, for example, been associated with poor perinatal outcomes, child abuse, dependence on welfare benefits and poor educational outcomes for women and their children (Butler et al., 1981; Simms and Smith, 1986). Yet, in recent years, there has been a steady trickle of research reports that suggest that the negative effects of 'teenage motherhood have been overplayed and that most mothers and their children fare well' (Furstenberg et al., 1987; King and Fullard, 1982).

This chapter argues that a negative focus on mothers under 20 is common because little attention is paid to the circumstances in which most mothers under 20 live. As a consequence any problems they experience are attributed to age rather than to structural factors such as their employment histories and prospects. The attribution of the 'problem of young motherhood' to youthfulness serves to individualize it, and as a result any difficulties seem to be young women's own fault.

The chapter first discusses current discourses about motherhood in the under-twenties age group and considers whether their negative orientation is justified. Not surprisingly, this negative focus is produced by people who are not, themselves, 'young mothers' but rather are 'outsiders'. There is generally a disjunction between 'outsider' and 'insider' perspectives. In the case of issues like early motherhood, which are constructed as social problems, outsider perspectives constitute the dominant social construction and are more likely to be explored and taken seriously than the accounts produced by mothers under 20 themselves (Seidman and Rappaport, 1986).

Having considered outsider perspectives, the chapter moves on to discuss the various ways in which young women who are mothers construct insider accounts of their lives. It uses data from a longitudinal study, done at the Thomas Coram Research Unit (TCRU), of women who were aged between 16 and 19 years when they gave birth in 1985 and 1986. Seventy-nine women (both black and white and of varied ethnicities) were interviewed in depth and 103 women were asked for basic demographic data in late pregnancy. The study is described more fully in Phoenix (1991).

A consideration of outsider perspectives

Reasons for becoming pregnant
It is often claimed that mothers under 20 become pregnant for dubious reasons, such as to get council housing or welfare benefits. There is, however, no evidence that teenage women, either in the USA or in the UK, have such motives for becoming pregnant, and young women's stories of their conceptions and decisions to give birth do not include such instrumental reasons (Phoenix, 1991).[1] Clark (1989) explicitly asked young women whether they had become pregnant for such instrumental reasons. They 'expressed derision or disbelief . . . It seemed laughable and tragic to them that anyone would "use" a baby to get a flat or house' (p. 11).

Moral panics about women (particularly single women) becoming pregnant in order to get welfare benefits are more common in the USA than in the UK. As a result, various studies from the USA have attempted to find a link between welfare policies, levels of welfare benefits and the incidence of 'teenage motherhood' and 'lone motherhood'. Wilson and Neckerman (1987) reviewed these studies but failed to find a relationship between welfare provision and poor women's childbearing.

If women are to become pregnant for personal gain they have to do so deliberately. Yet instrumental reasons for giving birth directly contradict another popular stereotype of mothers under 20 as women who become pregnant accidentally and hence irresponsibly. Mothers under 20 are reported to have high rates of accidental rather than 'planned pregnancies' (Morrison, 1985; Simms and Smith, 1986). Yet teenage women report that they become pregnant for a variety of reasons (Phoenix, 1991), just as older women do (Oakley, 1981). It is, therefore, unsatisfactory to categorize women who become pregnant in their teenage years as doing so for irresponsible reasons to do with instrumentality or ignorance or to socially construct them as becoming pregnant for clearly different reasons from mothers who are over 20.

Childrearing styles

Negative social constructions of motherhood in the teenage years are partly produced and partly confirmed by research findings which suggest a 'gloomy adumbration' of outcomes for 'teenage mothers' and their children (Wells, 1983). The childrearing styles of mothers who are under 20 have also come in for criticism in research reports. Mothers under 20 have, for example, been reported to be deficient in knowledge of child development (Fry, 1985), to have childrearing styles that are less 'child-centred' than those of older mothers (Crnic et al., 1983; Landy et al., 1984). Their children are reported to be more at risk of abuse and of non-accidental injury than the children of older mothers (Butler et al., 1981; Chilman, 1980).

These negative research findings are echoed in media reports of child abuse which produce yet more negative constructions of mothers under 20. When mothers are teenagers then youth is emphasized, but where abusive parents are older, age is treated as irrelevant and does not feature. The taken-for-granted nature of beliefs that 'young mothers' are inadequate to the task of childrearing is illustrated in the casual way in which such assumptions can be called upon, as in this review of a book on Hitler: 'Still, in his horrible way, Hitler was pointing to a problem that is constant and, in today's "underclass" very serious. How do you stop single teenage mothers from breeding up tomorrow's football hooligans?' (Stone, 1989).

Is age the problem?

Negative findings such as those discussed above have been questioned on methodological grounds and in terms of their tendency to focus on problems, even when problems are rare (Carlson et al., 1986; Furstenberg et al., 1987; Lamb and Elster, 1986). For example it is still commonplace for research reports to assert that 'teenage motherhood' presents serious antenatal and perinatal problems even though many medical practitioners agree that, physically, women are well suited to childbearing in their late teenage years (Morris, 1981).

Analyses by Neville Butler and his colleagues (1981) on data from over 500 mothers under 20 and their children in a large-scale, nationally representative study clarify the difficulties of disentangling **correlation** from **causation** in studies of early motherhood. In keeping with many other studies, they found a range of problems associated with motherhood before 20. For example, in comparison with the children of older mothers, the children of younger mothers were more likely to suffer from complications in the perinatal period, to be admitted to hospital as a result of accidents and to gain lower scores on developmental tests. However, when other factors such as parity were considered, differences either disappeared or were greatly reduced. Four-fifths of the mothers under 20 were having their first child (and were hence at greater risk of birth complications) as compared with older mothers who were more likely to be having a second or subsequent child. Similarly socio-economic factors such as overcrowding, the number of children in the household and number of household moves, were found to be more significant than age in predicting many negative outcomes. Although Butler and his colleagues (1981) conclude that 'the net result of a child of a teenage mother is disadvantage and often multiple disadvantage', they acknowledge that:

> The fact that the differences between teenage and other mothers were in general reduced by such attempts to control possible confounding co-variables supports the view that there is little specific biological effect of maternal age that could not be explained by other intervening variables; we just haven't allowed for the right ones. (vol. 2, p. 63)

Other researchers have also found that factors associated with social class are more important than age in influencing how teenage mothers and their children fare (for example, Broman, 1980).

Evidence that early motherhood is necessarily detrimental to mothers and their children is thus far from clear-cut. The negative findings which are frequently stressed tend to apply only to a minority of women. Why then is the negative construction of motherhood in the teenage years such a pervasive one? An important reason is that the characteristics that women in this age group bring to motherhood are often treated as if they were consequences of early motherhood when, in fact, they predate it.

Would the deferment of motherhood improve young women's life chances?

Women who become mothers before they are 20 years of age are predominantly from the working classes. They are more likely than their peers to leave school with few educational qualifications, to experience periods of unemployment and to be dependent on welfare benefits. They come from larger than average families of origin and are more likely to have parents who have separated. The men who father their children come from similar backgrounds (Lamb and Elster, 1986; Simms and Smith, 1986). Penhale (1989) reported that the experience of unemployment seems to have an impact on young women's childbearing. He found that women aged between 17 and 19 years who were unemployed at the 1981 census were more likely to have a child within the next five years than were their age peers who had been employed in 1981.

In the USA it is now well documented that (at least for young white women) drop-out from school, and hence the failure to gain qualifications, generally precedes pregnancy (Edelman and Pittman, 1986). Before they conceive, therefore, many young women have already had problems with schooling, they lack qualifications and are economically impoverished in comparison with their peers. This observation has led some researchers to suggest that young women who can least afford to are most likely to have children (Bolton, 1980; Bury, 1984).

Just as early motherhood cannot be simply considered a cause of poverty, neither can poverty be said to cause early motherhood. Penhale (1989) points out that while prior experience of unemployment was correlated with childbearing early in the life course, most young women who experience unemployment do not go on to have children in the next five years. Similarly, while poor socio-economic circumstances are a feature of early motherhood, only a very small proportion of teenage women (about 3 per cent) currently give birth each year. While many young people experience poverty and do not have 'proper jobs', most young women who lack money do not become mothers. Poverty is thus the context within which the overwhelming majority of instances of motherhood under 20 occur, rather than a causative factor.

For women who become pregnant before they are 20, the intersection of their employment and motherhood careers does not fit the conflictual model generally assumed. Their poor labour market experiences and prospects offer no good employment reasons for deferring motherhood. Neither are periods out of the labour market likely to have an adverse effect on their job prospects. Poor employment prospects for mothers who are in their teenage years are not the consequence of youth, but the result of structural factors. This point is illustrated by the fact that, in the study reported here, one-third of the women's mothers and a quarter of their fathers were reported to be registered unemployed. Many parents were employed in insecure, poorly paid occupations. For most women deferment of motherhood into the twenties is unlikely to make much difference to their ability to make independent provision for themselves and their children. The most likely benefit of such deferment may be to make them less likely to be seen as behaving 'pathologically' which, in itself, may make their lives easier.

Although motherhood early in the life course cannot be said to cause poverty, the fact that it is associated with poverty and hence with dependence on welfare provision lends apparent legitimacy to its definition as a social problem. The fact that teenage women who become mothers are now more likely to be single than to be married when they give birth is considered further evidence of its problematic status (Ineichen, 1986). These factors contribute to a perception of teenage women as being 'too young' to be mothers. The following sections consider young women's own views of whether they are 'too young' to be mothers together with their perspectives on marriage and motherhood.

Insider perspectives

Women who give birth in their teenage years are generally discussed only from the 'outsider' perspectives provided by researchers. Yet 'young mothers' have their own views about early motherhood, which do not always accord with outsider perspectives. Women interviewed in the Thomas Coram Research Unit (TCRU) study were, on the whole, conscious of how 'young mothers' are socially constructed. Recognition that they are devalued gave them some investment in defending themselves against these negative images. They rarely displayed any group identification with other mothers in the same group or in similar socio-economic circumstances. Yet almost all maintained positive views of themselves as mothers.

> I mean I stimulate her as much as I can, and I play with her . . . I mean I think I'm doing quite well at it . . .

> I think I cope really well with him. Like I'm always talking to him and trying to involve him in what I do. I think I'm good in that way . . .

Women used a variety of strategies to maintain positive social identities (see Skevington and Baker, 1989 for further discussion of this). They sometimes accepted conventional ideas and normative assumptions about motherhood, and marriage. If those views and assumptions defined their group ('young mothers') as pathological, they defined themselves outside the group by seeing themselves as exceptional and others as less deserving or worse than themselves. This strategy led some women to reproduce stigmatizing notions about other women (in similar circumstances to themselves) being the 'undeserving poor'.

> The ones that do need help never seem to get it . . . the ones that I know are doing a lot better . . . on social security than what I am, going about it the right way.

Alternatively they rejected the conventions and assumptions which defined them negatively and asserted their own beliefs in preference by, for example, asserting that their own age group of mothers was preferable to older age groups (see 'Too young to be mothers?' below). A further strategy was to attempt to forestall what they perceived to be likely criticisms of their age group of mothers. One woman, for example, asked how she thought she was coping as a mother replied, 'I think I am coping quite well. I don't leave him wi' anybody.'

These strategies for maintaining a positive sense of self could not easily be separated out. At one and the same time, for example, some women stated the advantages of being 'young mothers' while asserting that women of their age were young to be mothers but that they themselves would have no difficulties with it. Their accounts were far from unitary, but instead drew on a number of different discourses which were available to them (Henriques et al., 1984; Hollway, 1989).

Most women in the TCRU study and their children fared well in the first two years after birth. The majority of children scored above the norm on a developmental assessment just before they were 2 years of age (Phoenix, 1991). The aim of the sections that follow is not to assess how women and their children were faring but to consider how women presented their ideas about motherhood, particularly 'young motherhood' and marriage and motherhood.

Too young to be mothers?

All the women in the study reported here considered that they were young people but most rejected the idea that they were too young to be mothers or that people would look down on women who have children while still in their 'teens simply because of their age. Nearly three-fifths (58 per cent) said that they believed they were having their first child at an average age. Two-fifths thought that they were younger than usual, but only just under a quarter thought it was possible that people might look down on them for no other reason than that they were having children early in life. This group of mothers is, however, increasingly unusual because the average age at which women give birth to their first baby is increasing and is now in the mid-twenties. It may, therefore, be that women were simply giving accounts which were likely to preserve their self-respect while protecting them from having to face the fact that negative attitudes about 'young mothers' are widely held. This does not, however, seem the most likely explanation because the women interviewed were not unusual within their own social networks.

Two-fifths of respondents' own mothers had first given birth before they were 20 and it was usual for them to know siblings, friends and peers who had also had children in their teenage years. In order to get an understanding of how common it was for women's social networks to include other women who also became mothers in their teenage years women were asked about the ages of their friends and relatives with children and those children's ages. It emerged that many did not know the exact ages of friends and so it was often not possible to be specific about whether a friend or relative gave birth at 19 or 21. The researchers' preoccupation with the issue of 'teenage motherhood' was not shared by most women. In addition most women did recognize that their age group of mothers was socially stigmatized. However, they did not consider that such stigma was appropriate to them or to women in their own social networks.

The variety of discourses women drew on to explain their ideas about age and motherhood can best be illustrated by some examples. These include arguments about: the irrelevance of age, comparisons with mothers known to be younger than themselves, problems with leaving childbearing too late, and the stigma of late motherhood (which many defined as not having children by the mid-twenties). The following two respondents simultaneously make use of two contradictory discourses. On the one hand they assert that age is irrelevant to childbearing and on the other that it is preferable to have children earlier than later. The second woman does this by appealing to psychological notions of children needing to be loved, and argues that love is possible at any age. She also refers to medical ideas about young women being physiologically ideally suited to childbearing.

> *Q*: Do you think that people look down on women who have their first child before they are 20?
> *A*: They might do yeah. I think they look down on women who don't have a child by 30, but there's no set time for anybody to have a baby by.
> *Q*: What do you think is the ideal age to have a baby?
> *A*: I think about now is all right . . . I don't want to get too old and have children. (19 years old)

> Yeah I think I'm young and people say I'm young, but I don't think it makes any difference really how old you are .. Whether you're 30 or 16 you can still give it as much love . . . She's 26 [sister] but she's getting on to have a baby when you think of it. The younger you are, the more likely that it's going to be healthier . . . (17 years old)

The following respondents compared their ages with younger women who were having children. The first rejects the notion that she is a 'young mother' and asserts that she has left childbearing late. The other two respondents accept that they are young to be mothers but find (different) ways of making youth a positive attribute.

> I think I've left mine quite late. All the girls I know – by 16 they've had their babies. (18 years old)

> Well my mum had me when she was 17. I find I am bit young to have a baby. But there are some girls here who are 15 years of age. I find that I am a bit young, but I can cope. (19 years old)

> Q: What would be the ideal age for you to have a baby?
> A: Twenty-five . . . Because you've had a bit of time to yourself. Twenty-five is a nice age. I'll be younger. It will be nice. My kids will be grown up and I'll still be young. (18 years old)

Not surprisingly, women stressed the problems of having children later as opposed to the benefits of having them earlier. Problems mentioned were physiological as well as psychological. Recurrent themes were being able to empathize with children (particularly in adolescence), retaining enough youth to be able to enjoy life after children left home and not being tied down.

It seems that women may have been responding to simplistic, unitary outsider views that it is automatically bad to be a 'young mother' which they may have thought were implicit in questions about age and motherhood. It would, however, be equally limiting if they simply asserted that all women should ideally become mothers in their teenage years. Their accounts are, however, more complicated than that. They do not simply accept or reject ideas about age and motherhood uncritically. Rather they choose those that most appeal to them and best suit their circumstances. Even if they accept that they are young to be mothers (and only a minority do so), they use familiar arguments and their own experiences to justify their situation. Arguments typically called upon for this purpose include comparisons with other, younger mothers and the advantages of being a youthful parent. Many sought to deny prescriptions about ideal ages for becoming mothers. As we have seen, this sometimes resulted in contradictory accounts because many women also felt that women should not leave it 'too late' to become mothers.

Where women did not have ready access to particular discourses they obviously could not make appeals to those arguments. Thus, being experienced in childcare was not usually cited as an advantage of being 'young mothers' even though four-fifths were experienced in looking after young children.

The meaning of marriage

One reason for the negative orientation to motherhood in the under-20s is that it is associated with women's single status (meaning not legally married). Single motherhood flaunts social conventions. Since three-quarters of British women who become mothers in their teenage years do so while single, it is not surprising that some mothers in this age group question the benefits of marriage. A third of the women interviewed in the TCRU study were legally married and another 10 per cent were cohabiting in late pregnancy. In general women were not positive about marriage and said that men got a better deal from marriage than women did. Two-fifths said that men benefited from marriage more than women, while only 7 per cent thought that women gained more from marriage. Even those who reported that marriage was extremely positive for women sometimes contradicted their direct accounts by highlighting only negative aspects.

> *Q*: What about advantages for men?
> *A*: They got someone to cook and clean and I think they rely on you and that's their benefit, they rely on you, and they think you're their slave. Well they don't think you're their slave, but they rely on you to wash and that, so they really haven't got any worries, I don't think. That's it, you've got to wash and make the dinner and that's hard luck if you don't because I can't. (17-year-old married woman)

Despite their negative views about marriage, the majority of single women (56 per cent) did consider that they would marry at some time. Only a quarter were adamant that they would never marry. A further fifth, however, were not sure if they would ever marry but did not discount the possibility. In this their views were similar to those of young women interviewed by Griffin (1985) and Lees (1986), who were negative about marriage but perceived no alternative for themselves later in life.

Respondents, both married and single, drew primarily on negative arguments to explain the meanings marriage had for them. They were one of the first generations whose parents had access to relatively easy divorce and some of those whose parents had separated cited this as a reason for not wanting to marry. Other arguments they used included restriction of freedom for women (but not for men) in marriage, dislike of the drudgery seen to be involved in women's traditional roles within marriage and the fact that cohabitation was perceived as being similar in many ways to marriage, without entailing the same disadvantages. The advantages mentioned for marriage were companionship and having someone to depend on for the management of money and for support. These were more likely to be mentioned by the third of women who were married than by single women.

The discourses women used in explaining their views on marriage were clearly historically specific. Women drew on current popular knowledge and debates to present their case. Thus feminist arguments that marriage subjects women to an exploitative division of household labour as well as to male domination within the household were much cited, although women did not consider themselves to be feminists (see Griffin, 1989 for discussion of how feminist ideas have permeated many young women's consciousness). Similarly, changes in divorce legislation and practice and removal of much of the stigma traditionally attached to cohabitation provided a context for women's feelings that marriage and motherhood were separable and cohabitation little different from marriage.

Women's silences about some issues they could have addressed were sometimes as informative as what they actually said. They did not, for instance, mention economic reasons for contracting marriage. Yet women who had married before conception were those with the most affluent partners (in comparison with other male partners in the study). It seems likely that high rates of unemployment among the young unskilled have made young men less attractive marriage partners than previously (Phoenix, 1991). It is, however, difficult for women to recognize that their decisions to marry or not may be affected by their male partners' economic prospects because marriage is now supposed to be contracted for emotional rather than material reasons (Gittins, 1986; Mansfield and Collard, 1988). So pervasive is the construction of the ideal marriage as companionate and loving that women could take it for granted that other people would recognize that if they married it would be the logical outcome of 'true (heterosexual) love'. This may well be one reason that some young women gave no particular reason for having married or intending to marry in the future.

Another possible reason is provided by Lees (1986) and Griffin (1985), who both suggest that since there are no clear alternatives to marriage, young women are likely to end up marrying by default, regardless of how negative they feel about marriage as an institution. The arguments women use and the discourses they construct to interpret their experiences can thus contradict the actions (such as getting married) they have either taken or anticipate taking in the future.

Employment and children's needs

In this study women were interviewed for the final time when their children were nearly 2. The normative assumption in the UK is that mothers of pre-school children should not be employed outside their homes because their children need to be with them. Although childcare manuals encourage mothers to see children's needs as congruent with their own (see chapter 4), mothers do not necessarily perceive such a congruence. Discussions of 'the needs of children' frequently ignore their mothers' needs. Those who advance the conventional argument that children need to be at home with their mothers rather than in daycare assume that women should sublimate their needs for income, stimulation and company to their children's needs (see chapter 10). On the other hand, developments in feminist theory which stem from the recognition that it is often stressful and boring for women to be at home with their children all day have led to the counter-argument that there is not necessarily an opposition between 'the needs of children' and those of their mothers (Oakley, 1974, 1981). According to this argument, mothers should be free to choose whether or not they return to employment because good alternative childcare is not detrimental to young children.

For the women in the TCRU study lack of labour market experience made it difficult for them to find jobs that were sufficiently well paid to enable them to pay for childcare. For just over half those interviewed, however, the discourse they drew upon protected them from having to face the problems raised by fruitless searches for adequately paid jobs and cheap childcare. In late pregnancy very few women (5 per cent) were actually in favour of maternal employment and two-fifths were openly hostile. When their children were 2 years old, 52 per cent of women said that they thought their children were still too young to be left with anyone else. Yet 19 per cent of those interviewed were in employment (half part-time) when their children were 21 months old and some others would have liked to be employed.

Many women's accounts demonstrate the conflict they experience about their own needs in comparison with those of their children. Where women subscribed to a conflictual model they gave what they perceived to be their children's needs precedence over their own.

> Well sometimes I feel that I would like . . . to go out to work to earn extra money and that but I also feel that I should be at home with her so she's more important. When she starts school I can start working. I *chose* to have her. It's my place to stay with her. (17-year-old married woman)

> Well I ought to be [at home with her] because you know she's young you know. You can't leave her somewhere else or with other people, but um I don't like to be at home full time . . . (married 19-year-old)

Male partners were also frequently reported to subscribe to normative expectations about mothers being at home with their children.

> *Q*: Do you feel you ought to be at home full time with her?
> *A*: Well yes . . . I'd like to until she's school age . . . [cohabitee] says oh it's nice because his sister's been at home with his mum . . . but I said I'd like to go back to work. I've sort of begun to miss it I suppose. But I think it's best to be with her. (17-year-old considering childminding in order to be at home)

Women could sometimes override cohabitee's and spouse's wishes, however, by subscribing to another set of discourses about children's needs; the need for children to socialize with peers.

> Paul don't really like me to work. He thinks I should stay at home with him until it's time for him to go to school, but I think . . . he does need other children, and I'm not prepared to give him any more at the moment (*laughs*). (18-year-old cohabitee)

It was even more fortuitous if women's own perceived needs or desires complemented what they believed to be their children's needs. The woman who advances the argument of wanting to be with her daughter (below) had actually taken up a hairdressing apprenticeship for a few months after birth, but had given it up on grounds of poor pay and missing her daughter.

> *Q*: Do you think you ought to be at home with her?
> *A*: Um I think . . . yeah until she goes to school – starts nursery, cos there's so many things you miss first two, three years of their lives you know and I'd like to spend that time with her at home . . . (18 years old)

By following conventional patterns in remaining at home with their young children, and believing that they should, some women were able to include themselves in the category 'good mother' and were thus able to distance themselves from social constructions of 'young mothers' as pathological. They were, after all, putting first what they understood to be the needs of their children. The positive side of this was that it allowed them to enjoy being with their children and the status they gained from motherhood without experiencing conflict about not providing adequate care for their children. This holding to convention could itself, however, be problematic for women and cause them concern if they felt that in some ways they were not providing for children's needs. While, for example, many were content to be single mothers, enjoyed their child and enjoyed motherhood, they were not always confident enough or perhaps did not have access to arguments that would enable them to reject notions that whatever the circumstances and regardless of the contribution fathers make, 'children need their fathers'.

> *Q*: Best things about being a mother?
> *A*: Just having him there plus he is a lovely child to be with. He doesn't cause me any trouble . . . I feel grown up.
> *Q*: Worst things?
> *A*: I'm frightened that he will grow up to be horrible – because he is separated from his father it might have an effect on him.
> *Q*: Do you ever feel that you could get more out of motherhood . . .?
> *A*: No I think I'm getting a lot out of it. Maybe if I was still with his father, motherly life and life in general would be better. (19 at birth of child)

Clearly then, the existence of negative views about single mothers and about 'young mothers' could generate anxiety and stress in mothers who were on the whole confident that they were doing well as mothers.

Conclusion

This chapter has considered 'outsider' and 'insider' perspectives on early motherhood. Both sets of accounts are socially constructed using discourses which make it possible to find contradictions within as well as between them. Despite the fact that there are commonalities between the two sets of perspectives, it is generally the case that 'outsider' perspectives construct motherhood in the teenage years negatively while young women themselves do not generally consider that they are too young to be mothers. Disparities in power between 'young mothers' and researchers and other professionals who pronounce on early motherhood are such that outsider constructions impinge on 'young mothers'' lives while insider constructions are rarely recorded.

Outsider constructions often fail to consider the ways in which structural constraints impinge on the lives of those teenage women who become mothers. The educational backgrounds and employment experiences of women who become mothers in their teenage years are such that their career opportunities and economic circumstances are restricted prior to conception. As a result, early motherhood cannot be said to have damaged the life chances of the majority of women who give birth in their teenage years. It is, therefore, not surprising that many consider they have little reason to defer motherhood.

Women can draw on a range of arguments to explain the meanings that motherhood holds for them. These arguments are culled from a variety of discourses currently available. The lack of well-paid employment for unskilled young people, developments in feminist ideology and its concomitant changes in how many women live, and trends in marriage and divorce have resulted in a broadening of the views young women are able to draw on when thinking about marriage and motherhood. Yet this widening of perspective does not necessarily change the status quo because it does not dramatically increase the alternatives open to women. Rejection of marriage as an ideal for women does not, for example, allow them to perceive any real alternatives to marriage in the long term. Similarly, those women who are not opposed to the idea of mothers with young children being employed, are mostly not able to find jobs which pay well enough for them to afford childcare. The ideas women call on to describe their situations reflect these contradictions in their position.

Women do not simply accept normative assumptions about motherhood, age, marriage and employment. Instead they subscribe to ideas that suit their particular circumstances and beliefs. Although broad themes can be picked out from accounts, different women chose different constellations of arguments. Nor did women use one set of discourses consistently. Most, for example, accepted feminist arguments about the effects of marriage for women. Yet many rejected feminist ideas on employment and motherhood. This illustrates the ways in which ideas gain popular currency because they accord with commonsense assumptions and people's own experiences and desires (which are themselves socially produced). (See Riley (1983) and discussion by Tizard (1990) of 'ideological gateways' for further consideration of this issue.) Since young women are in a devalued group of mothers, they have more investment in defending themselves against possible criticisms than may other groups of mothers. The women in this study did not do this by means of a strong group identification but instead chose to distance themselves from the negative assumptions associated with 'young motherhood'.

Note

1 Indeed, in their nationally representative study of over 500 women who became mothers before they were 20, Madeleine Simms and Christopher Smith (1986) found only one woman who said that she became pregnant in order to get housing.

References

Bolton, F. (1980) *The Pregnant Adolescent*. Beverly Hills, CA: Sage.

Broman, S. (1980) Longterm development of children born to teenagers. In K. Scott, T. Field and E. Robertson (eds), *Teenage Parents and their Offspring*. New York: Grune and Stratton.

Bury, J. (1984) *Teenage Pregnancy in Britain*. London: Birth Control Trust.

Butler, N., Ineichen, B., Taylor, B. and Wadsworth, J. (1981) *Teenage Mothering*. 2 vols. Report to DHSS. Bristol: University of Bristol.

Carlson, D.B., Labarba, R.C., Sclafani, J.D. and Bowers, C.A. (1986) Cognitive and motor development in infants of adolescent mothers: a longitudinal analysis. *International Journal of Behavioural Development* 9 (1), 1–14.

Chilman, C. (1980) Social research concerning adolescent childbearing: 1970–1980. *Journal of Marriage and the Family* 42 (4), 793–805.

Clark, E. (1989) *Young Single Mothers Today: a Qualitative Study of Housing and Support Needs*. London: National Council for One Parent Families.

Crnic, K., Greenberg, M., Ragozin, A., Robinson, N. and Basham, R. (1983) Effects of stress and social supports on mothers in premature and full term infants. *Child Development* 54, 209–17.

Edelman, M. and Johnson Pittman, K. (1986) Adolescent pregnancy: black and white. *Journal of Community Health* 11, 63–9.

Fry, P.S. (1985) Relations between teenager's age, knowledge, expectations and maternal behaviour. *British Journal of Development Psychology* 3 (1), 47–56.

Furstenberg, F., Brooks-Gunn, J. and Morgan, S.P. (1987) *Adolescent Mothers in Later Life*. Cambridge: Cambridge University Press.

Gittins, D. (1986) *The Family in Question. Changing Households and Familiar Ideologies*. London: Macmillan.

Griffin, C. (1985) *Typical Girls: Young Women from School to the Job Market*. London: Routledge and Kegan Paul.

Griffin, C. (1989) 'I'm not a Women's Libber, but . . .' In S. Skevington and D. Baker (eds), *The Social Identity of Women*. London: Sage.

Henriques, J., Hollway, W., Urwin, C., Venn C. and Walkerdine, V. (1984) *Changing the Subject: Psychology, Social Regulation and Subjectivity*. London: Methuen.

Hollway, W. (1989) *Subjectivity and Method in Psychology*. London: Sage.

Ineichen, B. (1986) Contraceptive experience and attitudes to motherhood of teenage mothers. *Journal of Biosocial Science* 18, 387–94.

King, T. and Fullard, W. (1982) Teenage mothers and their infants: new findings on the home environment. *Journal of Adolescence* 5, 333–46.

Lamb, M.E. and Elster, A.B. (1986) Parental behaviour of adolescent mothers and fathers. In A.B. Elster and M. Lamb (eds), *Adolescent Fatherhood*. Hillsdale, NJ: Erlbaum.

Landy, S., Cleland, J. and Schubert, J. (1984) The individuality of teenage mothers and its implication for intervention strategies. *Journal of Adolescence* 7, 171–90.

Lees, S. (1986) *Losing Out: Sexuality and Adolescent Girls*. London: Hutchinson.

Mansfield, P. and Collard, J. (1988) *The Beginning of the Rest of Your Life: a Portrait of Newly-wed Marriage*. London: Macmillan.

Morris, N. (1981) The biological advantages and social disadvantages of teenage pregnancy. *American Journal of Public Health* 71 (8), 796.

Morrison, P. (1985) Adolescent contraceptive behaviour: a review. *Psychological Bulletin* 98 (3), 538–68.

Oakley, A. (1974) *The Sociology of Housework*. Oxford: Martin Robertson.

Oakley, A. (1981) *From Here to Maternity: Becoming a Mother*. Harmondsworth: Penguin.

Penhale, B. (1989) *Associations between Unemployment and Fertility among Young People in the Early 1980s*. London: Social Statistics Research Unit, Working Paper no. 60.

Phoenix, A. (1991) *Young Mothers?* Cambridge: Polity Press.

Riley, D. (1983) *War in the Nursery: Theories of the Child and Mother*. London: Virago.

Seidman, E. and Rappaport, J. (1986) Introduction. In E. Seidman and J. Rappaport (eds), *Redefining Social Problems*. New York: Plenum.

Simms, M. and Smith, C. (1986) *Teenage Mothers and their Partners*. London: HMSO.

Skevington, S. and Baker, D. (eds) (1989) *The Social Identity of Women*. London: Sage.

Stone, N. (1989) The gas chamber mentality (book review). *Guardian*, 14 December.

Tizard, B. (1990) Research and policy: is there a link. *The Psychologist* 13, 435–40.

Wells, N. (1983) *Teenage Mothers*. Liverpool: Children's Research Fund.

Wilson, W. with Neckerman, K. (1987) Poverty and family structure: the widening gap between evidence and public policy issues. In W.J. Wilson, *The Truly Disadvantaged: the Inner City, the Underclass and Public Policy*. London: University of Chicago Press.

6

Perspectives on Later Motherhood

Julia C. Berryman

At one time there was nothing unusual about later motherhood – in many families sibling births spanned a generation, and grandchildren were often similar in age to their parents' younger brothers and sisters. Neugarten (1972) records that in the 1920s 42 was the average age at which women in the USA had their last child, and yet today only a small percentage of women have children later in life. This chapter looks at the perception of older mothers in the medical and psychological literature and shows how differently these disciplines construe such women.

The medical perspective on later motherhood tends to be problem-centred. 'Elderly' pregnant mothers are seen purely in terms of increased risks to themselves and their infants and this is the only aspect of later motherhood that is widely discussed. Psychological studies of women who become mothers later than usual are scarce, but those that are available suggest they have qualities which make them just as good, though different, from their younger counterparts. This chapter starts by discussing the relationship between fertility and age, and then considers the medical and psychological literature on later motherhood. Some findings of a preliminary study of becoming a mother after 40 by Kate Windridge and myself are presented (Berryman and Windridge, in press a, b).

When do women have babies?

Currently there is an identifiable pattern of childbearing. Over 90 per cent of women in England and Wales, at the present time, have their children before the age of 35. The majority of births are to women in their twenties (63 per cent) with a smaller percentage born to women in their thirties (20 per cent). Just over 8 per cent of births are to women under 20, and approximately the same percentage of births to women aged 35 and over (Birth Statistics, 1989). The average age of mothers for all births in England and Wales is currently 27.1 years and for first births (in marriage) is 26.5 years. This figure is the highest recorded age for this statistic since 1946.

There is a current trend towards later parenting. Birth rates have increased most in the age groups 35–39, and 40 and over – reaching their highest levels since the early 1970s (Birth Statistics, 1989). A similar trend has been recorded in the USA (Berkowitz, et al., 1990), where births in the 30–39 and 40 and over age groups have more than doubled since 1970.

There are biological limits on the age at which women can become mothers. Although fertility in men declines with age, there is no sharp drop in fertility such as that associated with the menopause in women. Nearly six times as many men as women become parents at 40 and over, although at 7 per cent they still make up only a small proportion of the total numbers of fathers (Birth Statistics, 1989).

The average number of children per family is now just two. However, this statistic is hard to interpret since the whole of women's childbearing years have to be considered to be certain that they have completed their families. Nevertheless, even allowing for the trend towards later motherhood, for those who are completing their families now, the average family size is unlikely to be increased to much above two children. As the average length of time between first and second babies is under three years (the median length is thirty-two months), most women complete their childbearing within a few years.

In summary, the majority of babies are born to mothers in their twenties who are likely to have one more child within about three years. Thus having babies is likely to be confined to a very short time within women's childbearing life, a period which can span forty or so years.

These figures show historical changes. Accurate historical birth records are hard to find. Most people are aware that the average family size in Victorian times and before was considerably larger than today, and new mothers who were also grandmothers were commonplace. In Scotland, Flinn (1977) records that 18.9 per cent of Scottish legitimate births in 1844 were to women of 35 and over, of which 6.6 per cent were to women between the ages of 40 and 49.

In the late 1930s when the birth rate was first recorded according to the age of the mother (age-specific fertility rate), women were more likely to have children later in life than they do now (Macfarlane and Mugford, 1984). Four per cent of births were to mothers aged 40 and over, and 15 per cent – or nearly twice as many as today – to mothers aged 35 and over.

There are also differences between countries. In Ireland, for example, birth statistics for the 1980s revealed that about 16 per cent of births (Dalen, 1977; Demographic Yearbook, 1988) were to women aged 35 or more, whereas this proportion was considerably greater in the 1950s and 1960s when about a quarter of births were to women of this age. These figures are probably related to what may be 'informal' contraceptive practices such as late marriage and abstinence during the fertile period.

Fertility and age
The statistics presented in the preceding section show that women have fewer babies as they get older. Whilst the reasons for this decline are likely to be many, one factor is undoubtedly the age-linked decline in fertility (Llewellyn-Jones, 1982, 1986). Data on the extent of the decline are patchy. Kern (1982) reports that by 35 'only half of all women can conceive; this figure is reduced to three to four percent by age 44'. Bourne (1989) describes a less dramatic decline; he reports that providing they have intercourse at the rate of three or more times a week, three-quarters of women between the ages of 36 and 40 who wish to become pregnant will do so. At age 20 a higher percentage of women get pregnant (95 per cent) eventually and they do so more quickly (two-thirds within six months). Cartwright (1976) reports that in her sample of women aged 35 and over who became pregnant 40 per cent did so in six months, but as many as 47 per cent took two years or longer. Of course, these figures relate to women who became pregnant, and they do not reveal the fertility of women in the population as a whole nor the proportion of women who do not become mothers because they have problems conceiving or carrying a pregnancy to term.

The General Household Survey (1989) suggests that women between 40 and 44 years who have a child already are more likely to believe that they could have another one (34 per cent), whereas few childless women of this age believe they are likely to conceive (5 per cent). It is noteworthy in this context that termination rates of women aged 40 to 44 years were until 1982 higher than birth rates (Birth Statistics, 1989). This figure is unlikely to be accounted for solely as a result of the identification of congenital defects, and may possibly be an indication that women believe they are less fertile than in fact they are at this stage of life.

In the study Kate Windridge and I conducted (see below), age itself was not a major factor in determining how quickly women became pregnant. When conception rates for all babies (planned and unplanned) were compared, first-time mothers took very significantly longer to conceive, with a mean of nearly four years. This is explained by the high level of fertility problems they reported. Women who had children already conceived more quickly than did women having their first babies after 40. This was the case both for their first children (born when they were, on average, 26 years old) and their later babies born when they were over 40. There is little evidence, therefore, of a decline in fertility. It is often assumed that women having babies later in life are having their 'first and last delivery'. However, Blum (1979) argues that this view is erroneous since more than a third of mothers aged 35 or more at their first delivery had more than one pregnancy and delivery during the five-year period of the study. Approximately 10 per cent of mothers in our Motherhood in Later Life study had more than one '40-plus' child.

The right time to have children

The general consensus in both academic and popular books on pregnancy, birth and parenthood is that there is a 'right time' to have a baby. Price (1977) pointed out that there is 'prejudice against the older parent'. Obstetricians and gynaecologists stress that the twenties are the best time to have a baby, and this message is clearly conveyed in the use of the term 'elderly primigravida' which has been applied to women aged 30 and over (Llewellyn-Jones, 1982). Popular books corroborate this view, with accounts of first-time motherhood from the early thirties upwards included as examples of 'elderly', 'older', 'late', 'now or never', 'up against the clock' mothers. These books and the medical literature also refer to the risks of having children 'too young' (see chapter 5). There are also prescriptions about a good time to have a baby in terms of how long women have been in a relationship with the baby's father; too short a time and too long may be seen as problematic (Bostock and Jones, 1987; Fabe and Winkler, 1979; Kitzinger, 1982; McCaulay, 1976; Michelson and Gee, 1984; Price, 1977; Shultz, 1979).

For women with fertility problems, one further reminder of the 'right time' to have a baby may come when they attempt to adopt. In Britain many adoption societies have age limits – and these vary from about 30 upwards. These limits seem quite arbitrary to many would-be adopters, and are hard to defend on the grounds of couples being unable to parent adequately at such an age as many foster mothers are older women (Shaw, 1986).

Problems for older mothers and their children

Pregnancy and birth complications are widely discussed in relation to older motherhood. Most general texts refer to them (for example, Bourne, 1989; Llewellyn-Jones, 1982) and reports of these go back many years. Davidson (1912) records that 'children of old parents are also often delicate and wanting in vitality, as though themselves prematurely old'. Mansfield (1988) notes that American medical students at the turn of the century were taught that childbirth was more difficult for older mothers and that in the 1940s older first-time mothers were said to be a 'hazard during pregnancy and labour'.

In her view of 'midlife childbearing', Mansfield (1988) lists eight pregnancy outcomes which are commonly linked to later childbearing: these are (a) pregnancy-induced hypertension (toxaemia); (b) placental complications; (c) prolonged labour; (d) delivery by caesarean section; (e) perinatal mortality; (f) maternal mortality; (g) infant mortality; and (h) low birthweight. Mansfield excluded Down's syndrome from this list since its link with increased maternal age is generally thought to be beyond question. In a review of 104 studies, Mansfield (1988) argues that the majority (61 per cent) were methodologically inadequate and hence of questionable value. In the better designed studies, only caesarean sections were found to be more common in older mothers, and it has been suggested that this probably reflects the tendency of physicians to opt for caesareans because of concern about a women's age, rather than because of other possible complications (McCaulay, 1976).

These findings are supported by those of Berkowitz et al. (1990), who also show that age does not 'appreciably increase the risks of adverse outcome in singleton gestations'. More specifically, they found that the risks of pre-term delivery, perinatal death and poor infant state at birth as measured on the Apgar test[1] were not significantly higher in women of 30 years or over. Older mothers were, however, more likely to have caesarean section deliveries, and infants were more likely to be admitted to intensive care units. Specific antepartum and intrapartum complications were more likely to be found in the older age group.

The older mothers in our study were asked to indicate the occurrence of a wide range of physical changes and conditions commonly associated with pregnancy, and to note which were problematic for them. Our findings did not indicate that older women necessarily experienced more problems than younger women. Mothers with more than one child did not report more problems with their later, 40-plus pregnancies than they did with their first pregnancies (at a mean age of 26). First-time mothers did not record any more pregnancy problems than mothers expecting second or subsequent babies.

In contrast, Down's syndrome[2] is probably the most widely known problem that is linked to increased maternal age (Nortman, 1974). The risks of having a Down's syndrome baby increase from 1.13 per 1000 live births at 30, to 9.19 cases at 40, and 30.84 for 45-year-old mothers (Mansfield, 1988). Maternal age is also associated with a range of other, less well known, problems in children. These include a variety of congenital malformations many of which are due to genetic disorders (in particular, trisomy) (Nortman, 1974). Schizophrenia (Dalen, 1977) and leukaemia (Gardner et al., 1990) have been linked to maternal age. Problems such as anorexia are also more common amongst the children of older mothers, and although the links have not been clearly established, there are some suggestions that younger children in families with older mothers are more likely to be school-phobic (Berg et al., 1972; Halmi, 1974).

Medical intervention during pregnancy

Advances in medical technology have provided older mothers with a range of techniques, such as chorionic villus sampling and amniocentesis,[3] which can be used to detect some genetic abnormalities in the fetus. They can reveal some abnormalities early enough for women to decide whether or not to continue with their pregnancies. These procedures themselves give rise to a new set of problems. Firstly, there is the risk of false diagnosis and of miscarriage triggered by the procedures themselves. Secondly, the expectation that such a procedure will be carried out puts a question mark over what is probably an otherwise normal pregnancy. Katz-Rothman (1986) terms such pregnancies 'the tentative pregnancy'; women experience their pregnancy differently from those not undergoing such interventions. For example, the perception of fetal movements is often delayed, and Katz-Rothman believes that women hold themselves back from such pregnancies lest they are destined to be terminated. On the one hand, these procedures may create stress for women, which may in themselves lead to greater pregnancy and birth complications, but on the other hand they may create a false sense of security and lead women to believe that because no genetic abnormalities have been detected, their babies will be perfect (Barbour, 1990; Mansfield and Cohn, 1986; Reid, 1990; Richards, 1989).

Many women in our study expressed fear of having a Down's baby, but some felt that the risks were greatly over-rated. One mother commented, 'I wish that the fact that 97 per cent of children are born perfect had been stressed to me.' Older women whose babies had been born prior to the availability of pre-natal diagnostic techniques commented that they were glad so much less was known in their day. It is difficult to balance the positive and negative aspects of such interventions but current approaches tend to overemphasize the risks and problems.

The advice offered in handbooks and guides comes solely from a medical perspective, and the over-riding aim seems to be the achievement of a problem-free pregnancy and birth and a perfect baby. Thus the implication is that a woman should not embark on the process if the outcome is likely to be anything less than this. A recent British Medical Association free manual for pregnant women states in its section for 'Mature Mothers', 'don't see too much of the event through rose-tinted spectacles', and discusses the risks of abnormalities and the likelihood of being 'taken for "Granny" at the school gate' (Jeffries, 1985). This seems to be unnecessarily pessimistic (and patronizing) in its advice. Modern medicine can cope better than at any time in history with the possible complications of pregnancy and birth – so that it seems curious that such stress is placed on the problems of later maternities.

One final point should not be ignored. Although most women would agree that their ideal pregnancy outcome is a perfect baby, there are undoubtedly many who do not necessarily wish to reject one that is imperfect. There is a danger that if the consensus is to abort imperfect fetuses, then it is less acceptable to proceed with a pregnancy in the knowledge that the baby may not be perfect. As medical advances improve pre-natal diagnostic techniques, these may place greater pressures on women who do not want these procedures, or who do not wish to act on the information which they provide. Society needs to consider carefully just exactly what impact these advances may have on attitudes towards disabilities, and on the parents' right to give birth to a disabled infant (Reid, 1990; Richards, 1989).

Psychological perspectives on later motherhood

Thus far, research on later motherhood has centred around the medical view of it. Motherhood has been viewed solely in terms of biology, and the mother has been regarded as the person who nurtures within her and gives birth to a baby. Her readiness for the experience in psychological terms and the skills which she brings to her new role as mother have not been considered, and yet being a mother, or being the one who 'mothers' a child, has been a concern of psychological research for many decades. This section considers the evidence which shows how later motherhood is experienced, and reviews some of the research that contrasts older and younger mothers' experiences of motherhood and approaches to childcare.

Reactions to later pregnancy and motherhood
In a study of the effects of maternal age in women aged from 16 to 38, Ragozin et al. (1982) found that greater satisfaction with parenting was related to increased maternal age. They argued that older mothers were more committed to the 'parenting experience'. This idea is reflected in the popular books which propound the view that later babies are probably carefully considered and planned babies. It is often said that they are more likely to be born to women with successful careers behind them who have probably delayed parenting for career reasons (Kitzinger, 1982). Alment (1970) believes that the older pregnant woman 'is likely to be better informed about her pregnancy . . . than her younger counterpart', but does not see this as necessarily a good thing because 'her awareness can deprive her of the protection of blissful ignorance which is part of the inborn optimism of the young primigravida' (p. 374). Thus, knowledge may be valued by some medical professionals, but for others the 'blissfully ignorant' patient may be preferred to the one who is better informed, reflecting some of the contradictory messages put across in childcare manuals (see chapter 4). A contrasting view comes from Hayden (see McCaulay, 1976, p. 19), an obstetrician who is 'all for women over 40 having babies' because he argues that such women seek pre-natal care, 'attend more carefully' and 'make more visits to the obstetrician than the younger age group'.

Eichholz and Offerman-Zuckenberg (1980) point out that mothers over 35 (especially those expecting first babies) are more likely to have fulfilled themselves prior to the birth, and thus are less likely to want their children to do this for them. Frankel and Wise (1982) found that the older mothers in their study (aged 33 and over) had all postponed childbearing voluntarily, whereas the younger mothers (in their twenties) had made less conscious choices about when to bear their children and felt less control in their lives. The younger group stressed the 'enormous sacrifices' of motherhood, in particular the isolation, financial stress and feelings of restlessness. The older group, with established careers, were seen as more 'accepting' and 'less conflicted'. Nevertheless, older mothers were more anxious when the children were young, and Frankel and Wise comment that the fear of losing a long-awaited baby may be more intense when parenting is delayed.

Welles-Nystrom and de Chateau (1987) echo this. They compared first-time mothers in their twenties with those in their thirties, and also found that the older group had a higher proportion of planned babies (81 per cent compared with 54 per cent). During early pregnancy, older mothers were more anxious, and after the birth they were described as more anxious and cautious. This was interpreted as an indication of their concern over their ability to 'master motherhood' or as a realistic view of older motherhood given the medical approach/model outlined earlier. However, anxiety was not necessarily seen as a problem because it was thought that it might indicate a desire to make a positive transition to the new role.

As Ragozin et al. (1982) suggest, older first-time mothers may have more experience of non-parenting roles, and this may increase their commitment to parenting once they become mothers. They may thus be less likely than younger mothers to see motherhood as involving 'sacrifices'. For example, older mothers of pre-term babies were more satisfied and expressed more pleasure in parenting than did younger, less educated mothers.

Delayed parenthood is often assumed to be more common in women from the higher socio-economic groups (Llewellyn-Jones, 1982). Wilkie (1981) suggests that it is a strategy adopted by 'women interested in careers'. Like Wilkie, Kern (1982) found a high percentage (70 per cent) of professional and highly educated women in her sample of older mothers. Wilkie notes that an interest in their careers is not a sign that women identify more with careers than with family roles. One of the effects of delaying parenting is, however, that such women have fewer children than do 'on-time' mothers. It seems probable that as a greater number of women are likely to enter the workforce in the 1990s (Women and Men in Britain, 1989), the trend towards later parenting will increase.

Older mothers and parenting
There are relatively few studies of parenting which consider maternal age. Reis (1988) reports that although very young mothers are less knowledgeable about the key stages in child development they are often considered to be more relaxed, warmer and better able to cope with the demands of childcare (Sears et al., 1957). Older mothers may experience more fatigue (Kern, 1982), but greater tolerance has also been attributed to them (Eichholz and Offerman-Zuckenberg, 1980); and Sears et al. (1957) suggest that older mothers are less likely to use physical punishment and ridicule to control their children.

Increased maternal age has been linked positively to the intellectual development of the child (for example, Ragozin et al., 1982; Zybert et al., 1978), and this association exists independently of other confounding variables such as social class and mothers' education. Seth and Khanna (1978) report that older mothers tend to discourage dependency but to encourage verbalization. Ragozin et al. (1982) suggest that the greater commitment to motherhood of older women (and especially older first-time mothers) may be related to their increased sensitivity to their baby's cues and their fostering of children's social, emotional and cognitive growth.

The picture of older mothers that emerges from popular and academic literature is of women who are likely to be from a higher socio-economic group, to be financially stable and, in particular for first-time mothers, to be 'career' orientated women who may have delayed childbearing for career reasons and have opted for motherhood at the eleventh hour. It has also been suggested that later babies are much more likely to be planned babies than the babies of 'on-time' mothers. Findings from our preliminary study indicate a lack of support for this view of older mothers.

Motherhood in Later Life study

Women were recruited to this study as a result of responses to advertisements in magazines and periodicals. The only qualification required was to have given birth on or after their fortieth birthday, hereafter described as '40-plus'. Three hundred and forty-six women participated in the research, the majority of whom had had their '40-plus' babies within the past five years. One hundred were first-time mothers. Some women had more than one child born since they were 40. The average number of children born to mothers with previous children was 3.57, and the mean age at the first birth was 26.24 years with the average gap being ten years between the first and the '40-plus' child. Some older children were grown up and in one case the gap between the first and the '40-plus' child was nearly 29 years.

Most of the mothers were in non-manual or professional occupations, with secretaries and teachers being well represented. The majority of respondents were married and/or in a stable relationship but a few had opted for single motherhood (in at least one case through artificial insemination).

Mothers were interviewed about the following areas of their experiences.

1 Conceiving their '40-plus' babies: the time taken to conceive, the occurrence of fertility problems and whether the baby was planned.
2 Reactions to becoming pregnant, their own and other people's.
3 Experiences and problems of pregnancy, including tests offered and conducted because of their age.
4 Experiences of later motherhood, including the impact on their lives, work and careers.
5 Family life and childcare, including the involvement of fathers and the reactions of older siblings.
6 Women with previous children were also asked to compare their experiences of post-40 pregnancy and motherhood with their experiences at a younger age and in particular with their experience of first-time motherhood.

Planning and reactions to pregnancy

Less than half the mothers had worked within a year of the arrival of their '40-plus' baby, and many of those who worked did so only on a part-time basis. Only 5 per cent recorded that they delayed having their '40-plus' child for career reasons, thus the view that the career is a major factor in the timing of these later babies was not upheld. Women who had '40-plus' babies were concerned about financial security but their careers were not major issues or priorities. Most women did not see their role in the family as being that of a financial provider.

Less than half the babies were planned and, as has been noted, fertility problems were much higher amongst first-time mothers: 40 per cent of these women had sought advice on fertility problems. These two findings provide a very different pattern of later motherhood from that which is widely assumed. Welles-Nystrom and de Chateau (1987) found that over three-quarters of the women in their study, aged 33 and over, planned their babies, but for women in this study who were somewhat older, there was much less evidence of planning.

Gynaecologists recognize 'the last fling of the ovaries' (Bourne, 1989, p. 505) as a phenomenon occurring at about 39. Perhaps women of 40 or so have such low expectations concerning the likelihood of a pregnancy (especially childless women as was indicated earlier) that contraception is not so widely or effectively practised. The high abortion rate amongst '40-plus' women (Birth Statistics, 1989) may also reflect this as well as general ideas about the inappropriateness of later motherhood.

The reactions of women in the later motherhood study varied. Most mothers and their partners were happy on first discovering the pregnancy (over two-thirds in both groups). The responses of family and friends, however, were often quite the reverse; '40-plus' motherhood was often seen as inappropriate and shock, horror and disgust were not uncommon reactions. Price's (1977) comment that our society is prejudiced against older parents was certainly evident.

After the birth

What was the experience of these older mothers once their '40-plus' baby was born? One outcome which is generally considered to be desirable was that older mothers breastfed for longer than average. About two-thirds opted to breastfeed, a similar proportion to that found in national surveys, but they tended to breastfeed longer than younger mothers (Department of Health and Social Security, 1974, 1980, 1988). Mothers having first babies after 40 breastfed for about six months, somewhat longer than women over 40 having second or subsequent babies who breastfed for about five months. This is two or three months longer than most younger mothers.

Physical exhaustion is often predicted to be a problem amongst older mothers (for example, Kern, 1982), and this was explored in these '40-plus' mothers. Sixty-three per cent of first-time mothers thought that they would be more tired with a '40-plus' child (compared with how they might have felt having one in their twenties), whereas less than half the second-time mothers indicated this. One-third of women mentioned sleep as a high priority when they had time without their child. Romito (1988) observed that breastfeeding mothers are more tired than bottle-feeding mothers, so perhaps the longer period of breastfeeding recorded in '40-plus' mothers was partly responsible for the high level of fatigue reported. No objective assessment of fatigue was made in this study, and it would be of interest to record the amount of sleep taken by new mothers and contrast it with their pre-pregnancy sleep rates.

Physically it is generally assumed that older mothers 'take longer to get back into shape' (Einon, 1988), and this was the case for '40-plus' mothers when compared with the same data for 'recovery' from pregnancy and birth for mothers with children already. Women were asked how long it took them to get 'back to normal'. Of course, the nature of 'normality' is highly subjective, and it is likely that each woman's expectations are influenced by her prior experience of pregnancies. First-time mothers may have higher or less realistic expectations of what they may achieve than mothers with children already. Nevertheless, women appeared to have no difficulty in answering this question. First-time mothers said it took them about eleven months on average to 'get back to normal', compared to seven months for women with children already and five and a half months for women whose first children were born a decade or so earlier. Women were asked to comment on the occurrence of a range of physical changes, symptoms and conditions, and to note if these had caused problems. First-time mothers noted more changes, but not more problems than mothers with children already. Mothers with children already reported more changes and problems compared with their first pregnancies. There is some evidence therefore that women having children after 40 may take longer to get back to normal than younger women, but these results may be influenced by their greater commitment to breastfeeding, to the parenting experience and to their ideas about normality.

Childcare arrangements

Older mothers are considered to be more financially stable than younger mothers, so how does this affect their approach to childcare? Are they more likely to have paid help with their babies? McCaulay (1976) noted that 'the era has passed when women have to choose between motherhood and/or "working" at a job', and she suggested that women over 35 are probably leading the way in combining motherhood and employment. If this was true for the US mothers in the 1970s, is it also the case for '40-plus' mothers in Britain? In the study reported here less than half of the mothers went back into employment within a year of the birth of their '40-plus' baby, and only one in six of the first-time mothers and one in twelve of the mothers who already had children said that the arrival of their '40-plus' baby made no difference to their career in paid employment.

Mothers were the major carers of their '40-plus' infants, and a third of the first-time mothers left work permanently as a result of their baby's arrival. One-fifth of women with children already did so. Most women saw a family arrangement in which father works full-time and provides income and mother has main care of the child and home as their best choice and two-thirds of women rejected strongly a family arrangement in which both parents worked full-time and there was paid help to care for the children and do housework. Clearly McCaulay's vision of the older mother combining domestic and career roles is not shared by the '40-plus' mothers of this sample, and the majority of the latter lived in 'traditional' types of family setting.

The contribution of fathers

Fathers played a relatively small part in the day-to-day care of and activities with their infants: mothers reported that fathers' main activity with their children was 'playing with' them and that first-time fathers spent more time in activities with babies than they did where women already had children. First-time mothers were more likely to have some paid help with their child (though this was still a small minority) than were mothers with previous children, but the latter had significantly more help from other relatives and friends. Fathers' help with housework and childcare has increased somewhat in recent years, making comparisons of the time fathers spent with babies born a decade apart difficult to interpret. Any increase in involvement may be merely a reflection of other trends (Grossman et al., 1988). In this sample fathers tended to be younger than their partners, especially the fathers of first-born children, who were on average three years younger. Generally, husbands are two and a half years older than wives (Marriage and Divorce Statistics, 1989). Thus for the older first-time mothers the age structure of the family was different from that of the average married couple.

Approaches to childcare and feelings about later motherhood

Women were asked a range of questions about their relationship with their new baby and their approaches to childcare routines, discipline and eating habits. In general there were few differences between first-time mothers and those with previous children, despite the greater experience of the latter. In fact, children born when women were in their twenties or thirties were more likely to be described as 'difficult' babies than were '40-plus' babies. Most mothers favoured having a routine with their child, and opted for a fairly firm approach to controlling or disciplining, and few children were described as fussy at meal times. Overall, the majority of mothers in both groups described their child as 'easy' or 'fairly easy'. In general, first-time mothers felt that with age came greater patience, whereas the majority of women with previous children felt that they were more relaxed than with their first-borns.

The feelings of older mothers about later mothering and their needs outside motherhood were also explored. The overwhelming response to motherhood was very positive. These older mothers frequently stated that they were more 'ready' for the demands of a baby, and they did not miss the reduction in their social lives. Significantly more first-time mothers noted that they would like more time away from their infants for themselves and to be with their partner. Women with previous children on the other hand found that the need to 'go out', experienced after their first babies were born, was a priority which they appeared to have outgrown. Women felt that they had a great deal to offer a later baby, and over 90 per cent enjoyed the experience. Although a minority felt that their greater age could be a disadvantage in areas such as engaging in sports with their children, the majority did not view the large generation gap as a problem. Without more information it is not possible to know whether the age difference between mothers and children and between later born children and older siblings could become more significant in later years.

Given the methods of recruitment, it is clear that these women are not representative of all older women who become mothers after 40. Nevertheless, only a tiny minority (2 per cent) noted that it had been a bad experience (one mother said that had a termination been possible, she would have chosen to have one). It seems likely that although these babies were not all planned, the option of not proceeding with the pregnancy was there for the majority and indeed many women were shocked to be offered the option of a termination by their doctor on the basis of their age. Perhaps it is going too far to say, as one of Kern's (1982) subjects did, that later motherhood is 'an endless joy', nevertheless '40-plus' mothers clearly found later motherhood to be highly rewarding and an experience which they would not have missed.

This study did not attempt to assess how the children of older mothers feel, but the mothers clearly considered their experience to be positive. Over half of those with grown-up children believed that they had a unique and special relationship with them. Price (1977) may be right when she notes that the 'disadvantages' for children of older parents may be more in the minds of the parents than in the minds of their children.

Conclusions

From the medical perspective, later motherhood is seen purely in terms of increased risks, and although much of the research has been strongly criticized (Mansfield, 1988; McCaulay, 1976), there is now a growing recognition that 'Many doctors deplore trends towards having babies later in life' and 'urge women not to postpone having children' (Birke et al., 1990, p. 67). The increased 'medicalization' of human reproduction has not only made women feel that having babies is an unnatural state, a 'disease' or 'disorder', but it has also undermined their role in reproduction. This is especially the case for those who opt for later motherhood. By defining women of 30 or more as 'elderly' or 'older', it is clear to women that they are viewed as problems from the outset. Indeed, they are even advised by the British Medical Association that they should not view their condition 'through rose-tinted spectacles' (Jeffries, 1985). If they had no anxiety about their pregnancies, then comments such as this one may well engender it.

Wendy Savage, who has long campaigned for a woman's right to decide how her pregnancy and delivery should be managed, has stressed that 'if you're surrounded by people who don't expect your body to work, it won't!' (Savage, 1990). This remark was made in a discussion on the trend towards more caesarean section deliveries, but it might equally well apply to a discussion concerned with older mothers. The expectation is, on the basis of their age alone, that such women will have problems, and Savage argues that this becomes a self-fulfilling prophecy.

In the study of older motherhood, whilst most women agreed that there was an ideal age to have a child, there was no consensus on when that age was. Responses ranged from 'it depends' (on personal factors appropriate to the individual woman) to ages in the 20s and 30s and 'every age'. Women's answers to questions such as these were highly influenced by their own experience. One mother, who had at least one child in each decade from her twenties to her forties, felt that she could not give an ideal age because she 'felt OK with all of them'. Perhaps the answer is that the right time is when a woman would welcome a baby whether planned or otherwise. There are no guarantees about parenthood at any age, yet the evidence indicates that older mothers may have skills as a result of their greater maturity which can contribute to their abilities as parents. This view is reinforced by women's reactions. In the perception of women themselves, having a baby later in life is a very positive experience. Whether planned or not, women feel that they have a lot to offer their child, and most are unconcerned about the larger than average generation gap.

The notion that 30 or over is old for a pregnancy is a particularly recent phenomenon. Perhaps if the trend towards later parenting continues then, by sheer force of numbers, the perception of such mothers will change. For the present, I would argue that what is important is that information about the whole experience should be more accessible. In other words becoming a mother is much more than just becoming pregnant and giving birth, and information on the psychological and sociological aspects of motherhood at any age and at any stage in the life of the child, needs to be just as widely available as that on the medical aspects of pregnancy and birth. If this were the case, women, and indeed all those concerned with pregnancy, birth and motherhood, would be better able to balance the problem-centred approach to later motherhood with the more positive findings of research in psychology and sociology.

Notes

The author would like to thank Ms Kathryn Noble for typing this chapter and all the many 40-plus mothers who took part in the Motherhood in Later Life project. The research on this project was supported by the Research Board of the University of Leicester.
1 The Apgar test is a test of newborn infants' physiological state. It is done on all babies born in Britain one minute and five minutes after birth.
2 Down's syndrome is a chromosomal disorder in which there is an extra chromosome on the 21st pair of chromosomes (trisomy 21). A normal individual has 23 pairs of chromosomes and each parent contributes one of each pair; in trisomy one parent gives 24 chromosomes because one pair amongst the 23 fails to disjunct. The result is mental handicap.
3 Amniocentesis and chorionic villus sampling are two pre-natal tests. Amniocentesis is carried out between 16 and 20 weeks of pregnancy and consists of inserting a long needle into the uterus (with the use of ultrasound for guidance) so that a small amount of amniotic fluid can be withdrawn. This fluid contains some fetal cells which can be grown in a culture so that chromosomal disorders and inborn metabolic errors of the fetus can be identified. The results take up to four weeks to become available. Chorionic villus sampling (CVS) is a test which is carried out between 8 and 12 weeks of pregnancy and is used to diagnose chromosomal abnormalities and inherited disorders. The test involves aspiration of a small sample of chorionic villi, the tissue developing around the placenta, from which chromosomal analysis can be performed. The results of this test are available within a few days.

References

Alment, E.A.J. (1970) The elderly primigravida. *The Practitioner* 204, 371–6.
Barbour, R.S. (1990) Fathers: the emergence of a new consumer group. In J. Garcia, R. Kilpatrick and M.P.M. Richards (eds), *The Politics of Maternity Care*. Oxford: Oxford University Press.
Berg, I., Butler, A. and McGuire, R. (1972) Birth and family size of school-phobic adolescents. *British Journal of Psychiatry* 121, 509–14.
Berkowitz, G.S., Skovron, M.L., Lapinski, R.H. and Berkowitz, R.L. (1990) Delayed childbearing and the outcome of pregnancy. *New England Journal of Medicine* 322, 659–63.
Berryman, J.C. and Windridge, K. (in press a) Having a baby after 40. I. A preliminary investigation of women's experience of pregnancy. *Journal of Reproductive and Infant Psychology*.

Berryman, J.C. and Windridge, K. (in press b) Having a baby after 40. II. A preliminary investigation of women's experience of motherhood. *Journal of Reproductive and Infant Psychology.*

Birke, L., Himmelweit, S. and Vines, G. (1990) *Tomorrow's Child: Reproductive Technologies in the 90s.* London: Virago.

Birth Statistics (1989) *Birth Statistics 1987.* Series FMI no. 16. London: HMSO.

Blum, M. (1979) Is the elderly primipara really at high risk? *Journal of Perinatal Medicine* 7, 108–12.

Bostock, Y. and Jones, M. (1987) *Now or Never? Having a Baby Later in Life.* Wellingborough: Grapevine.

Bourne, G. (1989) *Pregnancy.* London: Pan Books.

Cartwright, A. (1976) *How Many Children?* London: Routledge and Kegan Paul.

Dalen, P. (1977) Maternal age and incidence of schizophrenia in the Republic of Ireland. *British Journal of Psychiatry* 131, 301–5.

Davidson, H.S. (1912) *Marriage and Motherhood: a Wife's Handbook.* London: T.C. & E.C. Jack.

Demographic Yearbook (1988) *Demographic Yearbook 1986.* New York: United Nations.

Department of Health and Social Security (1974) Present day practice in infant feeding. *Report on Health and Social Subjects* no. 9. London: HMSO.

Department of Health and Social Security (1980) Present day practice in infant feeding. *Report on Health and Social Subjects* no. 20. London: HMSO.

Department of Health and Social Security (1988) *Present day practice in infant feeding.* Third report. London: HMSO.

Eichholz, A. and Offerman-Zuckenberg, J. (1980) Later pregnancy. In B.L. Blum (ed.), *Psychological Aspects of Pregnancy, Birthing, and Bonding.* New York: Human Sciences Press.

Einon, D. (1988) *Parenthood: the Whole Story.* London: Bloomsbury.

Fabe, M. and Winkler, M. (1979) *Up Against the Clock.* New York: Random House.

Flinn, M. (ed.) (1977) *Scottish Population History: From the 17th Century to the 1930s.* Cambridge: Cambridge University Press.

Frankel, S.A. and Wise, M.J. (1982) A view of delayed parenting: some implications of a new trend. *Psychiatry* 45, 220–5.

Gardner, M.J., Snee, M.P., Hall, A.J., Powell, C.A., Downes, S. and Terrell, J.D. (1990) Results of case-control study of leukaemia and lymphoma among young people near Sellafield nuclear plant in West Cumbria. *British Medical Journal* 300, 423–34.

General Household Survey (1989) *General Household Survey 1986.* An Inter-departmental Survey Sponsored by the Central Statistical Office. London: HMSO.

Grossman, F.K., Pollack, W.S. and Golding, E. (1988) Fathers and children: predicting the quality and quantity of fathering. *Developmental Psychology* 24, 82–91.

Halmi, K.A. (1974) Anorexia nervosa: demographic and clinical features in 94 cases. *Psychosomatic Medicine* 36, 18–26.

Jeffries, M. (ed.) (1985) *You and Your Baby: Pregnancy to Infancy.* London: British Medical Association, Family Doctor Publication.

Katz-Rothman, B. (1986) *The Tentative Pregnancy.* New York: Viking Penguin.

Kern, I. (1982) '. . . an endless joy . . .': The joys of motherhood over 35. *Papers in the Social Sciences* 2, 43–56.

Kitzinger, S. (1982) *Birth Over Thirty*. London: Sheldon Press.

Llewellyn-Jones, D. (1982) *Everywoman: a Gynaecological Guide for Life*. London: Faber and Faber.

Llewellyn-Jones, D. (1986) *Fundamentals of Obstetrics and Gynaecology*, vol. II: *Gynaecology*. London: Faber and Faber.

Macfarlane, A. and Mugford, M. (1984) *Birth Counts: Statistics of Pregnancy and Childbirth*. London: HMSO.

Mansfield, P.K. (1988) Midlife childbearing: strategies for informed decision making. *Psychology of Women Quarterly* Special Issue: Women's Health, Our Minds, Our Bodies, 12, 445–60.

Mansfield, P.K. and Cohn, M.D. (1986) Stress and later-life childbearing: important implications for nursing. *Maternal Child Nursing Journal* 15, 139–51.

Marriage and Divorce Statistics (1989) Review of the Registrar General on Marriages and Divorces in England and Wales 1987. Series FM2 no. 4. London: HMSO.

McCaulay, C.S. (1976) *Pregnancy After Thirty-Five*. New York: Dutton.

Michelson, J. and Gee, S. (1984) *Coming Late to Motherhood*. Wellingborough: Thorsons.

Neugarten, B. (1972) Social Clocks. Paper presented at the American Psychoanalytic Association, New York, December. Quoted in Tuirini, P. (1980) Psychological crises in normal pregnancy. In B.L. Blum (ed.), *Psychological Aspects of Pregnancy, Birthing, and Bonding*. New York and London: Human Sciences Press.

Nortman, D. (1974) Parental age as a factor in pregnancy outcome and child development. *Reports of Population/Family Planning* no. 16. New York: Population Council.

Price, J. (1977) *You're Not Too Old to Have a Baby*. New York: Farrar, Straus and Giroux.

Ragozin, A.S., Basham, R.B., Crnic, K.A., Greenberg, M.T. and Robinson, N.M. (1982) Effects of maternal age on parenting role. *Developmental Psychology* 18, 627–34.

Reid, M. (1990) Pre-natal diagnosis and screening: a review. In J. Garcia, R. Kilpatrick and M.P.M. Richards (eds), *The Politics of Maternity Care*. Oxford: Oxford University Press.

Reis, J. (1988) Child-rearing expectations and developmental knowledge according to maternal age and parity. *Infant Mental Health Journal* 9, 287–304.

Richards, M.P.M. (1989) Social and ethical problems of fetal diagnosis and screening. *Journal of Reproductive and Infant Psychology* 7, 171–86.

Romito, P. (1988) Mothers' experience of breastfeeding. *Journal of Reproductive and Infant Psychology* 6, 89–99.

Savage, W., quoted in McKee, V. (1990) Childbirth choices: is there a backlash against natural birth? *Good Housekeeping* 135, 54–5.

Sears, R.R., Maccoby, E. and Levin, H. (1957) *Patterns of Child Rearing*. Evanston, Ill.: Rowe Peterson.

Seth, M. and Khanna, M. (1978) Child rearing attitudes of the mothers as a function of age. *Child Psychiatry Quarterly* 11, 6–9.

Shaw, M. (1986) Substitute parenting. In W. Sluckin and M. Herbert (eds), *Parental Behaviour*. Oxford: Basil Blackwell.

Shultz, T. (1979) *Women Can Wait: the Pleasures of Motherhood after 30.* New York: Doubleday (Dolphin).

Welles-Nystrom, B.L. and de Chateau, P. (1987) Maternal age and transition to motherhood: prenatal and perinatal assessments. *Acta Psychiatrica Scandinavica* 76, 719–25.

Wilkie, J.R. (1981) The trend toward delayed parenthood. *Journal of Marriage and the Family* 43 (3), 583–91.

Women and Men in Britain (1989) Research and Statistics Units, Equal Opportunities Commission. London: HMSO.

Zybert, P., Stein, Z. and Belmont, L. (1978) Maternal age and children's ability. *Perceptual and Motor Skills* 47, 815–18.

7

Challenging Motherhood: Mothers and their Deaf Children

Susan Gregory

To diagnose a child as disabled is to alter the way society deals with that child, both formally through special institutions and informally in the way members of a society react to disabled children. By association too, the diagnosis of disability in a child has implications for the mother in the way in which she constructs her particular tasks because the images of motherhood available to her are based on healthy able-bodied children. To be a mother of a disabled child is to be different – a mother because she undoubtedly has a child, yet somehow not a mother in terms of the conventional notions of motherhood which pervade our society. This chapter attempts to explore the way that such mothers construct the task of mothering a disabled child. It does this firstly by examining the received wisdom about disabled children available to mothers in books and magazines on babies. It then focuses more specifically on deaf children and looks at the impact of children's deafness on their mothers.

The impact of disability

In order to understand the impact of the disability of a child on the mother it may be helpful to consider the construction of motherhood prevalent in Western society. The extent to which books on pregnancy and motherhood describe contemporaneous perceptions, attitudes and mores is difficult to evaluate and, as Mechling (1975) points out, such data are not without their problems. It cannot be assumed that these books either reflect practice or influence it. However, it is likely that these images are ones which society approves of, or at least condones, and they provide an easily accessible source of information for both the literate mother and social researcher (see chapter 4). In the context of this chapter books on pregnancy and childbirth are important in that they highlight the ambiguous attitude of society towards disability.

Books on pregnancy readily available to mothers talk of the possibility of disability but clearly establish that it is something to be avoided, that it should not be allowed to happen. Advice is given on how to prevent this through care over diet, through limiting or excluding drugs and alcohol, and the avoidance of contact with particular illnesses which are related to disability. The advice given by Einon in *Parenthood: the Whole Story*, a book widely available, is typical of many:

> By the time you are sure you are pregnant, the embryo is starting to take shape. It is delicate and vulnerable. Drugs, diet, smoking and exposure to chemicals may influence its development . . . Although with care you can reduce the risks to your baby you cannot eliminate them . . . Eat sensibly, take exercise, don't smoke or binge on alcohol and coffee and take drugs sparingly or not at all. (Einon, 1988, p. 19)

And later:

> At a slightly later stage, things can go wrong which produce profound disabilities without killing the embryo . . . The development of the eyes and ears can be disrupted by Rubella, but blindness or deafness are not fatal to the embryo or child . . . For most of us these are the stuff of nightmares. The care taken to reduce the risks to a minimum is well worth taking. (p. 60)

It is a generally held view that many mothers will be afraid that their baby will be born disabled, and while such fears are sympathetically discussed in books on pregnancy, they are also presented as neurotic and irrational. However, termination is discussed as a legitimate and acceptable possibility should there be evidence that the undesirable is likely to occur. Einon again:

> It is possible to discover whether or not the child you are carrying has chromosomal abnormality before birth and abortion is normally offered to anyone in this position. (p. 18)

The overall message is that disability is unlikely, undesirable and to be avoided at all costs. While the basic theme here is that care should be taken to avoid giving birth to a disabled child, there is an implicit message that it is the mother's responsibility to take all necessary steps to avoid it, with the corollary that if anything does go wrong the mother may feel somehow to blame.

Yet, while books on pregnancy and birth include some discussion of disability, mother-and-baby books designed to help and advise the new mother are, in contrast, strangely reticent on this subject. In the positive, sanitized world of the baby book, reference to such families or children is rare. Yet this is not because disability is uncommon, for two out of every 100 babies will be born with impairments that will be disabling within this society. The relative silence is, therefore, more likely to be because disability is at variance with the idealized notion of motherhood and babies endorsed by such books. But this silence serves to exclude mothers of disabled children from inclusion in the category of motherhood as constructed in our society. For mothers of disabled children, this occurs not through being told explicitly, but because they find themselves and their situation invisible; their exclusion is a result of omission.

If one looks at any of the currently available baby books and magazines intended for mothers, one is struck by the relative absence of any mention of disability in the vast majority of them. The Reader's Digest *Mother and Baby Book* (1989) has a section on special problems around birth such as prematurity, jaundice and the death of a baby, but nowhere mentions children growing up with a disability. The *Complete Mothercare Manual* (1986) mentions the possibility of disability early in the book as a potential problem, but the reader is then referred straight through the book to the list of useful names and addresses at the back, making it seem that the book itself is not for mothers of disabled children who must seek information elsewhere. Penelope Leach in her popular book *Baby and Child* (1979, reprinted 1985), addresses disability briefly (in only half a page) and she, too, suggests that parents follow up the 'useful addresses' given at the back of the book. One of the best sellers in the field, sold by Marks and Spencer, *The Complete Book of Babycare* (Nash, 1980), fails to list disability in the index. Apart from the section on pregnancy, the only two references to disability I could find were on deafness: 'Any doubts about a baby's hearing should be mentioned to a doctor promptly' (p. 178), and on 'mental retardation' (sic):

> The development of social responses and the general understanding of situations is a measure of the baby's intellect. Mentally retarded infants, for example, are usually so slow to learn skills that their milestones are generally delayed. By about six weeks a normal baby smiles in response to his mother. (p. 180)

The dismissive style of these brief inclusions and the fact that there are no more mentions of disability later in the book, seems to convey the message to mothers of disabled children that they are not part of the assumed readership of the book and thus not within the remit of the 'Complete Babycare' under consideration. The consequence for the mother is her exclusion from the category of mothers as it is constituted by books (and also by magazines on childcare), for disabled children are excluded from these pages.

There are, however, two childcare books that do refer more extensively to disability. These are both by male doctors – Dr Hugh Jolly (1977) and Dr Benjamin Spock (1971) – and within them disability is treated as illness, in that the topic is clearly located in the sections dealing with illness and sickness. While it is outside the scope of this chapter to discuss this issue in detail, such a medical model of disability is itself problematic, within its implications that disability is illness to be treated or cured. It is a model increasingly rejected by disabled people themselves (Finkelstein, 1985; Oliver, 1990).

What images remain for these mothers, to whom the unthinkable happens and who are excluded from the popular discourse on motherhood which is silent on their situation? Having a disabled child leads mothers to enter a new domain. The available images are portrayals of unremitting bravery and devotion; stories in the popular press about disabled children generally focus on sacrifice and heroism. The child becomes the focus of appeals for money as fund-raising efforts such as 'Children in Need' create disabled children as objects of charity, where basic needs are provided for not as of right, but by people raising money by particular, and often ludicrous, activities such as swimming in vats of custard. Thus in being portrayed in need of philanthropy and pity, mothers of disabled children are further placed outside the popular conception of motherhood. There is a contradictory aspect of the images of sacrifice and heroism which presents a paradox to mothers: a disabled child is undesirable, but a mother of a disabled child is portrayed as loving and accepting her own child unconditionally.

I propose to explore these notions further by looking here specifically at deaf children and their mothers, at the impact of the child's deafness on the family, and the way in which motherhood is construed in the various kinds of information available. I will also consider the ways in which normalization is such a powerful device that mothers are pressured to present their children in a particular way. The notion of 'normal development' is central to current conceptions of mothering and a reason for the exclusion of mothers of disabled children from babycare books is that they cannot easily be incorporated into this discourse. It will emerge that one of the implicit goals offered to mothers of deaf children is that of normalization – to make their child be, or seem to be, as 'normal' as possible (for a further discussion of normalization see Urwin, 1985).

Most of the material presented below comes from two related research studies of families with deaf children. In the first, carried out in the early 1970s, I interviewed 122 mothers of deaf children of 5 years and under. The sample comprised all such children diagnosed as having a hearing loss at the time of the study in five East Midland counties; the refusal rate was low and thus the sample can be taken as representative (Gregory, 1976). In a recent follow-up study, 101 of these families were selected for further interview[1] of whom eighty-three were traced and the mothers interviewed (Gregory et al., in preparation). Following the work of John and Elizabeth Newson, both studies used a guided interview schedule where the interview follows a specified format, but the structure of the questions and the general nature of the prompts allows the interviewees relative freedom in answering and elaborating as they choose (see Newson and Newson, 1963, for further details). Most interviews took four to five hours and the quotes included here are from transcripts of the interviews. In addition, I have included some material from published accounts by mothers of deaf children.

The meaning of diagnosis

Most deaf children, over 90 per cent, are born to hearing parents, the majority of whom have no prior experience of deaf children. Deafness is rarely diagnosed at birth unless there is a major and very rare physical abnormality of the ears. If newborn infants are 'at risk' various screening techniques may be employed, but even then diagnosis will take place over a period of weeks. Diagnosis is most likely to occur during the second year of life, often at mothers' instigations because they are concerned about the children seeming different or being slow in talking. As with other disabilities which are not diagnosed at birth, mothers thus have an initial period of 'ordinary' motherhood.

It is at diagnosis that hitherto ordinary mothers became abnormal, as mothers of deaf children, and for most mothers this is a highly significant time. For some of the mothers interviewed, I have reported their reaction close to the time of diagnosis and again several years later, when their offspring were in their twenties. While consistency is not a feature of all memories of child-rearing, those concerning diagnosis show it to a remarkable extent. In common with other specific identifiable happenings, these events are remembered with particular clarity and probably indicate the impact that the diagnosis had at the time.

Not surprisingly, for many it is a distressing time, as this mother of a 6-year-old deaf boy describes:

> We knew really, but I was heart broken, we knew when he was being tested; it was a shattering time that was; it was terrible but the thing is you have to keep telling yourself and make yourself try and accept it. The thing is I don't think you ever really do fully fully accept it. I'm always waiting for one morning I'll get up and Colin will be all right, if I was dead honest about it, but really I know he won't be.

Interviewed eighteen years later, when her son was 24, she still remembered her initial reaction:

> We were young, naive, we were absolutely stunned and absolutely broken hearted. It was awful. I mean it could make me cry now thinking about it. It was awful.

The models most frequently used to construct parents' feelings around the time of diagnosis are derived from the work of Kubler-Ross (1970) based on reactions to death and dying, where she specifies the mechanisms of denial, anger, bargaining, depression and grief. The period of diagnosis is seen as a period of loss of the expected hearing child and a need to accept the deaf child. Moses (1985), in talking about the diagnosis of deafness in children, says:

> Most parents find disability to be a great spoiler of their dreams and fantasies about who or what their child was to be. Most dreams require an unimpaired child; therefore the initial diagnosis of disability often marks the point when a cherished and significant dream has been shattered . . . Ironically, often the people who are needed to facilitate grief instead discourage it. Rather than accepting the denial, guilt, depression, anger and anxiety which are the natural part of the grieving process, those closest to the bereaved individual may view these affective states as psychopathological. (pp. 86–7)

While some mothers undoubtedly feel these powerful emotions and go through such stages of adjustment, with others it is far less clear that this is the case. There is a danger that the expectation of grief and despair may become prescriptive, that all reactions are accommodated to this model, preventing attention to other equally significant reactions. Also mothers who do not go through such stages and do not publicly admit feelings of grief may, with the widespread adoption of such a model among professionals, be seen as pathological.

Diagnosis of deafness in a child is rarely a sudden or completely unexpected event because it takes place over an extended period of time. Often the mother is the first to suspect and fights to have her suspicions recognized. Her suspicions may arise either through the child obviously not hearing some significant event, or more likely through delay in the child developing spoken language. In either of these cases there is likely to be a long period of suspicion or anxiety on the part of the mother before the diagnosis is confirmed. It may, in fact, take some months for mothers to get their fears taken seriously. Reports of periods of six months to one year from the mother's first suspicions to getting a diagnosis are not uncommon. Doctors and health visitors often see their task as reassuring mothers of young children because new mothers are perceived as susceptible to irrational fears. Such reassurance arouses complex emotions in the mother. For, having taken the courage to voice her fears, to hear the news she most wants to hear – that they are groundless – while herself still believing them to be valid, can only be stressful.

The response to eventual diagnosis in such cases is likely to be relief at being taken seriously. The mother of a girl aged 4 years said:

> I was just sheer relieved to know it wasn't me going mad, at first. So many people had stood in my path and said 'You're whittling, you're worrying there's nothing wrong with her, she'll talk when she's ready', I thought if it went on much longer at home and the child was supposed to be normal, I'd go off me rocker. So really it wasn't so much finding fault with anybody, or how it had been handled, it was just relief to know at long last we did know there was something wrong, and what is was and we could tackle it.

Interviewed sixteen years later, when her daughter was 20:

> It's so difficult to remember what it was like at the time I think. When you felt there was something wrong all along and you couldn't put your finger on it, knowing something is a relief in a way – it takes the worry out of it – and the wondering whether you were imagining it or going mad, or wondering was it this or was it that, when somebody says it's that, that's one big relief.

Another very common reaction, which also contained elements of relief, is that of being grateful there is not something perceived as more seriously wrong with their children or that the diagnosis is not of a less acceptable disability. As these two mothers of 3-year-old deaf boys said:

> Relieved, to tell you the truth. Because I was worried they would say he was retarded to tell you the truth. That was another hurdle we could have done without.

> Well, I think the fact I'd realized this before. I think in a way, rather
> than – I don't know whether it's awful to say this or not – but rather
> the fact he should be mentally retarded, it was a relief in a way that
> it was deafness. At least I thought we might get somewhere.

While for many mothers the shock is profound at the time of
diagnosis, others are caught up in seemingly trivial details of the
implications, as this mother recounts some years after the
diagnosis:

> The funny thing is when I look back on it – when I was told he was
> deaf and would need to wear hearing aids – I thought 'how will he
> manage when he's on the beach with his trunks on?' – to hide them
> I suppose. I didn't think of anything else. I wasn't even worried even.
> I look back and think if that was all I had to worry about. I have to
> laugh, I was so young.

The danger of having a model of expectations of reactions to
deafness (or anything else) is its prescriptive nature, as indicated
by the mother who said 'I know I should feel guilty but I don't'.

For the majority of mothers, diagnosis brought with it
particular feelings of responsibility, that having brought this child
into the world they were responsible for his or her well-being and,
in addition to this, often they had to reconsider their plans for the
future. This was sometimes expressed as a realization that they
could not easily choose to go back to work straight away, or that
they would have to make particular efforts in bringing up their
child, as indicated in the following:

> At last I saw the extent of my responsibility towards Sarah. If ever she
> was to catch up she must receive a continuous stream of information
> for all her waking hours. As I looked around me, I saw a world which
> jostled to be described, a world which I must share. (Robinson, 1987,
> pp. 44–5)

Public worlds

While diagnosis is initially a private matter, mothering takes place
in both the private and public domains, and after diagnosis the
mother has to re-define her status as the mother of a deaf child.
For most mothers, the diagnosis brings with it a feeling of being
different, of being set aside.

> I used to find on holiday I felt Carol's handicap more, when we were
> at the sea and watching other children, than at any other time. Apart
> from all the day-to-day things, you felt that when you were on holiday
> you ought to be the same as everybody else but you weren't.

Breaking the news to others is sometimes more difficult because the diagnosis was not at birth and so people had come to know the child as all right, for the mother may not have shown her early fears and doubts to others. This mother of a young adult man clearly remembers how it was:

> I think if he was diagnosed right from birth, if they could do that, you haven't got – and it is stigma, as much as it sounds silly, to say to someone 'my baby's deaf'. Whereas if you are sort of told – I know it is traumatic whatever the time – but you haven't got the trauma then of letting someone see them running round for two years and then they say, 'Did you know Mark was deaf?' It takes a lot to say it and it takes a lot for you to actually say it to somebody else. It takes a long time to accept it yourself without having to communicate it to everybody else, you know. Whereas I think if it is known from the start and people – it is easier for you. They think: 'Oh yes a fine baby but you know he is deaf and they are doing everything they can', that sort of thing, rather than having to take the step and say 'yes well, I have taken him there and he is deaf'. It's a lot to say it.

One of the main immediate problems for many mothers is how to present this information to others. The mother of a deaf child has to take the responsibility for managing such a situation though this is clearly difficult: 'Well I either blurted it out at the beginning so that they knew or I avoided it, and it just depended on my feelings at the time.'

For some mothers there is a stigma attached to having a deaf child but the issue is not simply this. It is felt that telling people puts the receiver of the information in a difficult position because they will be embarrassed and not know what to say.

> People are embarrassed I think they're guilty. You know they feel rotten that you've got a handicapped child and they haven't. They don't want a handicapped child but they wish you hadn't got one.

> It's not that you feel lonely but other mothers are too embarrassed to say anything.

Voysey (1975) points out the mother of a disabled child needs to develop a comprehensive account of her situation both for herself and to put it to other mothers. She is, in Goffman's sense, 'the wise' someone who is herself without stigma, but bound up with the stigmatized (Goffman, 1968). The public presentation of the family is usually the mother's concern.

For mothers in general, their children's overt behaviour may reinforce or contradict the public image they are attempting to create and maintain. Thus children may be unwitting partners in the construction of an acceptable public presentation. When the child is disabled this may be complicated by the child's lack of conformity to the idealized norm. Moreover, when children are deaf the areas of doubt increase as it is not clear to anyone what the appropriate image is. This can be compounded by the fact that deafness is invisible, there are no outward signs to the casual observer that the child is different.

Some mothers respond by going out less and less:

> Before we had the children we used to have a lot of family get-togethers and we don't now and I feel a lot of it is because of Christopher.

While others resist such change:

> When Stephen was a baby I felt I wanted to shut me and him away . . . and it took me a long while to come round. Now he goes where I go and if I meet someone he comes along as well.

Many mothers were concerned about their public image for somehow the deafness meant more rather than less was expected of their children. Because they wanted their children to be accepted, greater conformity in behaviour rather than less was required of them, imposing additional pressures on mothers:

> We were so conscious of this thing so many people said, you know, if a child has got some disadvantage they have to be extra special in other respects to be accepted, which is jolly hard but it's true. I always dressed her as nicely as I could and we did our best to ensure she behaved nicely – not that she always did – but we did our best. She was good at table, you could have taken her anywhere for a meal, and you still could – she is not at her best at home, she sits with her elbows on the table but you can take here anywhere and she will behave . . . She is very good. You could be proud of her. You could take her out anywhere.

> I've always said to Peter 'you've got to behave normally'. If you're badly behaved nobody wants to know. If you behave satisfactorily you will be accepted and your deafness won't be so bad. If you're horrible, nobody wants to know. You've got to be acceptable. Certain deaf people expect special attention. I don't think a deaf person should. I think you should be as normal as possible, and just be acceptable.

Mothers may also lose the support network of other mothers because the child is different and because other mothers do not know what to say or how to handle the situation. The following mothers comment as they look back on the early times following diagnosis:

> You feel so alone, you and your child versus the world. Nobody wants to know. You always feel it's you they're getting at.

> You feel isolated when other people were . . . Mums had got hearing

kids and you were the odd one with a deaf child. There were no clubs where you could go to.

Well you are so isolated. They are so different, you can't communicate with other mothers in the same way, and the children can't. They're normal in the way they develop physically I suppose, but in their habits . . . You haven't got anything to talk about when they say 'Oh she said so-and-so and so-and-so today'. You see, there's nothing.

The involvement of professionals

Mothers of disabled children are likely to receive explicit specific advice on bringing their children up. The status of this advice is different from that usually given to mothers, in that it may be unsolicited and it will certainly be difficult to reject, as disability makes a child a legitimate focus of public concern. Moreover, the mothers may be particularly vulnerable to such advice, as there is little other information available. However, professionals by definition are middle class and the advice pervaded by middle class ideologies, with implicit expectations of parenthood and childrearing which may not be shared by the parents. Even in 1981, a leaflet was published specifically for parents of deaf children containing the following advice:

It is useful to have a bedtime routine, one you follow every night. Children respond well to routine. (McArthy et al., 1981, p. 18)

Everybody needs time away from their children, if the husband wife relationship is to blossom and there is already a danger of the hearing impaired child becoming the focus of all family life. (p. 23)

Tantrums occur when there is a clash of wills, the parental and the child's, and it is necessary on points of discipline that the parental will is achieved. If there is a family rule that something is not done then it is not done today, tomorrow or ever. (p. 17)

Such advice based on assumptions about routine, discipline and the need for child-free periods for parents carries strong ideological messages that the parents may not share.

A particular theme of the advice given to parents of deaf children is an emphasis on educational goals and language development. The major manifestation of deafness is a difficulty in developing spoken language. While some have argued that, with good auditory training and hearing aids, good spoken language is possible, for most profoundly deaf children it remains an unobtainable goal. In a major study of deaf school-leavers Conrad (1976) found that half left school with speech that was hard to understand or effectively unintelligible. Markides, more recently (1983), in writing about profoundly deaf children, has concluded 'that the speech of the large majority of these children is unintelligible to the man (sic) in the street'. Such difficulty with spoken language is indicative of a more general problem with communication by speech as deaf children also have relatively poor lip-reading skills and reading ability. The picture is not the same for the small number of deaf children who have deaf parents and learn sign language as a first language – a point I shall return to later.

Currently controversy surrounds the best way of bringing up deaf children. Should the parents learn and use sign language with their children or communicate only by spoken language? The controversy is fierce as the following quotations from recent publications concerned with the education of deaf children show:

> Our examination of the communication options available for use with deaf children confirms our conviction that for the majority, the overwhelming majority of deaf children, the oral-auditory approach offers the best chance of developing language and providing the means of communication. Through an oral-auditory approach, therefore, we believe the child is offered the most satisfactory preparation for life in the wider society. (Lynas et al., not dated but published in 1988, p. 32)

> When children are born, they are predisposed to learn a natural language. Natural sign languages are learned easily through normal language acquisition processes by deaf children who are exposed to them at an early age. For this reason, natural sign language is the best vehicle for providing access to socio-cultural information during early childhood and to the curricular content of education at all ages. (Johnson et al., 1981, p. 15)

While the controversy *per se* is not a focus of this chapter, it is of critical importance to mothers and the context within which mothering takes place. For the vast majority of mothers of deaf children, who are hearing, issues about how to communicate with their children and how to prepare them for communicating with other people are critical. Communication, after all, is at the heart of the mothering process which is essentially concerned with cultural transmission.

Most families with deaf children will be visited weekly by a peripatetic teacher of the deaf. One of the problems for both parents and adviser is the very existence of such a service presupposes that there is advice that can be given, and thus a correct way to bring up deaf children and foster language development. A further implication is that not carrying out the advice will have adverse consequences. Thus a failure on the part of the child to develop language skills can be blamed on the mother for there was a correct way to do things which she must, by implication, have failed to achieve. Often the mothers were unable to carry out the advice, despite desperate efforts:

> When I talk to the teacher I feel guilty that I'm not playing *my* part, you know. Although I do constantly try . . . You know they say 'You should try so-and-so' or 'You could try so-and-so with Tim, or do so-and-so with Tim'. But you can't do that with Tim. I don't care what anybody says, you cannot do it. That child will not do a thing you know. The times we've tried, you know and he's gone to bed and I've cried and cried to John [husband] and John says, 'Ooh you are silly'. But I say, 'John I must try and help him' and he says, 'You've done all you can for him you know'. But I cannot help him, I just cannot help him. I've tried so hard. John says, 'You're trying too hard, you're upsetting yourself'. You just can't, I've tried.

The impact of any failure to carry out the advice is magnified by the vulnerability of mothers of disabled children to professional ideologies and advice. For mothers with non-disabled children, advice usually occurs within the context of a wider commensurate group of friends, relatives and acquaintances with whom they can share discussions of common childrearing experiences. The incidence of disability inevitably means that mothers with deaf children are unlikely to know others in a similar position. Their only knowledge about practice will be mediated by professionals whose knowledge is more often gained from relevant literature or observation than from first-hand experience of living with disability. Thus there is a reliance on knowledge in the public domain which may neither facilitate professional goals nor fulfil the mothers' hopes.

Theory into practice – the advice on early development

The professional advice given to parents of disabled children has similar origins to that given to parents of children without disabilities, much of which is validated by reference to contemporaneous developmental psychology. The introduction of video recording into the study of the mother–baby interaction enabled psychologists to examine and re-examine the same sequence of behaviour over and over again. This highlighted two things: firstly babies being altogether more purposively active and more competent than had previously been thought and secondly the subtlety of the interaction between mothers and children. One effect of this kind of research has been to attribute wider responsibility to mothers. While the influence of Bowlby (1953) has been to make them responsible for social development and created the need for ever-present mothers, research in the 1960s and 1970s made them responsible for cognitive development as well. The suggestion was that the optimal development of children requires the formation of complex interaction skills and the development of joint action and joint reference which depends not only on the presence of mothers but on the quality of their interaction with their children.

Advice resulting from this perspective focuses on stimulating children and sensitivity to them. It emphasizes the quality rather than the quantity of interaction. Although research studies may reveal specific aspects of mother–baby interaction, the situation they describe is extremely idealized and context-dependent. Riley (1983), for example, draws attention to this isolation of the mother–child pair from the wider social community:

> It speaks only of the activities of a timeless ahistorical desert island mother child couple, watched at its communicatings as in a bell jar. (p. 20)

She draws attention to the pressures on mothers as a result of attempts to use such studies to point to 'good mothering':

> The responsibility attributed to mothers widened: they are seen as responsible, not only for emotional development, as in earlier 'attachment' work, but also for facilitating the child's communicative capacities – its humanity. (p. 25)

Methods of observation in research influence not only descriptions of the data but the data themselves. The discrepancy between naturally occurring behaviour where mothers have to look after other children, attend to domestic duties etc., and behaviour elicited during research can be acute. My concern here, however, is with deaf children, where advice based on traditional studies of child development is particularly problematic. There has been a recent shift in counselling parents of deaf children from ideas of bombarding children with spoken language to a need for more intensive and elaborate communications. Mothers are expected to engage with their children in intensive play and language stimulation, and when not playing to convert general household activities to opportunities for communication. However, there are clearly problems in such advice for it involves mothers being asked to spend a great deal of time with their deaf children. Just as research studies have isolated the mother–child pair, so the advice treats them in isolation and ignores other relationships within the household, and other demands upon the mother.

Because a mother is responsible for the quality of the interaction, any perceived failure of the child's development can be interpreted as her failure to establish and maintain a 'good' relationship with her child. Yet it is clear from working with such families that because of the nature of the disability, interactive play may be more difficult with deaf children. Because they do not hear, deaf children may make sense of their world in unexpected ways. Many of the approaches of the mother are not responded to by the child in the way mother intends (see Gregory and Barlow, 1989).

Sometimes the professional advice can be at variance with the intuitions of the mother. The advice puts a high emphasis on using all the means available to get the child to speak. Withholding things until the child makes a vocal request is a popular strategy advocated by professionals.

> One evening, Ray and I are clearing up in the dining room after tea. There is a bowl of tangerines up on the bureau out of Ben's reach. He toddles in and points. He loves oranges. 'Do you want an orange?' Ray signs, bringing one up close to his face. 'OK, then, say "orange", orange, look. Do you want an orange? Say "orange"!' We know that he can; he has said it before. But this time, Ben does not say 'orange'. His face expressionless he turns and walks out. I follow him with the orange. He doesn't want it; he won't even look at it, even though I offer it unconditionally on the palm of my hand, at his level not mine. Close to tears I take it back in the dining room and replace it in the bowl. What are we doing to this child? (Fletcher, 1987, p. 99)

In the normal course of events, such communicative activities occur within the context of the general interaction, and arise naturally from it. By making such activities ends in themselves the fundamental nature of these processes is destroyed. Divorcing structure from content, translating fun into teaching, distorts the interaction for both mother and child. By attempting to make this implicit tacit knowledge explicit, the nature of that knowledge inevitably changes. By making actual language learning explicit, language becomes a goal of interaction rather than a product of it and the nature of the communication itself becomes different. This became apparent to the following mother when she saw her own actions through the eyes of her husband and mother. She had been encouraged to take all opportunities to convey information to her child through speech:

> Already this morning I had lost my temper with my mother who was staying with us, but even then I used the argument for giving language. 'We're *angry* Sarah,' I said. 'These are *tears*.' I lifted her finger and she touched my face. 'I'm not happy. I'm *unhappy*.' I couldn't miss such an opportunity. Sarah had to know what feelings were. I had to grasp every chance there was. Mick [her husband] and Mum had stared

at me in utter disbelief as I turned from them and went into the lounge. (Robinson, 1987, p. 57; italics in original)

Furthermore, the mothers are asked to do two contradictory things, often simultaneously. While in general terms they are asked to be responsive to their child, the specific advice that they are given inhibits this by including many prescribed activities which necessitate the mother being conscious of her own behaviour, whether it be getting the child to attend to her or getting the child to listen. This effectively removes her attention from the child and from focusing on, and responding to, his or her initiatives.

The idea that there can be a straightforward relationship between research findings and practical procedures is illusory and it may be that theory and practice remain essentially incommensurable. A powerful example from another area of disability is a study of children with Down's syndrome which tried to implement behaviours from the laboratory in the home. In concluded firstly 'that the greatest caution must be exercised when extrapolating from laboratory research findings to more natural situations particularly when intervention and remedial strategies are involved' and secondly that 'when intervention strategies are introduced great care must be taken in monitoring the effects on the parental feelings, and of not upsetting the adaptive and interactive process for short term illusory gain'. The language of theory has yet to develop an adequate account of practical knowledge, has yet to translate 'knowing how' into 'knowing that' in a way that maintains the integrity of both, and this may well not be possible.

The power of the norm

Implicit in the advice given to parents of disabled children is the generally unquestioned assumption that the normal is the ideal. Although this is advocated as a goal for the child, and advice to mothers is often couched in terms of behaving normally, often that is the opposite of what she is being asked to do. This paradox is clear from the following mothers' descriptions of their 'normality':

Well, treat him normally, really. I mean you've not got to sort of . . . I know you protect them more, but they've told me you must treat them like a normal child. I mean, there's obstacles you've got to get over. I mean, you can't treat them as a normal child because they can't talk, they can't hear. But you've got to do your best and that's all you can do.

The most important thing to realize is that they are perfectly normal children, they just can't hear, and not to think well they'll never be able to do anything, because they can do anything they set their minds to. I think that's the important thing, particularly when you are first told, because it's awful, shattering, [. . . you need] to cling to the hope most definitely that they are perfectly normal children, they just cannot hear. That's the way I've tended to bring Josie up.

I think as N. . . [her husband] says, you've got to accept the fact. There was a lot in *Talk* [the magazine of the National Deaf Children's Society] at one time about this business of saying 'you shouldn't think I have a deaf child, but I have got a normal child who happens to be deaf'. The fact is that the child is deaf means that it is not normal. Let's face it. You might as well accept it. It's never going to be exactly the same as everybody else because it is deaf. It can be helped to lead as normal a life as possible but it is never going to be completely normal because it is missing one sense. Just as no blind child is ever going to be able to lead a totally normal life.

Perhaps the ambiguity was most closely expressed by the mother who said: 'I think he's got to be treated more normally than a normal child.'

But even if we were to accept the goal of normality, the fundamental fallacy is that by behaving normally, in a situation that is essentially different, mothers can produce 'normality'. Moreover, the paradox of all advice that stresses normality is that 'normal' mothers do not normally *treat* their children 'normally'.

Deafness as disability?

Until now in this chapter, deafness has been treated as a disability, which is the way it is viewed by most hearing people, including hearing mothers of deaf children; this reflects administrative and legislative categories. However, the Deaf community offers an alternative construction of deafness, that Deaf people constitute a linguistic and cultural minority group. They point to the fact that Deaf people spend much of their time with other Deaf people and that they have their own language, which in the UK is British Sign Language, which exhibits linguistic features common to other languages. Gradually Deaf people are reclaiming their history (see, for example, Grant, 1990; Jackson, 1990) in a similar way to other oppressed groups, such as women or those from ethnic minorities. To this end they use 'Deaf' rather than 'deaf' to refer to those people who identify with the cultural aspects of deafness rather than the audiological ones. Audiological distinctions imply deficiency and disability whereas a cultural definition is affirmative and positive. It is beyond the scope of this chapter to discuss whether such constructions are really mutually exclusive. The Deaf community suggest that deaf children of deaf parents do not have the communication problems described here and point to societies where deafness has not been a problem, such as on Martha's Vineyard, in the USA, where a significant proportion of the population was deaf and as the title of a book about the Vineyard indicates, 'Everyone here spoke sign language' (Groce, 1985). Oliver reports a recent conference in Bristol where Paddy Ladd, a leading member of the British Deaf community, responded to a challenge from the floor that many parents regarded the birth of their deaf children as tragedies. He said that he understood this and was sorry, but could only add that the Deaf community regarded the birth of each and every deaf child as a precious gift (Oliver, 1989).

Undoubtedly, many deaf children will, as adults, be active members of the Deaf community. Yet the notion of a strong Deaf community rather than offering a positive solution to hearing mothers, presents a further dilemma. In acknowledging their child is Deaf, they are in a sense losing their child to a different language and cultural group, for part of childrearing is the sharing and developing of a common culture. As one mother said:

> You feel, actually, with young deaf children, cheated in a lot of ways because they do not learn nursery rhymes. I mean, Carol has never taken to tunes or anything like that has she? You know how you sing little songs to them and that. You can never do that . . . All the little funny things you tell children. It was ages before Carol understood a joke, ages.

For many Deaf people, their deafness is an integral part of their identity, and being Deaf is a positive experience and they take pride in their own unique language and culture. Yet in a society where difference is constructed as deviance and where motherhood is constructed around notions of normality, many hearing mothers find it difficult to embrace a different culture and community for their children.

Conclusion

This chapter has looked at the challenge of motherhood for mothers of disabled children. It has discussed prevalent ideologies of motherhood and the dilemmas these pose for such mothers in establishing their maternal identity. In discussing these issues I have drawn on my research into deaf children and their mothers. While deafness has been used as an example of disability, it has been suggested that this is not an inevitable construction. It is used here because it is the way it is commonly construed in the non-deaf world; many Deaf people take issue with that view. It is possible to conceive of a pluralistic, multicultural society in which to be a mother of a deaf child is not the challenge that is described here. But while motherhood is constructed around the notion of normal development, mothers of children who are different face a series of dilemmas. To embrace the ideology of normalization carries with it the danger of failure, but not to do so can mean exclusion from motherhood as it is generally understood.

Yet, perhaps the final word belongs to two of the mothers for whom this challenge has been an issue of day-to-day living, rather than an academic discussion. Many of the mothers interviewed in the studies reported here suggested that strength and understanding had come from confronting these issues in their daily lives:

> I wouldn't have developed the way I have I'm sure. It's made me into a stronger and more determined person. I think it makes you more tolerant.

> I used to think in more simple terms, that to live with deafness was an enormous strain. But I am sure it has got its positive side. I certainly feel my involvement in teaching and counselling now is greatly informed and improved in quality because I have had to think through these things – I have had to live with it.

Notes

The research reported in this paper was supported by grants from the National Deaf Children's Society and the Leverhulme Foundation.
1 Excluded were families from ethnic minority groups, who it is hoped will be the basis of a separate study, and children who were fostered at the time.

References

Bowlby, J. (1953) *Child Care and the Growth of Love*. Harmondsworth: Penguin.

Conrad, R. (1976) *The Deaf School Child*. London: Harper and Row.

Einon, D. (1988) *Parenthood – The Whole Story*. London: Bloomsbury.

Finkelstein, V. (1985) Paper given at the World Health Organization meeting, 14–28 June, Netherlands.

Fletcher, L. (1987) *Language for Ben*. London: Souvenir Press.

Goffman, E. (1968) *Stigma: Notes on the Management of Spoiled Identity*. Harmondsworth: Penguin.

Grant, B. (1990) *The Deaf Advance*. East Lothian: Pentland Press.

Gregory, S. (1976) *The Deaf Child and His Family*. London: George Allen and Unwin.

Gregory, S. and Barlow, S. (1989) Interaction between deaf babies and deaf and hearing mothers. In B. Woll (ed.), *Language Development and Sign Language*.

Monograph no. 1. International Sign Linguistics Association, Centre for Deaf Studies, University of Bristol.

Gregory, S., Bishop, J. and Sheldon, L. (in preparation) *The Young Deaf Child Grows Up* (working title).

Groce, N.E. (1985) *Everyone Here Spoke Sign Language*. London: Harvard University Press.

Jackson, P. (1990) *Britain's Deaf Heritage*. East Lothian: Pentland Press.

Johnson, R.E., Liddell, S.K. and Erting, C.J. (1981) *Unlocking the Curriculum: Principles for Achieving Access in Deaf Education*. Working Paper 89-3. Gallaudet University, Washington, DC: Gallaudet Research Institute.

Jolly, H. (1977) *Hugh Jolly Book of Child Care*. London: Sphere Books.

Kubler-Ross, E. (1970) *On Death and Dying*. London: Tavistock Publications.

Leach, P. (1985) *Baby and Child*. Harmondsworth: Penguin (first published 1979).

Lynas, W., Huntington, A. and Tucker, I. (not dated but published 1988) *A Critical Examination of Different Approaches to Communication in the Education of Deaf Children*. Manchester: Ewing Foundation.

Markides, A. (1983) *The Speech of Hearing-Impaired Children*. Manchester: Manchester University Press.

McArthy, K., Nolan, M., Tucker, I. and Fulbeck, C. (1981) *Some of the Problems Encountered by Parents of Hearing Impaired Children*. London: National Deaf Children's Society.

Mechling, J.A. (1975) Advice to historians on advice to mothers. *Journal of Social History* 9 (1), 44–63.

Moses, K.L. (1985) Infant deafness and parental grief: psychosocial early intervention. In F. Pavell, T. Finitzo-Hieber, S. Friel-Patti and D. Henderson (eds), *Education of the Hearing Impaired Child*. London: Taylor and Francis, pp. 86–102.

Mothercare (1986) *The Complete Mothercare Manual*. London: Conran Octopus.

Nash, B. (ed.) (1980) *The Complete Book of Babycare*. London: Octopus Books (marketed under the St Michael label for Marks and Spencer).

Newson, J. and Newson, E. (1963) *Infant Care in an Urban Community*. London: George Allen and Unwin.

Oliver, M. (1989) Conductive education: if it wasn't so sad it would be funny. *Disability, Handicap and Society* 4 (2), 197–200.

Oliver, M. (1990) *The Politics of Disablement*. London: Macmillan.

Reader's Digest (1989) *Mother and Baby Book*. London: Reader's Digest Association (first published 1986, reprinted with amendments 1989).

Riley, D. (1983) *War in the Nursery: Theories of the Child and Mother*. London: Virago.

Robinson, K. (1987) *Children of Silence*. London: Victor Gollancz.

Spock, B. (1971) *Baby and Child Care*. London: New English Library (first published in the USA 1946, revised and new English edition 1971).

Urwin, C. (1985) Constructing motherhood: the persuasion of normal development. In C. Steedman, C. Urwin and V. Walkerdine (eds), *Language, Gender and Childhood*. London: Routledge and Kegan Paul.

Voysey, M. (1975) *A Constant Burden*. London: Routledge and Kegan Paul.

8
Sons and Daughters

Jacqueline McGuire

Traditional developmental psychology views mothers as 'people who influence their children'. The study of child gender fits with this tradition. Mothers' behaviour is scrutinized to discover whether the upbringing of girls and boys differs and whether mothers' perceptions might lead to the differences which are identified between girls and boys. Although much is now said about the complex inter-relationship between individuals in a relationship, each influencing the other, there is still an underlying assumption that mothers play a very influential role in the way their children develop.

This chapter attempts to turn the issue round and discuss one way in which the child might influence the experience of mothering. Is the experience of mothering a daughter different from that of mothering a son? Material collected in a study of first-born London boys and girls in their third year, from fairly traditional two-parent families, is used to illustrate how mothering might be influenced by child gender. Before discussing detailed findings from this study, reasons why one might expect child gender to be of relevance to mothers are reviewed briefly, concentrating in particular on studies of women with young children.

Mothering and child gender in developmental psychology

In some respects children's gender is very trivial considering all the factors that may influence the experience of motherhood and the meaning of motherhood in women's lives. However, a child's gender is perceived to be a significant factor and in the majority of Western societies, despite growing awareness of feminist ideas, women more often describe a preference for boys than girls (Moss et al., 1980; Williamson, 1976).

Studies indicate some of the practical implications of preferences for women in different cultures and classes: boys who could work in their father's business or in the fields, or girls who could help with the housework and childcare (Williamson, 1976).

However, there is also mention of the mother–child relationship. Girls are thought to provide companionship, to be easier to raise, or more likely to complement the values of their mothers.

Different theoretical areas of psychological study have suggested various ways in which gender is likely to be important for parent–child relationships. Attachment theory forms the basis of much research on children's socio-emotional development (see chapter 10). However, although attachment theory considers the impact of some child characteristics, such as early biological vulnerability (Horowitz, 1987), child gender has rarely been a major focus. For example, Bowlby (1969) refers on only nine pages (out of 378) to sex differences in behaviour, principally to proximity-seeking in animals such as sheep and monkeys rather than humans. Bowlby notes a trend for females to stay closer to their mothers. Most of the research shows that in stressful, anxiety-provoking situations the behaviour of girls and boys is very similar, and only occasionally are girls reported as staying closer to their mothers (Maccoby and Jacklin, 1974). This may very well be a result of their mothers' behaviour. Mothers tend to perceive girls as less competent, or in more need of protection and supervision, and encourage greater proximity (Newson and Newson, 1986). While attachment theory does not address gender explicitly, it provides a basis from which to infer some of the ways in which a child's gender could influence a mother's relationship with her child.

In contrast, the behaviourist approach to understanding mothering has looked principally at the extent to which boys and girls are presented with different learning situations and girls are encouraged to behave in a more nurturant manner than are boys (for reviews see Henshall and McGuire, 1986; Huston, 1983; Lewis, 1986). Reviewers disagree about the extent to which mothers behave differently with girls and boys. In many studies mothers appear to differentiate less than fathers, leading to the conclusion that gender is not a major factor influencing their relationships with children (Newson and Newson, 1986). However, girls and boys are dressed differently from an early age and use different toys and playthings. The toys which are commonly provided for girls, but very rarely for boys, are strongly related to the 'traditional' role of mother, i.e. dolls (babies), household items for cleaning and cooking and for childcare (McGuire, 1988; Weinraub et al., 1984). Thus mothers have the opportunity to influence daughters in many subtle ways by the use of these toys or by the kinds of household activities which they share together. These interests may influence mother–daughter relationships, bringing mothers closer to daughters than to sons.

The importance of a parent's gender to a child has been emphasized in accounts of the development of gender identity. Once a young child begins to behave in a gender-typed way the same-sex parent is assumed to be a principal source of information about gender-appropriate behaviour. As children look towards same-sex models, one could predict that women's experiences of motherhood would vary, depending upon their child's gender. Girls might express a stronger desire for joint activities with their mothers, from early in the pre-school period, as gender awareness emerges. Depending upon the mother, this might lead to a closer relationship, but it might also introduce more possibilities for conflict.

Psychoanalytic explanations also address the development of gender identity, gender differences in child behaviour and same-gender identification between parent and child from the child's viewpoint. The same-sex parent is assumed to be of particular importance once the child's gender identity has been established. Before that time, prior to the stage of Oedipal conflict, the primary importance of the mother for her child, and vice versa, is considered to be the norm for both girls and boys.

Chodorow (1978) and Eichenbaum and Orbach (1986) take a somewhat different perspective and highlight the relevance of the child's gender for the mother. Chodorow seeks to explain why women raise daughters with mothering capacities and the desire to mother but sons whose nurturant capacities and needs are systematically repressed. Drawing from clinical case studies, she notes that over-intense 'hypersymbiotic' relationships are described frequently between mothers and daughters while they occur rarely between mothers and sons. These mothers display a form of pseudo-empathy with their daughters, from early on in life, appearing to be responsive and attentive, but in actual fact responding to their own needs rather than their children's. As a result mothers' relationships with their daughters are more intense, competitive and emotionally conflicted than are those with sons. In the long run, she suggests this kind of mothering will impede girls' development of self and of an identity separate from their mothers'.

Chodorow views such clinical cases as exaggerated forms of normal development. She suggests that because mothers are the same gender as their daughters and have been girls themselves, they tend not to experience infant daughters as separate from themselves in the same way as mothers with sons. This primary identification with and women's experience of their daughters as extensions or replicas of themselves is expected to have long-lasting effects upon the mother–daughter relationship as well as the eventual parenting behaviour of the daughter. Chodorow hypothesizes that mother and daughter will continue to feel alike in fundamental ways. Mothering in her terms involves a double identification for women, both as a mother and as a child.

A different line of research, but one which may be useful for an analysis of mothering sons and daughters, considers the child's temperament and links the behavioural expression of temperament and gender (Rendina and Dickerscheid, 1976). Thomas and Chess (1977) describe three main types of child behaviour – easy, difficult and slow to warm up – and explore how the 'goodness of fit' between the parent and child may be relevant to the child's adjustment. In other words, a calm, quiet parent may not cope well with a child who always has to be dashing about or reacts dramatically to any new event. Similarly a very active parent, always doing things and visiting new places, may find a quiet, shy or 'slow to warm up' child equally frustrating. While the temperamental divisions do not appear to be gender-related, one could think about them interacting with perceptions of appropriate behaviour for girls or boys. Problems may occur for a parent if the child's behaviour does not 'fit' their idea of femininity or masculinity.

There are some aspects of each of these approaches which are relevant to understanding women's experiences of mothering. In general, however, psychologists have focused on mother–child interactions, while ignoring mothers' experiences. The remainder of this chapter looks at the experiences of one group of mothers, at home with their young children, to examine ways in which their child's gender may be relevant to their day-to-day interactions.

Background to the study

The sample, contacted at mother-and-toddler clubs in an outer London borough, was of forty families with first-born children between the ages of 24 and 33 months. All were white, British-born, two-parent families, half of whom had boys and half of whom had girls. None of the mothers worked full-time, though a quarter had part-time jobs. All the fathers were working outside the home, 57 per cent in working class occupations and 43 per cent in middle class jobs, as classified by the Registrar General's definitions. This family constellation is common in Great Britain and the USA: at the time the study was carried out only 5 per cent of women with children under 5 were in full-time paid employment outside the home (OPCS, 1980).

There were three sources of data: observations, transcripts of observed conversations and interviews with mothers and fathers. Two home observations were conducted for each child, each lasting an hour. The situations were manipulated only in terms of excluding times when visitors were present and trying to ensure that the father was at home for at least one of the two sessions. Transcribed tape recordings give contextual information and interviews with mothers and fathers provide information about attitudes to childcare issues, gender-related topics such as the roles of men and women, and the parents' relationships with the child being studied. (Further details of the method can be found in McGuire, 1983, 1988.)

Identification

Mothers and daughters

Mothers were not asked directly whether they saw anything of themselves in their children, but some indirect information may be of relevance. One possible way in which the identification of some mothers and daughters is demonstrated is in terms of their preference for a child of the same sex. Mothers of sons may have felt that something was lacking in their relationship with their children since almost half recalled wanting a girl and several raised the concept of maternal identification with a daughter, suggesting that it would be easier to bring up a girl because they would understand them better. This may have been wishful thinking since many mothers were at that time finding their sons difficult to cope with.

> I felt unsure about bringing up a boy. I felt I knew more about girls having been one, I didn't think I would be able to understand a boy so easily, or cope with him.

> I definitely hoped for a girl. I thought I would cope better, they would be like yourself, you would have more in common so it would be easier.

Women who had given birth to daughters, however, did not show much evidence of identification with their children, although they often spoke in a manner congruent with Chodorow's idea that it is more difficult to be mother to a daughter than a son.

However, the concept of 'goodness of fit', discussed by temperament theorists, may be important to the development of mother–daughter identification; not only the 'fit' between the temperament of mother and child, but also the goodness of fit between women's ideas of femininity or typical girls' behaviour and that of their own child. When they were given a chance to say briefly what their child was like, negative or difficult characteristics were attributed more to daughters than to sons.

> She's very difficult at the moment, she's vicious, pinches and bites and kicks, she's a right tomboy. (Susan)

> She's very difficult, a trying child and very bad tempered. (Kelly)

This latter mother went on to comment, 'I am like that as well, that's the trouble'. She appeared disorganized and seemingly unhappy with her situation as a full-time mother. In view of her depressed state, and other stresses such as her husband working long hours and having two children less than a year apart, her identification with her difficult, stubborn daughter may have been particularly stressful. Their conversations were very confrontational, with neither giving in easily. For example, as Kelly's mother was trying to tidy toys up before supper, she attempted to get her daughter to help:

> M: Oh there's the bathroom to do. Out of the way, out, out, out!
> C: Out of the way, out of the way.
> M: Let's get these toys up. [*M came to the bathroom, C was in there with her sibling, age 10 months.*]
> M: Get out of the way, get out of the way! [*M moved sibling into the hallway, C stayed in the bathroom.*]
> M: Out, come on then, out, out, yes.
> C: No!
> M: Yes!
> C: No!
> M: Yes!
> C: No!
> M: Yes!
> C: No!
> M: Out, come on!
> C: No.
> M: Yes.

In order to try to break the deadlock, Kelly's mother attempted to enlist help with the younger child, perhaps using the pronoun 'We' to emphasize their joint duty to care for the baby, but with very little response from her daughter:

> M: Here Kelly. Find Pamela's dummy for me. There you are, that's a job you can do. Where that's gone heaven knows. We'll want that for tonight.
> C: Pamela's lost it.
> M: Yeah, I know Pamela's lost it.
> C: You find it then. Doo, doo, doo, doo, doo.

Kelly then continued to taunt her sister, shutting the bathroom door in her face after calling out 'You're not coming into my house, you can't get in'. Her hostile behaviour may have been an indication that, prior to her young sister's birth, she and her mother had shared a close and involved relationship (Dunn and Kendrick, 1982).

Kelly and her mother appeared to have a very difficult, tense alliance. Kelly's own behaviour suggested that it was in some ways very close, possibly like the extreme cases which Chodorow refers to, with mother–daughter identification and a strong need for each other, accompanied by a great deal of tension. Kelly stayed close to her mother but they shared little physical contact. So while she ranked second, out of forty children studied, in the number of times she followed her mother about, and fifth in terms of the numbers of approaches made to bring herself physically close to her mother, Kelly did not cling at all, by climbing onto her mother's lap or leaning against her. This contrasts to many other children in this study, for whom approaching mothers and seeking physical contact were highly related.

Kelly's relationship with her mother may also be an example of a situation where a mother identified with her daughter, but felt unhappy about what she saw 'in the mirror', since it was not her ideal of femininity.

In contrast, for Tammy and her mother there seemed a very good 'fit' between expectations and child behaviour, and between child and mother. Her mother spoke glowingly of Tammy, highlighting traditionally 'feminine' aspects of her behaviour:

> She has a very nice temperament. She's lovely, and she's a pleasure to be with, a happy little girl. She's not aggressive, she's sociable and she loves people and children. She's very affectionate, gentle and loving.

> She's dainty and delicate with toys. She doesn't like to get dirty, she loves new clothes, always looking in the mirror and she loves dolls and babies.

Her daughter behaved very differently from Kelly. She was the least likely of all the girls to seek her mother out, probably because her mother sought her out very frequently and told her daughter where she was going whenever she left the room. She seemed prepared to be involved in all Tammy's activities, making many suggestions for what to do and giving close direction and help during play, ranking second or third out of the 40 mothers for all these behaviours, as the following excerpt shows. Tammy wanted to put her walking reins on the cat, but he was not to be found:

M: Go and put the reins on teddy instead.

C: Reins on teddy.

M: Yeah, Mummy will come and join you when she's finished the drying up, or bring teddy in the kitchen. [*Tammy ran to fetch teddy and brought him into the kitchen.*]

C: Teddy, teddy out sitting room.

M: You're bringing teddy to the kitchen? All right darling.

C: Teddy.

M: Are you going to put the reins on teddy?

C: Yes.

M: Go on then, you'll have to work out how they go, Tammy.

[*Tammy tried briefly to put the reins on while they discussed putting them on the cat. Then her mother went to help and worked for three minutes getting the reins fixed.*]

C: I taking him walk.

M: You're going to take him for a walk? Well, lucky teddy. Right, go on then, now he's ready for a walk. Are you going to hold his hand too? You can hold the rein and you can hold teddy's hand, take him for a walk.

C: And Mummy take him for a walk?

M: Have I got to come too?

C: Yes.

M: Go on then, I'll follow him. Where are you going? Where are we going then?

This relationship may contrast with that between Kelly and her mother in another way, possibly showing the mother's intense need to be a 'good' mother, to model appropriate behaviour for her daughter, or to satisfy her own needs.

> I do gear my day to her, but it's our choice to have her, so you make it the most important thing in your life.

When asked about mothers with young children taking paid employment she said:

> It's a great pity for whatever reason, it's especially a pity if they don't need the money. It's sad that a woman should feel so depressed and lonely that she would want to leave her baby with others.

This was an extremely intense relationship with little observable conflict; the kind of relationship which Dunn and Kendrick (1982) found to be altered by the birth of a sibling.

In these cases women may have been studying their daughters' behaviour and comparing it with their ideal of feminine behaviour and then reacting to that comparison. These cases suggest that mother–daughter identification is possible. But it may be necessary to look at how their own and their daughters' behaviour conforms to women's perceptions of appropriate feminine behaviour and how satisfied women are with their role within the family.

Mothers and sons

Classic psychoanalytic theorists would expect mothers of young boys to identify with them in the same way that they identify with daughters, but Chodorow would predict a distancing between mothers and sons, even in the early years, and possibly maternal attempts to foster father–child relationships. Findings from this study indicate that mothers with sons do express loving relationships in different ways from mothers with daughters. They are less likely to cuddle or sit close together. Yet mothers with sons are more likely than girls' mothers to describe their sons in completely positive ways. They tend to emphasize what they see as their sons' masculinity but to minimize its negative aspects and to refer to mutual affection.

> My beautiful son, he's loving and nice. He picks you flowers and kisses you better. He's very, very boy, manly, a boyish boy, a good boy, not really naughty, mischievous in a nice way.

> A little pickle, he knows what he wants. He loves company, people, fun, a proper little boy really. He's quite a lovable little chap, he likes a cuddle.

> He could be a bully if he got his own way, say at playschool, but apart from that he plays all right. He's very loving, comes to give you a cuddle, and has to kiss people goodbye.

Mothers with sons also seem to direct boys towards their fathers, talking about the fathers when they are not at home, and encouraging boys to play with fathers when both parents are present. Fifteen mothers of boys made reference to fathers compared with ten mothers of girls. Fathers of boys are often mentioned as someone who would come home to praise or admire their sons. Fathers seem to be mentioned particularly in joint mother–son play when 'masculine' interests such as cars are being used or discussed. In this example the child's father and three male relatives are all brought into imaginative car play:

M: I think your new car's in there.
C: Here it is.
M: Here it is, your new car. You forgot to show it to Daddy. Daddy was playing with it when you were asleep.
[*They play with small cars and a garage for more than ten minutes, during which time both his grandfathers are imagined as the little figures, and an uncle, plus the boy himself.*]
C: Grandad, he's going to walk now.
M: Is he walking?
C: Stop. Get car. Get Lee's car. Got Lee's car.
M: Where's Lee's big car? Are you going to work now and get some money?

C: Fall down. [*Little people down the ramp.*]
M: You go in your big car.
C: Fall down man.
M: Are you going to work like Daddy?
C: Go work Daddy.
M: Where's your big car gone?
C: This money.
M: Oh, he's got some money. Has he been at work?
C: Daddy, been work Daddy.
M: Oh, he's been to work with Daddy.

This conversation not only enables Lee to identify with his father by acting out his behaviour, it also provides information about the father's role within the family. In the following example, Nathan's mother regularly introduces the idea that his father is the person he should be trying to please, a strategy which could enhance father–son identification at the expense of that with the mother. For example, after directing him towards Duplo she says:

M: See if you can make your train again.
C: Train.
M: Then when Daddy gets home we'll show him what Nathan's made.
C: Made.
M: Yes [*pause*].
M: Are you going to make a train Nathan? To show Daddy?
C: Daddy, Daddy, Daddy, Daddy, oh, oh, oh. [*Starts to play with Duplo.*]
M: Oh Nathan, that's lovely. Has Nathan done that?
C: Uh Mummy, Mummy [*holds pieces out to her, for help*].
M: Did you do that all on your own? [*Ignores request.*]
C: Mummy?
M: Yes? No, I'm not doing it. You're going to do it to show Daddy.
C: Daddy.
M: Yes.
[*Later on during the observation, during joint play*]
M: What will Daddy say to Nathan? Do you think he'll say 'Good boy Nathan, that's lovely'? Do you think he'll say that?
C: Ah, ha, ha.
M: Nathan? Do you think he'll say 'good boy Nathan'?
[*C throws some toys and laughs.*]

Interestingly, although 'Daddy' has been evoked as the person the constructive play was for, he is not mentioned when discipline is needed. When the child throws the toys she says 'No, I don't think it's very funny. You're not meant to throw things', making it clear that she sets the rules for appropriate behaviour.

In contrast, girls' fathers are referred to in different ways. Several fathers are mentioned as a threat, someone who would not like what they were doing, in their presence or absence. For example:

M: No you're not climbing on there.

C: Just get the tea pot.

M: No, you know Daddy doesn't like you to, come on, Cindy. Don't sit on the arm [of the sofa].

C: Uh?

M: Don't sit on the arm. Sit on the seat or go and sit on your chair. Do as you are told. [*C continues to sit on the sofa arm.*]

M: Do as you are told. I told you to get off the arms. [*C continues to sit on the sofa arm.*]

M: Please, Cindy, do as you are told!

C: No.

M: Right! [*To father*] You tell her.

[*Father glares at C, and she gets off the arm at once.*]

It is possible that establishing the father as the authority figure for girls but not for boys is a strategy designed to strengthen identification between mothers and daughters, and between fathers and sons. It highlights the power structure within the family of a dominant man and submissive woman.

In the following example, Vicky's father is present but rarely speaks or plays. During the short time they do play with blocks, Vicky's mother intervenes frequently, moving materials, suggesting activities and reprimanding her daughter for activities which the father ignores. He is, however, referred to as the authority figure.

M: Come here, I haven't finished your nose. Come here there's a good girl, come on [*pulls Vicky towards her*]. Don't have a tantrum, let Mummy do your nose.

C: [*squeals and rolls on the floor*] Aaah, haaaaa aaaah.

M: Daddy's going to sort you out. Do you want Daddy to come and sort you out? Mmm? Do you? He'll come and sort you out won't you Daddy? He will, he'll come and get you.

She finally manages to wipe Vicky's nose, and Vicky's father then mildly says 'Go and get some toys then', with no mention of the misbehaviour. In fact, he only made six statements to his daughter during the hour he was observed, none of which was disciplinary, while Vicky's mother made on average twenty controlling verbalizations per hour (such as 'stop that right now', 'You mustn't bite your nails') and a further fifty-two directives (such as suggesting activities, telling how things worked), plus a great deal of praise and criticism. Her interventions when Vicky misbehaved could have many interpretations, such as feeling that Vicky's behaviour was a reflection of the inadequacy of her mothering, that it was a mother's place to discipline girls, or as a kind of competitiveness. It might be designed to highlight the child's bad behaviour for her husband, to weaken her husband's attachment to, or indulgence with his daughter.

When questioned about who was stricter, this mother responded that she was. However, it was more typical for the girls' mothers to say that fathers are stricter, although in reality, fathers were observed to discipline girls less than mothers, and less than they did boys.

It seems therefore that these women perceive, and want their daughters to perceive, men as arbiters of discipline and control. Girls are likely to learn that their father is the source of discipline within the family, since their mothers talk as if they were, even though the men were not observed to play a disciplinary role with their daughters. This could enhance mutual mother–daughter feelings, placing them both in an inferior position and slightly distanced from the father. In contrast, the women with sons appear to increase the opportunities for father–son identification.

Attachment behaviour

One of the behaviours thought to indicate children's attachment to caregivers is the extent of their proximity seeking. While this is most clear-cut at times of stress, it is also observable in routine interactions. Attachment theorists describe a tendency for young females to remain closer to their mothers than males. This could influence the quality of the mother–child relationship in both positive and negative ways. It may be rewarding at times to feel that you are very special and that a child needs you. However, a busy mother also needs to be able to make time for herself, to complete work in the house or to relax. Tammy's mother described her as 'More clingy than some other kids', although the observational evidence suggested quite the opposite. However, in general, the girls in this sample were more 'clingy' than the boys and tried to maintain proximity to their mothers by approaching mothers, following them, clinging for attention and requesting attention or joint activities such as play or reading.

The mothers were asked how they felt about clinginess, and slightly more of those with a daughter talk in terms of irritation or annoyance. This might be due to the lower amount of proximity seeking shown by boys, but mothers' feelings are not necessarily related to what is observed. For instance, the mother of one of the least clingy girls reports: 'Yes, she does go through phases, she hangs onto my skirt or legs, she's always there.' Asked how she felt about it she said, 'I can only keep my sanity by saying "It's only a phase". I get irritated but there's nothing you can do.' Mothers with more clingy daughters express similar feelings:

Yes, she does cling a lot, especially since the baby has been born, wanting to be picked up and cuddled. It gets on my nerves, especially when I have them both and I'm trying to watch TV. (Kelly)

Yes, she's fairly clingy, I would like her to be more independent, it gets me down. (Lynn)

If I go into another room, she has to keep coming to check. My shadow I call her, always bumping into her. (Nancy)

Boys' mothers tend to speak in a more indulgent way about them, including mothers of two boys seen to follow their mothers or to demand attention:

He has his days, more since the baby was born, but not a fantastic amount. He likes to feel I'm there but he doesn't cling. (Mark)

Yes, he likes a lot of cuddles, he comes to get me sometimes, but he's usually over it in a couple of minutes. (Sam)

These different reactions of mothers to proximity seeking in boys and girls are reflected in the observational data. Boys who sought out their mothers were more likely to receive kisses and hugs than those who were more independent. But, in contrast, clingy girls did not receive more attention but were more likely to be criticized, to be distracted or to be disciplined physically. The same pattern was observed for mothers' responsiveness to children's demands for attention. While mothers of daughters and sons were equally likely to agree to a request for joint play, they were more likely to stop what they were doing and attend to a child's handiwork or read to sons than daughters. This pattern suggests a certain level of irritation or annoyance with the desire for attachment from daughters, but a more relaxed situation between mothers and sons.

From this study it is not possible to draw any conclusions about whether the child behaviour follows on from parental treatment or vice versa, since they were not seen over an extended time interval. However, one can develop some hypotheses based upon how the mothers spoke about their children, and the ways in which they handled stressful situations, as the following excerpts, one with a girl and the other with a boy, demonstrate. In both cases, the mother wanted to finish some ironing. The boy's mother is able to achieve this. Her son wanted some attention, but she is able to provide it by giving ideas, directions and information, without stopping her work. John had been playing Lego with his father while his mother ironed. His father left the room to get on with cooking the supper and John continues to play:

C: Broken door, broken door, broken.
M: Put it back on then, can you put it on?
C: Daddy, Daddy do it?
M: Daddy's gone to peel the potatoes for your dinner.
C: Mummy do it. Uuuuh, aaaah.
[*His mother ignores this and continues ironing, C plays with Lego for four minutes with only one or two comments.*]
C: Red one, blue one, came off.
M: What came off?
C: That one came off.
M: Well put it back on then.
C: Red one [*puts the piece back on*]. Not mend it.
M: That won't go up there, will it?
C: Uh?
M: It's not meant to go on top of another lorry.
[*Pause as C works on Lego*]
M: Ah, that goes there, doesn't it?
[*His father comes into the room and parents discuss food, father leaves and mother continues ironing.*]
C: Bridge! [*It is broken.*]
M: Oh.
C: Too big, uh uuh uuh . . .
M: Too big? It's only a little bridge now isn't it? You mend it. Can you mend it? [*C pulls it apart.*]
M: Ooh, goodbye bridge.
C: That came off, it came off.

At this point, having finished her ironing, his mother comes over to help and plays with John for a couple of minutes. John appears to be used to keeping busy while his mother works. She seems to give him attention in the form of tuition and instructions, but is able to continue with her own activities. This was the general pattern with boys; mothers gave them more information during play, asked more questions, and gave more directions.

The scene with John contrasts sharply with that in which another mother also tries to finish some ironing, but experiences a non-stop barrage of fussing from her daughter, Julie. For about fifteen minutes Julie sat in the kitchen trying to get her mother to stop, with various requests, while her mother became increasingly annoyed:

M: You go and get your purse and put them [coins] in there and then you can go to the shops [make-believe] and spend it.
C: No. Uh huh . . .
M: Can't you? With your basket and your shopping bag.
C: No want to, uuuh uuuh . . .
M: Where are you going?
C: Nowhere, [*whining*] eeh eheh eeh heh . . .
M: Well if you're not going to the shops you don't need any money do you?

C: No, don't want to do it, eeeh eeeh eeh. I want my Mum do it [*cries*].

M: Now stop that crying.

C: Don't want to go, eeh eeh eeeh . . .

M: No, you're not having anything, stop crying.

C: No want my uuh uuuh uuh . . .

M: Come out from under there [ironing board], come on.

C: Uuh uuh uuuh . . .

M: Come on out.

C: Don't want to, uuh uuh uuh . . .

M: Do you want a smack?

C: No.

M: Well stop this.

C: Get Mummy's p's [pennies].

M: No, you go and play with your house.

C: Noooo.

M: Go and read a Miffy book.

C: Nooo, I don't want to [*cries*], uuuh uuuh uuuh . . .

M: You're being silly, come on!

The conversation continues in this way until it is discovered that Julie had wet herself. Her mother stops to attend to this, cuddles her and reads to her for five minutes. On two occasions she tries to resume her ironing, suggesting jigsaw puzzles and starting one off, but Julie continues to fuss until the ironing is completed.

The persistence suggests a pattern of the mother acceding to the child's requests for attention and joint time, but also a high level of maternal irritation, which corresponds closely to the relationships between girls' proximity seeking and maternal discipline or criticism. It is very likely then that the style of attachment more typically seen in young girls, wanting a great deal of proximity even when there is little obvious stress, may have a far-reaching impact upon how mothers feel and act with them. In addition, the different reactions of mothers may lead to more clinging behaviour in girls.

Power and control

Appearance

The final issue to be discussed is power and control within mothers' relationships with their young children, relating it in particular to ideas about femininity or masculinity. A confrontational yet involved style was more typically shown by women with daughters than those with sons. The mothers tended to make more suggestions to girls about what they should do, they criticized girls more, prohibited and threatened more. All these behaviours could be interpreted as mothers attempting to establish more control over girls than boys. This is clearly demonstrated in battles over choice of clothing.

Maccoby and Jacklin (1974) dismiss differences in the way that girls and boys are dressed as trivial compared with other aspects of childrearing. However, it led to many conflicts for these 2-year-olds. Mothers of both boys and girls said they encouraged children to choose their own clothes. However, they report differences in how they manage disagreements about clothing. Mothers of girls are more likely to have the final say than mothers of boys. The following comments give an idea of how girls are 'helped' to make up their minds about how they should look:

> I always go through the drawer and get an outfit, even knickers and that, I like them to match. She has to wear it even if she doesn't like it.

> She would [choose], but she always wants trousers and I don't like her in trousers. I like little girls in dresses.

> I always take her to the wardrobe and she points. If I don't like her choice I pretend it's to do with the weather. She isn't adamant yet about anything specific.

Comments made by the boys' mothers are tempered, giving the impression that their sons generally have things more their own way, possibly reflecting the attitude that boys can look a bit odd or scruffy while the neat appearance of girls is important. It must also be recognized that fewer alternatives are available for boys' clothing. This difference, reflecting a societal attitude towards gender, may interact with mothers' greater involvement with daughters and their inclination to assert themselves more clearly.

> Over shoes he's adamant and won't wear wellies. He wants running shoes all the time. We have some new expensive shoes that he won't wear at all.

> I won't force him to wear clothes that he don't want.

> I like him to look like a little boy, with dungarees and little shirts with checks. I ask him what he wants. He gets quite upset so I'd let him wear it.

> He throws a fit, wants his trousers with Spiderman on, and he will get clothes out of the drawer. Normally I have to give in.

A statement made by another mother, discussing discipline rather than clothes, summarizes the way the boys seem to be treated, emphasizing mothers' desire for them to make their own decisions:

Some days he knows what he wants and he won't be easily dissuaded. I try to control him, but I don't want to break his spirit.

It seems, therefore, that perceptions of femininity and masculinity interact with encouragement of independence, in the case of clothes, so that mothers exert their will over daughters more than with sons. This is likely to be a source of ongoing conflict throughout childhood, unless (or until) daughters are 'persuaded' to have the same ideas as their mothers about appropriate appearance.

Toys

The different kinds of toys given to girls and boys provide another way in which the children's gender may influence women's experience of mothering. Boys' toys are predominantly vehicles and sport equipment, and many mothers rarely involved themselves with these toys, concentrating instead upon more neutral activities such as drawing, painting or puzzles. Most of the toys bought for girls related to feminine activities, girls owned more than one doll, many of them baby dolls with all the necessary equipment such as buggies, baths, clothes, plus housekeeping equipment such as vacuum cleaners and cookers. With some girls there was quite a lot of make-believe caretaking but none with boys. Joint make-believe mothering led some mothers to become very involved and even to take control of the play situation.

Interactions with boys, using 'masculine toys' tend to include more sharing of ideas, and the mothers sometimes express a lack of confidence. For example John's mother, after working on a Lego structure commented, 'Oh, I'm no good at bridge building, am I?', and reported on her incompetence when her husband came into the room, telling him, in front of their son, 'My bridge collapsed'. What was more notable, however, was how very few of the women used the boys' toys, suggesting that they are not comfortable with that kind of play. In two cases, mothers personalized the play by introducing family members, one constructing two grandmothers and a baby sister, sitting in the park, with Lego and the other making grandfathers and uncles the occupants of the small cars. It would seem likely that women with young boys try to relate their son's activities to their own interests, but do not become intensely involved in masculine kinds of play, perhaps leaving that to fathers. The play context is consequently one in which mothers behave differently towards their sons and daughters, imposing themselves more obviously on their daughters' play than their sons'.

Conclusions

Conclusions from such a small sample of women with children of one age group and raised in one type of family can be drawn only with caution. However, certain themes in their experiences may be relevant in a broader sense. Women attempted to control and direct and were more critical of daughters. Daughters, in turn, stayed closer to their mothers and demanded more attention. The relationships between maternal and child behaviours pointed to some degree of ambivalence in mother–daughter relationships.

It could be argued then that women with daughters had higher expectations as a result of identifying with them from early infancy; though it could also be due to more clearly defined ideas about how girls should behave. Mothers' critical remarks during 'mothering' play and their strong feelings about how girls should look both point to the influence of sex-role stereotypes rather than wanting the girls to be like themselves.

Mothers with sons were less controlling and made more allowances for them. They talked very affectionately about their sons, but boys did not stay as close to their mothers. One possible reason for this may be that boys' mothers make more efforts to foster father–child relationships. They may therefore feel ambivalence, wanting to stay close to their sons but at the same time feeling it is important to be more separate and to give father–son identification time to develop. Overall, they played a more hesitant role with boys, using their toys very infrequently, expressing lack of skill when they did, and giving their sons more opportunities to make their own decisions.

In many ways, superficial observations of these mothers with their children did not suggest that children's gender had a significant impact. Looking beneath the surface, however, being the mother of a daughter seems to lead to more conflict and tension, more need to be involved but also more irritation when daughters make demands on them. Mothering a son may be more relaxed in many ways; mothers feel perhaps that they do not have total responsibility, as husbands will be more involved, so boys' identities are treated with more respect and allowed to develop with less interference. It appears to be relevant to women's perceptions of themselves as mothers that they consider that fathers are more likely to be involved in rearing sons while with daughters mothers are more likely to have to shoulder sole responsibility. This could lead to greater satisfaction from the level of commitment necessary, but also more anxiety and doubt about their performance as mothers.

References

Bowlby, J. (1969) *Attachment and Loss*, vol. 1: *Attachment*. Harmondsworth: Penguin.

Chodorow, N. (1978) *The Reproduction of Mothering*. Berkeley, CA: University of California Press.

Dunn, J. and Kendrick, C. (1982) *Siblings: Love, Envy and Understanding*. London: Grant McIntyre.

Eichenbaum, L. and Orbach, S. (1986) *Understanding Women*. Harmondsworth: Penguin.

Henshall, C. and McGuire, J. (1986) Gender development. In M. Richards and P. Light (eds), *Children of Social Worlds. Development in a Social Context*. Cambridge: Polity Press.

Horowitz, F.D. (1987) The psychobiology of parent–offspring relations in high risk situations. *Advances in Infancy Research* 3, 1–22.

Huston, A. (1983) Sex-typing. In P.H. Mussen (ed.), *Handbook of Child Psychology*, vol. 4. New York: Wiley.

Lewis, C. (1986) Early sex-role socialization. In D.J. Hargreaves and A.M. Colley (eds), *The Psychology of Sex Roles*. London: Harper and Row.

Maccoby, E.E. and Jacklin, C.N. (1974) *The Psychology of Sex Differences*. Stanford, CA: Stanford University Press.

McGuire, J. (1983) The Effect of a Child's Gender on the Nature of Parent–Child Interactions in the Home, During the Third Year of Life. Unpublished PhD thesis, University of London.

McGuire, J. (1988) Gender stereotypes of parents with two-year-olds and beliefs about gender differences in behavior. *Sex Roles* 19, 233–40.

Moss, P., Bolland, G. and Foxman, R. (1980) Transition to Parenthood. Unpublished report, Thomas Coram Research Unit, University of London Institute of Education.

Newson, J. and Newson, E. (1986) Family and sex roles in middle childhood. In D.J. Hargreaves and A.M. Colley (eds), *The Psychology of Sex Roles*. London: Harper and Row.

OPCS (1980) *Birth Statistics for 1978*. London: HMSO.

Rendina, I. and Dickerscheid, J.D. (1976) Father involvement with first-born infants. *Family Coordinator* 25, 373–8.

Thomas, A. and Chess, S. (1977) *Temperament and Development*. New York: Brunner/Mazel.

Weinraub, M., Clemens, L., Sockloff, A., Ethridge, T., Graceley, E. and Myers, B. (1984) The development of sex role stereotypes in the third year. *Child Development* 55, 1493–503.

Williamson, N.E. (1976) *Sons or Daughters: a Cross-cultural Survey of Parental Preferences*. London: Sage.

9

Mothering More than One Child

Penny Munn

Models of mothering are cultural representations of the particular reality of being a mother which provide information on expected maternal behaviour. The discipline of developmental psychology has been instrumental in constructing current models of mothering since the information and theories about children which it supplies define mothering (and motherhood) by implication. The assumptions of psychologists have been based on only a very small part of mothers' experiences. In particular, developmental psychology has neglected the situation of mothers with more than one child, concentrating instead on the description of the archetypal mother–child dyad. The topic of this chapter is the process of mothering more than one child, the relation this bears to currently popular models of mothering, and how such models would need to be extended to incorporate the fact that most mothers have to care simultaneously for more than one child.

Within psychology, the two major theoretical perspectives on motherhood are derived from attachment theory and from social identity theory (Boulton, 1983). In neither theory is adequate consideration given to the processes involved in mothering two or more children. Social identity theory has been used in the study of the development of an identity as a mother rather than an attempt to describe the changes in such identity after this transition. The major impact on the way in which developmental psychology has constructed mothering has come from attachment theory (Bowlby, 1969; see also chapters 8 and 10). Attachment theory initially focused exclusively on the young child's or the infant's experiences with the mother, to the extent that a mother's behaviour which is not directed to her infant is seen as problematic, and as a source of conflict to her. Bowlby writes:

> Behaviour that in some degree competes with infant care includes all the usual household duties. Most of these, however, can usually be dropped at short notice and so are quite consistent with mothering. Other activities are less easily shelved. Some of the most intractable are the demands of other family members, especially of husband and other young children. Inevitably, therefore, a mother experiences conflict, and her care of the baby may suffer. (1969, p. 241)

In attachment theory the relationship between mother and child is cast as romantic love and is described along dimensions of intimacy and exclusive availability of the mother to the baby. Such idealized notions of mothering are congruent with popular views of women as simultaneously nurturant and passive. This model of mothering is focused on the gratification of the vulnerable infant's needs, and the experiences of the infant are emphasized at the expense of those of the mother. Two aspects of reality are obscured by such a model; the dynamic interaction between maternal and infant experiences, and the family context within which the mothering experience is embedded. The majority of women who bear one child go on, quite soon afterwards, to bear another – yet current psychological models of mothering have very little so say about the processes involved in mothering more than one child. The assumption that mothers must experience 'conflict' when faced with any distraction from their infants comes from the inadequacy of current models of mothering, rather than from empirical study of maternal experiences throughout the entire span of motherhood.

The metaphor of mother–child love as a romantic attachment is accepted within our culture because it is a familiar, well-tried way of understanding relationships. Adults know what it is like to feel loved, rejected, jealous, and so on, and are able to use these experiences to empathize with infant experience. This does not necessarily mean that the metaphor is accurate, or appropriate to the actual experience of the infant. It does not follow that mother–child relationships must be exclusive relationships in which the presence of a third is problematic. Neither is it the case that mothers of more than one child necessarily experience an emotional tug-of-war. A metaphor is a representation of reality, and can be useful in building models of reality, but only if the limitations of any one metaphor are carefully observed (Craik, 1952). This metaphor of the mother–child dyad as a romantically attached couple has been useful in helping adults recognize that infants have feelings (a fact which was not always recognized), but it becomes less than useful if we begin to imagine that mother and child actually *are* a romantically attached couple.

Since current models of mothering assume mothers to be all-nurturant, and to have exclusive dyadic relationships with children, then it is inevitable that such models will ascribe jealousy to other family members in their relations with each other. Fathers are commonly held to feel envy towards their infants (a belief which prevents serious questions being addressed about the ways in which fathers negotiate entry into mother–

infant dyads), and sibling rivalry has long been considered the most salient dimension of a developing relationship between brothers and sisters. Yet relationships between siblings are important in their own right, and the impact which siblings have on each other is not adequately captured within such a framework, as Dunn and Kendrick (1982) have demonstrated. Their empirical description of the arrival of a second child and the early stages of a sibling relationship has made it plain that relationships between siblings exist along multiple dimensions, and show infinitely greater complexity than the single dimension of envy.

Study material

In this chapter, data derived from an empirical study of the growth of a relationship between siblings in early childhood are used to examine the inadequacies of the dominant model of mothering within developmental psychology. I shall take some theoretically important findings from this study and show that these may be used to address questions concerning maternal development.

The sibling study was carried out with Judy Dunn between 1982 and 1984 in the town and surrounding villages of Cambridge. Forty families were studied over a period of eighteen months. The sibling pairs were observed when the second-born children were 18, 24 and 36 months old. Observations totalled two hours at each time-point. Mothers were interviewed to give background information on themselves and on their children. The age of the older siblings at the start of the study ranged from 2½ to 6 years. All families were white and had two parents at the start of the study. Although over half the families were middle class (social class I/II, professional/managerial), social class ranged from I to V. Only one of the fathers was unemployed at the start of the study.

Accounts of the relationships between the siblings have been documented elsewhere (Dunn, 1985), as have empirical analyses of developments in prosocial behaviour and conflict between the children (Dunn and Munn, 1986a, 1986b), social rule understanding (Dunn and Munn, 1985), and the contribution of temperament to the sibling relationship (Munn and Dunn, 1989). It should be emphasized that this did not start out as a study of mothering or of mothers. The mothers were not interviewed about their experiences of mothering, but about their children. The purpose of this chapter is to use the findings from the study of the sibling relationship to suggest ways of conceptualizing the processes involved in mothering more than one child. Two very striking findings emerged from the data on the siblings: firstly, the rapid changes in the sibling relationship, and secondly, the differences between the younger children and their older siblings. Both these aspects of the siblings and their relationship have implications for our concepts of mothering within a family context.

Changes in the sibling relationship

The second child's transition from infancy to childhood proved to be a particularly interesting phase in the development of the family, although it is a transition which has attracted little previous research attention. We found that changes in the younger children were accompanied by changes in the relationship between children and their older siblings.

Over the course of the visits, the younger children changed from being little more than babies to being small pre-schoolers with a wide range of social and intellectual abilities. This time was one of very rapid change for the younger children; their use of language developed from utterance of one or two words to the use of complex sentences and verb forms. Their physical abilities in moving around and in manipulating their environment increased apace, and the increase in their intellectual capacities was demonstrated by the growth in their ability to sustain quite complex play bouts. With such rapid changes in the individual children, it was inevitable that their relationships with older siblings would show an equal degree of change.

When we looked at the playing and fighting that we had observed taking place between the siblings, there were no changes between 18 and 36 months in the amount of this interaction between siblings; the same amount of time was spent in play, and in conflict, at all three time-points. However the *nature* of the interaction between the two had undergone radical changes as the younger children became more competent. When the younger children were babies, it had been the older children who were responsible for maintaining the play; by the age of 3 the younger children took equal responsibility. At this time aggression became less frequent and verbal argument more frequent. In short, changes in the younger children's abilities were accompanied by changes in the relationship between the siblings (Munn and Dunn, 1989). The increasing competence and autonomy of children at this age also brings about changes in their relationships with their mothers (Mahler et al., 1975; Sander, 1965).

The focus of studies which document changes in early childhood is generally too narrow, and I aim to expand that focus to include a consideration of the mothers' experiences during this time of transition. The time of transition to be described consisted of a *series* of developmental events occurring in the younger child, rather than a discrete event such as the arrival of a new baby or the start of full-time schooling. Adjustments to this type of transition can be expected to occur over a longer time-span than is the case with discrete events.

From baby to toddler: the problems mothers face

It is apparent that one consequence of psychological models of romantic love and monotropic attachment in mother–child dyads is that the simple fact of having a pre-schooler *and* a baby to mother simultaneously rules out any possibility of matching a maternal ideal. Dunn and Kendrick (1982) have described the effect that a mother's tiredness after the birth of a second child has on a first-born's behaviour; those mothers who reported the greatest feelings of tiredness and depression had first-born children who showed the greatest levels of distress and disturbance after the birth. Even when the second child has moved on from the difficult early stages, there are still major constraints on a mother's time and attention which preclude an 'ideal' performance.

In comparison with the plethora of childcare manuals for new parents, little advice is provided for second-time parents (see chapter 4). Traditional advice to a second-time-around mother is to include the first-born as much as possible in the care of the baby; mothers who follow this advice may indeed find that it results in greater harmony between their children, but the *cause* of this is not entirely clear. This strategy is believed to avoid arousing the elder child's feelings of jealousy by minimizing mother–baby exclusivity. However, it is unclear as to whether it actually works in this way, or whether it is a strategy which simply promotes and supports the relationship between the two children.

With the younger child's shift from infancy to childhood, strategies such as these become less useful to mothers. The enjoyable baby has by this time changed into a demanding and difficult toddler, likely to offer both deliberate interference with an older child's play and deliberate naughtiness to a mother. By the age of 18 months, the younger children we observed were beginning to use the word 'mine', and by 24 months, many actively resented the 'help' offered by older siblings. The siblings' construction of the relationship – of themselves as helpful, magnanimous individuals in relation to their younger siblings –

was consequently challenged by these developments in the younger children. These changes in the younger children were tantamount to the arrival of a new person to the older siblings, and demanded changes in the strategies used by both mothers and first-born children. It is at this point – when the second child can no longer be accommodated as an infant – that the discrepancy between the reality of mothering two children and the model based on mothering one child is at its height.

Mothers' experiences of first- and second-borns

Spontaneous comments offered by the mothers clearly revealed that they evaluated their performance as mothers more negatively the second time around when they compared their second- and first-born children.

> I haven't had the time to spend playing with her and reading her books like I did with the first one. All that sort of thing has gone by the board somehow.

> This one hasn't really had friends and social occasions organised specially for her. I just haven't had the energy to do as much for her as I did for her sister. She's just had to tag along with what's organised for her sister.

> It doesn't seem fair really; he's always had to fight for attention, whereas his brother at his age had us all to himself.

These comments the mothers made on the differences in their own performance clearly indicated that the mothers felt they were 'under-performing' with the second children. They also remarked on the differences their second children and their first-borns had shown as infants. These differences between siblings, which often emerge very early, are also interesting to psychologists (see Dunn, 1985, for discussion). It was of particular interest for theories of mothering that there was no pattern whereby the second child was easier than the first, or vice versa. For some mothers, the experience of mothering the *second* child was far better than it had been with the first child:

> I had such a lot of trouble with the first one never sleeping, I dreaded having all that again. But when he arrived I had a pleasant surprise. He was completely different from his brother as a baby.

While for others it was the *first* child who had provided a better experience of mothering:

> When he [the second-born] arrived, I realized that I'd had a very easy time with the first one. Before he was born, I had no idea just how tiring a baby could be.

Whether these differences reflected inborn differences in the babies' temperament, or whether chance variation in the mothers' circumstances affected the infants, the fact remains that the experience of mothering the second child was often a very different one from that of mothering the first. It is possible, not only that each child differentially affects its mother, but also that a different *kind* of relationship is established with each child. This is not to say that mothers love one child more or less than another, but this was something that emerged as an issue which two of the mothers had dealt with in the second child's infancy:

> Before she was born, we couldn't imagine how on earth we were going to be able to give the same sort of love we'd given to her brother. It did worry us, but it wasn't difficult at all. We had as much love for her as we'd had for him.

> When she [first-born] was born, I thought I knew all about loving a child – but do you know, it wasn't until her brother was born that I realized what it was like to be really *close* to a child. It's not that I love him more than her – I love them both equally in different ways. It's just that I was much *closer* to him as a baby than I ever was to her.

Differences between first- and later-born children are often ascribed to parental learning. Some of the mothers mentioned confidence as a factor in their experience of the second baby, but this was cited only in reference to the very early stages of establishing physical care; being nervous, for instance, the very first time the first-born had been bathed or fed in contrast with the first experiences of caring for the second child. The traditional view of motherhood is that experience of one child carries over to the next. Clearly, this is the case for the physical tasks of giving birth, feeding and caring for a child; feelings of confidence and capability must make a big difference the second time around. However, a large part of mothering consists of discovering a unique individual and establishing a relationship with him or her. The individuality of the child plays a large part in the developing relationship between mother and infant, and this is a factor which is unaffected by parental learning. This is one aspect of childcare in which previous experience does not necessarily transfer from one child to the next, and may actually be unhelpful if expectations are inappropriate to the second child.

Mothers' management of the sibling relationship

The experience of having two children rather than just one involved not only the management of two rather different children, but also the management of the relationship between those children. Since both are often undergoing rapid changes, this is not always an easy matter. There are three aspects of the mothers' management of their children's relationships which are of particular interest. The first of these is the management of conflict, an inevitable accompaniment to rapid change. Although conflicts are an everyday (and in some views necessary) part of family life, in the idealized version of family life, fights do not happen. We should, then, find that there is a contrast between what mothers do and what mothers are supposed to do about fights. The second is the mothers' influence over the quality of their children's relationship, and the third is the mothers' role in the power relationships that develop between the children. These last two issues relate to the actual processes whereby mothers influence their children.

Sibling conflict
Conflict between the siblings was frequent; overall, the sibling pairs we studied averaged four conflict episodes in every hour they were observed, and the mothers commented on how difficult they found this. Many of them asked 'Do other people's children squabble as much as mine do?' and expressed relief at the information that all sibling pairs squabble. We found that the incidence of friendly and hostile interactions was unrelated, so the frequency of conflict was not a reliable indicator of the 'quality' of the relationship, nor of the negative feelings between the children. This finding challenges psychoanalytic theories which hold that sibling conflict is an expression of competition over the mother and mutual resentment between siblings. Advice based on such theories dictates that mothers should strive to divide themselves evenly between their children, avoiding in particular the anger and resentment of the older, more capable child. Furthermore, analytically oriented psychologists suggest that mothers should not intervene in their children's conflicts, as such intervention is held to simply fuel childish envy and rage, and to prevent an alliance developing between the children (Brazelton, 1976). Studies of dysfunctional families have demonstrated that training mothers in non-intervention strategies can reduce sibling hostility (Brody and Stoneman, 1983), but this does not necessarily provide support for the theory, since it is by no means apparent just how the effect is achieved.

We found that mothers intervened in over half of all the conflicts we observed. They not only felt justified in so doing, but were in fact providing important early lessons both in morality and in strategies for managing conflict. The mothers' interventions were frequently couched in terms of explanations and justifications of the rights and responsibilities that make up the social world. Mothers' language to children during disputes functioned as a device for indirect tuition in such matters as rights, responsibilities and reasons. Conflicts between siblings were, therefore, likely to elicit highly educational language from mothers.

Justification was used by children in disputes as early as 18 months, and increased over the subsequent year and a half. This increase in the use of justification was found in mothers' and siblings' use of such forms, as well as the younger children's, demonstrating how other family members adapted their linguistic strategies to the younger child's emerging skills (Dunn and Munn, 1987). Mothers' interventions in quarrels at 18 months were associated with the younger children's later behaviour in conflict. In those families where mothers intervened in quarrels most when the children were 18 months old, children's conflict behaviour at 24 months was often more sophisticated – both in teasing and in offering conciliation – than in families where the mothers tended to be non-interventionist (Dunn and Munn, 1986a).

The use of reason has been shown to be related to immediate childcare goals. Kuczynski (1984) has shown that parental use of reasoning strategies is associated with parents' having particular long-term childrearing goals, such as routine compliance to moral strictures, and that where parents are concerned merely with short-term compliance, reasoning is less likely to be used. Where there are two children to care for, mothers' short- and long-term goals may be linked in an interesting manner. The mothers' goal of ensuring that children's behaviour fitted into their family context was their primary aim – they were concerned to defend either their own or their first-born children's rights. Socialization (the deliberate teaching of values) was a secondary goal. The 'socializing' effect was a *by-product* of this adjustment on the younger children's part to all family members.

The mothers' task in managing sibling conflict consisted of far more than containing the older child's jealous feelings towards the younger. They were the source of social rules regarding rights and responsibilities which the children quickly learned. Their justifications during conflicts acknowledged their children's status as social and moral beings, and contributed to their further social development. Their treatment of conflicts between siblings, far from separating the children and resolving conflicts for them, as psychologists have assumed, served to establish and define the children's position in relation to one another.

Influence over sibling relationships

It was obvious that the mothers had some indirect influence over the relationship between their children. We saw many skilled and timely interventions in interactions that were about to become hostile, and much planning that forestalled negative feelings in the shape of well-timed suggestions for a snack or for a different activity. It was also noticeable that conflict often escalated after the observation, when the mothers were saying goodbye to the observer and thus had their attention drawn away from the children. Beyond this type of maternal influence, however, it was clear that the sibling relationship had taken on a life of its own by the time the second-born children were 3 years old. Both children knew each other very well by this time, and had built up a shared history of interactions that had become relatively independent of their relationships with their mother. While the mothers had contributed to this shared history, the children themselves had made the major contribution. Some of the mothers had commented on this to the first-born children, warning them that the second-borns, who were mere babies at the time, would in the future offer retaliation for their nastiness. In fact, we found that those older siblings who behaved most positively towards their younger brothers or sisters at 18 months were those whose younger siblings were markedly positive towards them eighteen months later, thus bearing out mothers' predictions and commonsense notions of reciprocity (Dunn and Munn, 1986b).

Management of power relationships

By 'power relationship' I mean to refer to those aspects of a relationship which concern relative dominance between two individuals. In human relationships, physical size does not form the framework for dominance relationships, since aggression is controlled through complicated rules. Power, then, is not a matter of who can wrest what they want through physical force, but of who can use permitted channels of control to gain advantages. The mothers' management of the sibling relationship was constrained by their need to maintain their own relationships with each of the children while ensuring that the children respected each other's rights and got on reasonably well together. The maintenance of family position was an important part of the mothers' relationship with each of their children, and the strategies the mothers used in dealing with conflicts reflected this position-maintenance. Although younger children were just as likely as their older siblings to be aggressive, when mothers did intervene in conflicts they were twice as likely to prohibit the older sibling as they were to prohibit the younger child (Dunn and Munn, 1986a). This was 'unfair' in the sense of being strictly unequal, but such abstract notions of justice as equal treatment, regardless of power differentials, seemed to have very little relevance for these family relationships. It seemed to be more important to the mothers that the children should learn that judgement of what was 'right' was a personal, concrete matter. Such judgement took more account of the older children's greater knowledge and physical power than of abstract legalist rules.

In the following incident, for instance, the older child has suffered an unprovoked attack on his person and on his play activity:

> Brendan [6½] is building towers with his little brother's blocks. Danny [18 months] runs at him and kicks over the tower. Brendan protests, but before he can reason with Danny, Danny grabs his hair from behind in both hands and begins to twist it viciously. Mrs Y remains at a distance and calls out urgently to Brendan: 'Brendan! Brendan! Remember what we talked about. Keep still. Just take his hands and unhook his fingers. Don't hurt him now. Just unhook his fingers from your hair.'

This mother did not think it unreasonable that her elder son be required to take responsibility for his younger brother's aggression. During the interview she remarked that the experience of dealing with a young sibling 'teaches you how to manage power relationships', suggesting that she had a particular socio-moral agenda for her interventions in conflict.

Such behaviour obviously begins as natural protectiveness towards the younger children. That it extends beyond infancy suggests that mothers have clear ideas about the relative positions of their two children with regard to physical aggression and protection. These decisions remained in force long after the younger children were less physically vulnerable. For both children, the mothers' interventions made the subtle point that the wrongness of the action depended more on the person who did it than on any intrinsic quality of the action. Although younger children and older siblings often complained to the mother about the other's actions, we observed no incidents in which the older siblings complained about the unfairness of their treatment in comparison to that of the younger children. This may have demonstrated the effectiveness of the mothers' implicit lessons in family rules. In one of the few instances where a *younger child* used this type of argument, her mother was quick to point out the very different circumstances of her brother's behaviour.

Helen (24m):   I'd like a lemon.
Helen's mother: Well if you go and do a wee wee and then you can have some more lemon.
Helen: But Davy isn't.
Helen's mother: Yes I know. But Davy doesn't do wee wees in his pants. Does he?

One of the socio-moral lessons that the mothers were actively striving to teach, then, was a sense of the differences in treatment given to each person according to their circumstances and their position within the family. By constructing and maintaining such a framework for the sibling relationship, the mothers were actively contributing to the power relationship between their children, as the following mother explained:

I think Cathy [older sib] has taken us much too seriously. She's *never* hit Emma [younger sib] and now Emma's got to the stage where she knows Cathy won't retaliate. She plays on it, and she knows she can get away with most things.

The prohibition against aggression toward the younger child was accompanied by maternal expectations that the first-born children would be caring and supportive toward their younger siblings. At the final visit, when the younger children were 3 years old, almost all of the mothers emphasized this aspect of their children's relationship, reporting that the older children frequently used their superior ability to teach and help the younger ones.

In all three aspects – conflict management, mothers' influence on sibling relationships, and the management of power relationships between siblings – it has been possible to produce descriptions of mothering activities neglected by the currently available psychological descriptions of mothering. This neglect is a direct result of the consideration solely of decontextualized mother–child dyads. A description of mothering which goes beyond this to include the family context suggests a very different model of mothering from those generally found in the literature. A model of mothering based on ideas of romantic love assumes implicitly that a good mother will replicate a nurturing, romantic relationship with each successive child (see Ward et al., 1988, for an example). This entails an increase in mothering tasks in a simple additive fashion, and an equal division of mothering and nurturance between two or more children, independently of each. Within this model, the mothering tasks with regard to the developing sibling relationship are very simple; to care for each child and to avoid making either child jealous of the other.

When the reality of mothering more than one child is taken into account, a model of mothering emerges in which the tasks involved in the management of more than one child are very differently specified. Rather than caring for each child independently of the other, mothers actively promote a relationship between their children. This is done by explaining the children's needs and motivation to each other, and by instilling in each child an appropriate moral code. Mother–child relationships are not duplicated with each addition to the family, and maternal experiences are different with each successive child. Mothers monitor, keep track of and structure not only individual children, but also the relationship between their children. The moral language which mothers use to structure the social world of an individual child is also used to construct and sustain the relationship between their children. It is clear that it is not possible to maintain the nurturant passivity and emotional availability suggested by popular accounts of mothering if more than one child is being mothered. The tasks of mothering are not increased additively with each birth, but rather multiply in complexity.

Models of mothering and 'mother-blame'

When mothers are studied in the context of the family the complexity involved in caring for and maintaining relationships with children becomes evident. How far should mothers be held responsible for the quality of their children's relationships with each other? Without an adequate understanding of the processes by which mothers attempt to construct relationships within the family, it seems inevitable that they will be 'blamed' for any dysfunction within their own family. When we do not understand a thing, it is only too easy to produce simplistic explanations that do not aid understanding. 'Mother-blaming' theories are one example of such simplistic explanations of pathological development, a type of ascription of responsibility which is negative in the extreme. While psychologists have been concerned to consider mothers as the cause of their children's negative behaviour, far less attention is paid to mothers as the producers of healthy and positive behaviour in their children. One consequence of this is that we know comparatively little about many of the processes of early development. What we need to do now is to look critically at models that have guided investigation of mothers and children, and to discard aspects of those models that do not match reality. One result of a realistic theory of motherhood may be that a more balanced view of developmental influences can be adopted, and that mothers will be less often held wholly responsible for developmental outcomes which are as yet poorly understood.

Towards appropriate models of mothering

A prerequisite of an adequate theory of mothering is that it will include a well-articulated model of mothers' intentions, motives and identity. It is notable in attachment theory, in particular, that mothers are depicted as relatively bland in personality and devoid of motives or of privileged understanding of their own children. The only model presented to account for maternal behaviour within attachment theory entails a highly speculative analysis of mothers' relationships with their own parents (Grossman et al., 1988; Main et al., 1985).

A large body of social-psychological research is devoted to explaining and theorizing about adult behaviour in dyads, groups and organizations, but very little of the understanding derived from this research has been brought to bear on an understanding of mothering. The work presented here forms a beginning for a theory of mothering based on maternal practices. It locates mothering within a complex network of relationships, and describes some of the ways in which mothers manage the complexity of their children's relationships.

Further studies of mothers within a family context may clarify a number of issues: how maternal identity develops as family size increases, the effect that different experiences of caring for children have on mothers' ideas of themselves, and the ways in which mothers manage the complexity of families larger than two. Topics of particular interest would include the ways in which mothers learn the complex management skills necessary for their task, the sources of information that affect their decisions, and the factors that affect their performance. The task of balancing needs and personalities within the family is a learned skill which requires effort and time. It may consequently be affected in a predictable manner by stressors such as illness, poverty, or marital disharmony. Research directed at these issues would contribute to a theory of mothering which is more rooted in the reality of mothers' day-to-day experience; it would also provide information highly relevant to professionals working with both functional and dysfunctional families, such as health visitors, social workers and medical practitioners.

What would a well-articulated, empirically based theory of mothering look like? Although I have pointed out some deficiencies of present models of mothering, and described how empirical studies of families raise many questions that are pertinent to the issue, no alternative *theory* has yet been described. All that we have to measure any emerging theory are the benchmarks of empirical test that will identify the theory as appropriate. The first criterion is the match between mothers' experience and psychological theory. When mothers read the work of developmental psychologists and recognize their own experience, this will be an indication that such theories are realistic and appropriate. The second mark of an appropriate theory relates to its application by professionals. When professionals working with mothers can use the theories generated by developmental psychology effectively, to support mothers through difficulties and problems, and to enhance their mothering abilities, then we can be a little more certain that we are producing useful theories.

Note

The sibling study described here was carried out with Professor Judy Dunn. Her expertise in research methods, child development and sibling relationships was essential both for the completion of the study and for my training as a researcher.

References

Boulton, M.G. (1983) *On Being a Mother: a Study of Women with Preschool Children*. London: Tavistock.

Bowlby, J. (1969) *Attachment and Loss*, vol. 1: *Attachment*. London: Hogarth Press.

Brazelton, T. (1976) *Toddlers and Parents*. London: Macmillan.

Brody, G.H. and Stoneman, Z. (1983) Children with atypical siblings. In B.B. Lahey and A.E. Kazdin (eds), *Advances in Clinical Child Psychology*, vol. 6. New York: Plenum Press.

Craik, K. (1952) *The Nature of Explanation*. Cambridge: Cambridge University Press.

Dunn, J. (1985) *Sisters and Brothers*. Cambridge, Mass.: Harvard University Press.

Dunn, J. and Kendrick, C. (1982) *Siblings: Love, Envy and Understanding*. London: Grant McIntyre.

Dunn, J. and Munn, P. (1985) Becoming a family member: family conflict and the development of social understanding. *Child Development* 56, 480–92.

Dunn, J. and Munn, P. (1986a) Sibling quarrels and maternal intervention: individual differences in understanding and aggression. *Journal of Child Psychology and Psychiatry* 27, 583–95.

Dunn, J. and Munn, P. (1986b) Siblings and the development of prosocial behaviour. *International Journal of Behavioural Development* 9, 265–84.

Dunn, J. and Munn, P. (1987) The development of justification in disputes with mother and sibling. *Developmental Psychology* 23 (6), 791–8.

Grossman, K., Fremmer-Bombik, E., Rudolph, J. and Grossman, K.E. (1988)

Maternal attachment representations as related to patterns of infant–mother attachment and maternal care during the first year. In R.A. Hinde and J. Stevenson-Hinde (eds), *Relationships within Families*. Oxford: Oxford University Press.

Kuczynski, L. (1984) Socialisation goals and mother–child interaction: strategies for long-term and short-term compliance. *Developmental Psychology* 20, 1061–73.

Mahler, M.S., Pine, F. and Bergman, A. (1975) *The Psychological Birth of the Infant*. New York: Basic Books.

Main, M., Kaplan, K. and Cassidy, J. (1985) Security in infancy, childhood and adulthood: a move to the level of representation. In I. Bretherton and E. Waters (eds), *Growing Points in Attachment Theory and Research*. Monographs of the Society of Research in Child Development 50, serial no. 209 (1–2), 66–104.

Munn, P. and Dunn, J. (1989) Temperament and the developing relationship between siblings. *International Journal of Behavioural Development* 12 (4), 433–51.

Sander, L.W. (1965) The longitudinal course of early mother–child interaction. Cross case comparison in a sample of mother–child pairs. In B.M. Foss (ed.), *Determinants of Infant Behaviour*, vol. 4, London: Methuen.

Ward, M., Vaughn, B. and Robb, M. (1988) Social-emotional adaptation and infant–mother attachment in siblings: role of the mother in cross-sibling consistency. *Child Development* 59, 643–51.

PART 5

THE QUESTION OF EMPLOYMENT

10

Employed Mothers and the Care of Young Children

Barbara Tizard

Attachment and the employed mother

After the end of the Second World War a powerful opposition to the employment of mothers developed, based on the threat of supposed long-lasting psychological damage to their children. Earlier opposition to maternal employment had tended to dwell on the dangers of physical and moral neglect, but the new threat was much more potent. The principal theoretician of this movement was John Bowlby, a medically qualified psychoanalyst. Bowlby came from the heart of the British Establishment, the son of a baronet, looked after by a nanny, and educated at the Royal Naval College, Dartmouth, and Trinity College, Cambridge. Like all psychoanalysts, he believes that the root of personality development lies in children's early relationships with their mothers. But whilst Freud believed that a baby becomes attached to its mother because she gratifies its instinctual hunger and oral drives, Bowlby believed that attachment itself is instinctual. Further, whilst Freud believed that the Oedipal crisis and its resolution is the key to later development, Bowlby believed that it is the quality of the mother–child attachment in the first three years which shapes the child's later personality development.

Bowlby originally developed his theory to explain his findings that young delinquents who were 'affectionless', that is, incapable of love, had experienced prolonged separation from their mothers in the first few years of life. In his most famous book, *Maternal Care and Mental Health* (1951), Bowlby put forward the concept of 'maternal deprivation', a state of affairs in which the young child does not experience an essential need, that is a 'warm, intimate and continuous relationship with his mother'. He argued on the basis not only of his study of young thieves, but also of research by others in orphanages and hospitals, that maternal deprivation 'may entirely cripple the capacity to make relationships with other people'. He concluded that the damage is likely to be permanent, unless the situation can be reversed in the first few years of life.

For Bowlby, the age at which separation occurs is critical. Below the age of about 6 or 7 months babies do not appear to be disturbed by separation. After the age of 3, children gradually become less vulnerable to separation because of their growing capacity to understand explanations and to conceive of a future when their mother will return. But between about 7 months and 3 years young children are likely to show intense distress when separated from their mothers. Studies in residential nurseries and hospitals showed that they pass through a regular sequence of behaviour, in which distress is initially accompanied by protest, and then followed by despair and eventually by emotional detachment from the mother, resulting, Bowlby believes, from repression of the child's feelings of anger and anxiety. After reunion the detachment may persist for a while, to be succeeded by ambivalence to the mother, clinging, anxiety and hostility. Repeated or prolonged episodes of this kind he believed permanently scar development.

Why should the experience of separation be so traumatic to young children? Bowlby believed that this can only be understood in relation to the attachment to the mother that develops some time between the ages of about 7 and 12 months, and remains intense until about the age of 3. Attachment is the tendency for the child to show a marked preference for a specific person, to derive security from being near that person, especially when frightened, tired or ill, and to protest if they go out of sight. Bowlby believed that attachment is a biologically adaptive mechanism which, by keeping the young close to their mothers, enables them to survive. He pointed out that the same tendency for the young to cling to or be 'imprinted on' their mothers can be seen in many other animal species, where it clearly functions to protect them from predators. It is because separation is potentially life-threatening that it is such a frightening and traumatic experience for the young child. The attachment bond serves other important developmental functions, enabling children to learn from their mothers and providing a secure basis from which to explore and play.[1]

According to Bowlby, all children are biologically biased to form an attachment to the person looking after them, and will do so even if abused. It is only rarely, after repeated experiences of separation, that children become permanently emotionally detached and incapable of giving love. However, attachments vary in quality, and a child with no confidence that her mother will be accessible and responsive to her may be 'insecurely' attached.

To explain the long-lasting influence of this early attachment relationship, Bowlby (1973) postulated that children form internal working models of themselves and others, and that these persist, relatively unchanged, throughout life. Children in a warm, loving relationship with their mother will develop a model of themselves as lovable and of others as trustworthy. Children who had an insecure early attachment are likely to see others as untrustworthy, or rejecting, and to believe themselves incapable of being loved.

The concept of insecure attachment was further elaborated by Bowlby's colleague, Ainsworth (see Ainsworth et al., 1978), on the basis of experimental work with children of 12–24 months in the 'Strange Situation'. Briefly, the experiment involves taking mother and child to a strange room and observing the child's responses to a series of increasingly stressful events, including the introduction of a stranger, the mother's departure, leaving the child alone with the stranger, and reunion with the mother. Securely attached children explore freely when their mother is present, and use her as a secure base when a stranger appears. They greet her warmly on reunion, and are readily comforted by her. Children who do not behave in this way are said to be insecurely attached. When reunited with their mother they may be ambivalent or angry, or they may avoid or ignore her. Their attachment to her is real, but it does not provide them with security.

Although they saw separation from the mother as an important cause of insecure attachment, Bowlby and Ainsworth state that insecure attachment more commonly occurs in babies who have never been separated from their mothers, but who have been inadequately mothered. Ainsworth and her colleagues (1978) found that those babies who were securely attached at the age of 12 months had mothers who, at an earlier age, had been observed by researchers to be more affectionate to them, more effective in soothing them, and more often engaged in face-to-face behaviour and physical contact with them than other mothers. The mothers of ambivalently attached, clinging babies tended to be insensitive to their signals and inept in handling them, whilst the mothers of avoidant babies had been more rejecting than other mothers. Several follow-up studies by other authors (for example, Sroufe, 1984) have shown that security of attachment in infancy is a good predictor of later emotional and social adjustment. At the age of 3–6 years those children who had been classified as securely attached at 12 or 18 months were functioning better in nursery school, in terms of such qualities as social competence, independence and high self-esteem, than those who had been insecurely attached.

An important aspect of attachment for both Bowlby and Ainsworth is that it is 'monotropic'. This term was defined by Bowlby (1969) as 'a strong bias for attachment behaviour to become directed towards one particular person and for a child to become strongly possessive of that person'. For many years, Bowlby believed that the bond formed with the mother is different in kind from all others. 'The integrating function of the unique mother-figure is one the importance of which I believe can hardly be exaggerated . . .' (1958). It is this relationship which he stated was essential for the child's security, and it is disturbances in this relationship which he believed led to psychological disorder. Hence his insistence that mothering cannot in any real sense be shared. However, it is notable that in his most recent article (1988) he writes throughout of 'the parent' or 'parents', rather than 'the mother'.

Implications of Bowlby's theories for the care of children

Bowlby was in no doubt as to the importance of his demonstration of the role of mothering in mental health, which he described as 'a discovery comparable in magnitude to that of the role of vitamins in physical health' (1951). In evaluating this claim it is important to set Bowlby's contribution in a historical context. He was writing at a time when many children's homes and residential nurseries were grossly understaffed and when, even if this was not the case, care was dominated by considerations of hygiene rather than psychological need. Babies in institutions often received only essential physical care, children were shifted at frequent intervals from one foster home to another, and hospitalized for long periods without family contact. There is no doubt that the humanization of these practices owes much to Bowlby.

At this stage, Bowlby was almost entirely concerned with the welfare of children who come into long-term care. Others, however, immediately seized upon the implications of his writings for the employment of women. A World Health Organization report (WHO, 1951) stated that the use of day nurseries would inevitably cause 'permanent damage to the emotional health of a future generation', a dictum that was quickly to become very influential.

In his later writings Bowlby concentrated on the development of attachment theory, and made only scattered references to the implications of his theories for the care of children. However, he did express the view that 'to start nursery school much before the third birthday is for most children an undesirably stressful experience' (Bowlby, 1973). In his view, a mother with a young child should 'give him as much of her presence as he seems to want . . . [so that] he can satisfactorily regulate his own intake [of mothering]. Only after he reaches school years may there be occasion for gentle discouragement' (Bowlby, 1969).

It became accepted wisdom amongst doctors, teachers and social workers that women with children under the age of 3, or even 5, put them at serious risk by going out to work, that daycare or nursery schooling is harmful for children under the age of 3, and that even over this age it should only be part-time. Few people now realize that British nursery schools until the 1950s took children from the age of 2, and that full-day school was seen as important to allow for the valuable social experiences of communal meals, rest and a balanced day.

Since the effect of Bowlby's advice is to impose severe constraints on the activities of the mothers of young children it is worth considering why a whole generation of British and American mothers followed it, or felt intense guilt if they did not. One reason is, no doubt, that the prevailing post-Second World War ideology, quite independently of Bowlby's beliefs, was to discourage women from entering the labour market. But it is too simplistic to see this as the whole story. In the first place, much that Bowlby had to say rang true. Mothers know that young children pass through a stage of clinging to them, that they are likely to be distressed if left with strangers, and may be disturbed on their return home. If an important psychologist had apparently shown that this distress leaves lasting effects, many women were prepared to believe him. This was probably especially true of those who to some extent and at some level had absorbed a psychoanalytic approach.

A further reason for accepting Bowlby's views was that he challenged the inhumane approach of orthodox doctors at that time. By stressing the reality and importance of children's distress on separation their protests could no longer be dismissed as trivial, or as bad behaviour resulting from mothers' hysteria or past spoiling. In consequence, children's emotional needs began to be seen as at least as important as their physical needs, and as matters to be taken into account by doctors and administrators. Bowlby thus provided prestige and theoretical back-up for a more humane attitude to the care of children in hospitals and nurseries.

But along with this humanity went an insistence on the enormous importance for the children's development of their relationship with one particular person, the mother. His earlier requirement that mothers of young children must be more or less constantly available to them was demanding enough. But the message of his later work, and that of Ainsworth, that the child's future mental health depends entirely on the sensitivity of the mothering she receives in the first years of life imposed an even heavier burden. Whilst in principle it is simple, although in practice it may be difficult, to avoid separations, the obligation to be continuously and appropriately responsive is much more difficult and onerous. More generally, any theory that attributes the origin of adult neurosis to inadequate mothering in the early years may be said to champion children at the expense of imposing guilt on their mothers.

A critique of Bowlby's theory

Separation does not in itself cause harmful effects
Research since Bowlby's early studies has shown that delinquency and an inability to care for others does not result from early separation *per se*, but may develop in association with a variety of adverse factors. Separation *per se*, whether it lasts a month, a year, or is permanent, has not been found to have any direct long-term effects on development. It seems rather that any apparent adverse effects on the child are due to the train of adverse experiences that may follow separation, for example, being taken into care, or the pattern of chronic adverse experiences that may have preceded it, for example, abuse or marital discord (Rutter, 1981).

Bowlby's claim that even transient separations of a day or a week are in themselves inevitably distressing and damaging has also not been substantiated. Of course, these separations may cause intense distress, but the evidence suggests that this is only the case when separation from the mother occurs in combination with one or more of the following adverse factors: the absence of other people to whom the child is attached; the child is in a strange environment; the child is passed from one person to another, and no one person takes over the 'mothering' role, that is, gives particular attention, comfort and affection to the child (Robertson and Robertson, 1971). When these conditions are not met, distress is likely to follow, and repeated total separations, as when a child has frequent changes of foster homes, may well be damaging, although research evidence on this point is limited. There is certainly reason to believe that familiarity and continuity play an important role in early development (Tizard, 1986).

Daycare is not in itself psychologically damaging
One of the most widely known aspects of Bowlby's thinking is his opposition to daycare, and hence to the employment of women with young children. This attitude arises, of course, from his belief that even transient separations, especially if repeated daily, damage the security of children's attachment to their mothers, and hence their personality development.

Viewed historically and cross-culturally, the belief lacks plausibility. In agricultural and peasant communities grandmothers and older children have always played an important role in childrearing; wealthy women in all societies have employed nannies. Weisner and Gallimore (1977) found that of 186 contemporary non-industrial societies there were only five where the child was almost exclusively looked after by the mother. Of course, it does not follow that because a practice is nearly universal it is necessarily beneficial. Nevertheless, strong evidence would be required to prove the contrary. So far as current Western society is concerned, there is no convincing evidence of the detrimental effect of daycare. At whatever age children enter daycare, they develop attachments to both their mothers and to their caregiver, and their attachment to their mother is much the stronger (Clarke-Stewart and Fein, 1983).

However, Ainsworth and her colleagues (1978) have argued that while children who experience daycare may form attachments to their mothers, these attachments are likely to be insecure. There is other support for their argument. Most recently, Belsky (1988), in reviewing a number of US studies, has concluded that 'more than 20 hours a week of non-parental daycare during the first year of life' puts infants at risk of developing insecure attachments. These studies certainly show a difference between the behaviour of babies of employed mothers and non-employed mothers (though the sample sizes are small), but the interpretation of this difference is disputed. Clarke-Stewart (1988) has pointed out that the Strange Situation (see above), which is used to assess the security of attachment, may not be very stressful for the children of working mothers, who are more used to being left with strangers in a strange room. Hence the finding that they are more likely to ignore their mothers on reunion may therefore simply reflect their greater familiarity with situations of this kind, and their consequent greater independence from their mothers.

This interpretation is supported by the findings of European studies of slightly older children of working mothers. Although some research, both in the USA and Britain, has found a high rate of behaviour problems amongst children in nurseries, these studies appear to be of families with many problems. In Britain, for example, priority in admission to day nurseries is given to families with serious psychosocial problems, so it is not surprising that day nursery children tend to show behaviour difficulties (McGuire and Richman, 1986). But when the children studied come from families without any particular problems, pre-school children who have been in daycare as infants seem to do as well on general measures of intelligence, personality, self-confidence and emotional adjustment as other children. A recent study from the Thomas Coram Research Unit in London, for example, followed a large sample of children whose mothers returned to full-time employment, mostly to professional and managerial jobs, after maternity leave. The children were cared for by childminders, relations, or in private nurseries. At age 3, the only difference between these children and those who had been cared for by their mothers was that the children of employed mothers tended to be less timid and more sociable towards unfamiliar people, and more willing to share with other children. This was especially true of the children cared for in nurseries. There were no differences in 'problem' behaviour or aggressiveness between mother-reared and other children (Melhuish, 1990).

The early years are not decisive for development
Bowlby's claims about the long-term effects of the security or otherwise of early attachment on adult personality and relationships remain speculative. No one as yet has assessed the security of attachments in infancy, and followed the children into adolescence or adult life. But there is mounting evidence that theories of the permanent effects of early experience are too simplistic.

Methodologically, the issue is extremely difficult to study, since for the great majority of children the environment, the people caring for them, and the child's own temperament remain fairly constant. It may be this constancy, rather than the influence of early experiences, which accounts for continuities in the child's behaviour. Thus the finding that securely attached 1-year-olds, as assessed in the Strange Situation, tend to become cooperative, mature 3-year-olds may be due in part or in whole to continuities in the family environment, rather than solely to the quality of mothering in the first twelve months. There is, in fact, evidence that major changes in family circumstances, for example, the father's unemployment, or divorce, are associated with changes in the security of attachment (Campos et al., 1983).

Opportunities to isolate the long-term effects of early experience arise only in unusual circumstances. The classic example is when a drastic change of environment occurs after infancy, so that it is possible to see whether the effects of early adverse – or beneficial – experience are reversed. Most studies of such changes suggest that a large amount of reversibility can occur, and that children are often extraordinarily resilient (Clarke and Clarke, 1976).

Resilience was certainly evident in a group of six children who were studied after they had survived Nazi concentration camps, and later interviewed in middle age (Moskovitz, 1985). They had all been orphaned in the first few months of life, and thereafter had been given only basic physical care by a succession of camp inmates. They had been subjected to many terrifying experiences, including being present at camp hangings. On release, at the age of 3, all were severely malnourished, their language was delayed, and they were aggressive and hostile to adults, although closely attached to each other. In middle age, four of the six were interviewed by a psychologist familiar with their earlier behaviour and history. Two of the four were described as happily married, successful and effective in their work, with charming and warm personalities. A third felt very insecure and was subject to depression, whilst the fourth was still preoccupied with the insecurities and privations of his childhood.

Another dramatic example was the case of Czech twins who were reared in virtual isolation in cupboards and cellars from the age of 1½ to 7 years. When rescued they were severely retarded and disturbed, had almost no speech, and could hardly walk. However, a strong emotional bond between them was evident. After foster placement they became devoted to their foster mother. By the age of 14 their IQ scores were average and they were described as agile, gay and popular at school (Koluchova, 1976). It seems most unlikely that their early suffering had no long-term effects on the twins, and indeed there are instances of somewhat similar early deprivation where recovery was much less complete (Skuse, 1984). However, the extent of recovery in some cases throws serious doubt on the theory that even very severe adverse experiences *necessarily* have a devastating influence on development, if the children's situation markedly changes.

Less dramatic, but well-documented evidence about the long-term effects of lack of early mothering comes from my own follow-up study of children who were adopted from residential nurseries between the ages of 2 and 10. Before this time the children were looked after by a large number of constantly changing nurses – on average fifty by the time they were 4½ – who were encouraged to relate to them in a detached, 'professional', manner. In other respects the care of the children was good, and their intellectual development was average. By the age of 4½ 70 per cent of the children still in institutions were said by the staff 'not to care deeply about anyone'. It was notable that they had not formed attachments to other children (Tizard, 1977). Nevertheless, after adoption most of the children quickly formed reciprocated attachments to their new parents. At age 16, their relations with their adoptive parents in most cases continued to be good. But many, though by no means all, still had more problems relating to their peers than did the control children, and they also tended to be more anxious (Hodges and Tizard, 1989).

A characteristic of this and other follow-up studies of children who have suffered adverse early experiences is that a sizeable proportion of children seem to escape without any ill effects, even when they remain in an adverse environment throughout childhood. Thus Quinton and Rutter (1985) followed up women who had spent their childhood in care from a very early age. As adults, 30 per cent had marked psychosocial problems, and 40 per cent were rated poor parents. But 20 per cent were said to have no psychosocial problems, and 31 per cent were rated as good parents. The parenting difficulties that were found rarely amounted to neglect or abuse, and the ex-care women were as affectionate with, and involved in, their children as the controls.

Bowlby and Ainsworth argue that the resilience of some individuals does not invalidate their hypothesis about the effects of early maternal deprivation, any more than the fact that some children do not succumb to the polio virus invalidates the hypothesis that the virus causes polio. However, the evidence seems better explained by a 'transactional' model, which can account for both the continuities and discontinuities in development. According to this model, individuals and their environments have a reciprocal influence on each other. Whether early experience determines later development depends on later events, which can maintain, amplify, or counteract the influence of early experience. Quinton and Rutter (1985) were able to show that whether or not the women who had spent their childhood in care had current personality and parenting difficulties could be related to events occurring after early childhood, starting with whether their experiences at school had been positive, and extending to the supportiveness or otherwise of husbands and the number of socio-economic stresses under which they were currently living. It was not the case that the later events had been inexorably set in motion by events in the early years.

These and similar findings suggest that although early adverse experience often does have a marked influence on development, positive experiences occurring at least as late as early adulthood can lead to improvements in functioning. Equally, such evidence as there is suggests that, unfortunately, a secure early childhood is not an insurance against later psychological damage. Loss of a parent during adolescence, for example, or loss of a spouse as an adult, seems to predispose towards depression, irrespective of the early circumstances (Brown and Harris, 1978).

Is the early mother–child relationship of unique importance?

It has already been pointed out that attachment theory is potentially threatening to women because of its message that the child's entire future can be permanently damaged by 'inadequate' mothering in the first years of life. But women do not always dote on their babies. They may be under a variety of pressures which lower their responsiveness or sensitivity, for example, poverty, poor housing, the care of a large number of other children, illness in the family, or marital discord, or they may have ambivalent feelings towards their child. The effects of such psychosocial stresses on relationships have rarely been studied, but most mothers will have experienced their reality at times. It has already been argued that insensitive mothering is unlikely to have long-term significance for the child if the mother's circumstances improve. However, there is another reason for doubting whether a less than perfect relationship is of crucial significance – that is, the important contributions to the child's development which are undoubtedly made by a variety of other people. Ainsworth (in press) argues that attachment to the mother differs from other affectionate relationships the child may have, in that it provides a unique experience of security and comfort. However, as the studies below show, there is ample evidence that people other than the mother can provide children with a sense of security. Of these, the most obvious is the child's father.

Until about ten years ago there were virtually no studies of father–infant relationships, and there seemed to be implicit agreement amongst psychologists that fathers are of little significance in the early years. For example, no one commented on the fact that the children separated from their mothers in a hospital or nursery were also separated from their fathers and the rest of their families. Yet it now seems very obvious that considering the mother–child dyad in isolation is artificial – even in a small nuclear family other family members play key roles in the child's life, as may friends and neighbours. So far as fathers are concerned, it is well established that they are important attachment figures for most young children, and may be the child's most preferred person, despite the fact that fathers generally spend much less time than mothers with the infant (Kotelchuck, 1976). In the Strange Situation, some babies have been found to be securely attached to their fathers, but not to their mothers. The intensity of infants' attachment to their fathers seems to depend on a complex of factors, including the father's sensitivity to the baby's signals, his playfulness with the baby, and the amount of time he spends in face-to-face interaction with the baby (Chibucos and Kail, 1981). At a later age, research has shown that if one parent is emotionally unstable, the presence of a stable parent seems to a large extent to 'buffer' the child from adverse effects (Rutter, 1979).

The fact that children are likely to be attached to both parents does not mean that their relationships with them are identical. Most researchers have found consistent and striking differences between the patterns of mother–child and father–child interaction. Mothers tend to hold their children more, smile at them more, display more affection to them, and carry out more routine physical care than fathers do, whilst fathers tend to be more involved in play, especially physically stimulating and exciting play (Lamb, 1977). This traditional differentiation of parental roles may change when both parents work; one study found that working mothers stimulated and played with their babies more than mothers at home did (Pedersen et al., 1982). On the other hand, a Swedish study of fathers who looked after the child whilst the mother worked found that the fathers tended to interact with the children in a 'fatherly' way, rather than switching to a 'motherly' style (Lamb et al., 1982).

If they were considered at all, sibling relationships in the past were mainly viewed in a negative light by psychologists. Some earlier psychologists, such as Adler, believed that sibling rivalry was a major influence on development. But throughout what might be called the Bowlby period, sibling relationships received even less attention from psychologists than the father–child relationships. It is only in the past ten years that detailed studies of how young siblings interact have appeared, most of them based on observations made in the children's homes. One of the major contributors has been a British psychologist, Judy Dunn (1983, 1986, 1988). As chapter 9 indicates, siblings play a complex and important role in each other's development, a role in which rivalry is only one component amongst many.

Dunn points out that the special feature of sibling relationships is the variety of roles that they encompass. Older siblings are at different times teachers, familiar playmates, aggressors, comforters and protectors. Like parent–child relationships, sibling relationships tend to be highly charged with emotion, and siblings tend to be markedly ambivalent to each other. Yet several researchers who have observed in the home have found that unfriendly and hostile encounters between siblings tend to be considerably outnumbered at all ages by friendly and affectionate behaviour (Abramovitch et al., 1979).

There is no doubt that siblings are usually attached to each other, and display the same attachment behaviour, although at a lower intensity, that they do to their parents. This attachment develops during the first year of life: infants as young as 8 months may cry when their older siblings leave the room, and greet their return with pleasure. By the age of 14 months, many children go to their older siblings for comfort, and from the age of 2½ an older sibling can comfort a younger one effectively, and be used by them as a 'secure base' (Dunn and Kendrick, 1982).

As to peers, until recently, many psychologists believed that children under the age of 2 or 3 have little to contribute to each other. Yet as early as 6 months, babies will smile and vocalize to another infant, especially when they are well acquainted. After crawling develops, they may follow another child around, poking and touching her, although sustained interactions are usually beyond the capacity of children in the first year of life (Vandell and Mueller, 1980).

During the second year of life both the frequency and complexity of social acts with peers increase. By the age of 2, well-acquainted children may interact more with each other than with adults. Interactions with peers in the second year of life are not only more frequent and complex than in the first year, but also less often emotionally neutral. Conflicts, especially struggles for possession of an object, become common, but so does friendly behaviour. Between 18 months and 24 months children will hug and pat each other, share toys and display sympathy and helpfulness to peers, as well as to parents and siblings. By the age of 2, many children will attempt to comfort another child in distress, protect a victim and seek help for them (Zahn-Waxler and Radke-Yarrow, 1980). Familiar 2-year-olds can also provide each other with emotional support. One research project showed that pairs of 2-year-olds from the same nursery group were able to take in their stride the situation of being left alone in a strange room, which distressed children on their own, or those paired with an unfamiliar child (Ispa, 1981).

In the complete absence of parents, or parent-substitutes, very familiar peers will in some respects act as parents to each other. The six children kept together as a group in the Nazi concentration camp, referred to above, were found when released to have the same kind of intense attachment to each other that children normally have for their parents, and an absence of the jealousy and rivalry towards each other usually found in siblings. They refused to be separated, even for a moment, and were extremely considerate and generous to each other. Towards adults they reacted with cold indifference and hostility.

Children's social networks include many people to whom, in varying degrees, they may be attached – aunts, uncles, neighbours, grandparents, childminders, friendly shopkeepers, older and younger children. It seems likely that because of the different kinds of relationships each forms with the child, each plays a distinctive role in the child's development. These relationships do not develop out of the child's relationship with her mother; rather, they seem to develop concurrently, and even independently. However, they have been very little researched, although one study has shown that a close relationship with an adult other than the parents, most often a grandparent, tended to protect children from the ill-effects of a disharmonious marriage (Jenkins and Smith, 1990).

Implications

The evidence briefly summarized here suggests that young children are unlikely to suffer psychological damage if their mothers go out to work, although they may suffer initial distress. Indeed, they are likely to benefit from the greater variety of social contacts outside the family. Young children can and do become attached to those who look after them, as well as to other children. These attachments are not likely to weaken their attachment to their mothers, but can provide additional sources of comfort and security. Further, if children's relationships with their mothers are less than good, other long-standing relationships, for example, with fathers, siblings and grandparents, may serve as important protective factors. In addition, all these people, because of their different personalities, skills and relationship to the child, contribute something different to children's enjoyment and enrich their development. Further, Bowlby's belief that any separation from the mother in the early years is in itself likely to inflict permanent damage on the child's development is not supported by the evidence. This does not of course imply that the quality of daycare is unimportant, or that it does not matter who cares for children, or how many changes of care or adverse experiences they may have. Children may be resilient, but some environments stimulate development more than others, and children need the security of attachment to familiar people, who are responsive to their needs. But even if the children's relationship with their mothers is insecure, or broken by separation at one stage of development, there is little evidence that this will necessarily inflict permanent damage, provided that children are part of a social network which provides them with alternative sources of security.

All of us, including mothers with young children, have to balance our own needs and aspirations against our obligations to others. Some women's needs are best met by full-time mothering for varying periods of time. For others, denying their need to function in other roles and to escape from the tyranny of constant childcare will lead to resentment and lack of fulfilment. For forty years, in the West, women with young children who have chosen to work outside their homes have been made to feel guilty and have been viewed as inadequate and selfish mothers. However, there is now increasing recognition that if childcare of reasonable quality is available, the situation has potential benefit for children as well as for their parents.

Note

1 The reader will note that Bowlby's views on separation and attachment antedate and are different from the recent theory that if separation occurs in the period after delivery, the mother may fail to establish a bond with her baby (for example, Klaus and Kennell, 1982).

References

Abramovitch, R., Corter, C. and Lando, B. (1979) Sibling interaction in the home. *Child Development* 50, 997–1003.

Ainsworth, M.D.S. (in press) Attachments and other affectional bonds across the life cycle. In C.M. Parkes, J. Stevenson-Hinde and P. Marris (eds), *Attachment Across the Life Cycle*. New York: Routledge.

Ainsworth, M.D.S., Blehar, M., Waters, E. and Wall, S.L. (1978) *Patterns of Attachment*. Hillsdale, NJ: Erlbaum.

Belsky, J. (1988) Infant daycare and socioemotional development. *Journal of Child Psychology and Psychiatry* 29, 397–406.

Bowlby, J. (1951) *Maternal Care and Mental Health*. Geneva: World Heath Organization. (This was rewritten for the general public under the title *Child Care and the Growth of Love* (1953), Harmondsworth: Penguin.)

Bowlby, J. (1958) The nature of the child's tie to his mother. *Journal of Psychoanalysis* 39, 350–73.

Bowlby, J. (1969) *Attachment and Loss*, vol. 1: *Attachment*. London: Hogarth Press.

Bowlby, J. (1973) *Attachment and Loss*, vol. 2: *Separation, Anxiety and Anger*. London: Hogarth Press.

Bowlby, J. (1988) Developmental psychiatry comes of age. *American Journal of Psychiatry* 145, 1–10.

Brown, G.W. and Harris, T. (1978) *Social Origins of Depression: a Study of Psychiatric Disorders in Women*. London: Tavistock.

Campos, J.J., Barrett, K.C., Lamb, M.E., Goldsmith, H.H. and Steinberg, C. (1983) Socioemotional development. In M.M. Haith and J.J. Campos (eds), *Handbook of Child Psychology*, vol. 2. New York: Wiley.

Chibucos, T. and Kail, P. (1981) Longitudinal examination of father–infant interaction and infant–father interaction. *Merrill–Palmer Quarterly* 27, 81–96.

Clarke, A.M. and Clarke, A.D.B. (1976) *Early Experience: Myth and Evidence*. London: Open Books.

Clarke-Stewart, K.A. (1988) The 'effects' of infant day care reconsidered. *Early Childhood Research Quarterly* 3, 293–318.

Clarke-Stewart, K.A. and Fein, G.G. (1983) Early childhood programs. In M.M. Haith and J.J. Campos (eds), *Handbook of Child Psychology*, vol. 2. New York: Wiley.

Dunn, J. (1983) Sibling relationships in early childhood. *Child Development* 54, 787–811.

Dunn, J. (1986) *Brothers and Sisters*. London: Fontana.

Dunn, J. (1988) *The Beginnings of Social Understanding*. Oxford: Basil Blackwell.

Dunn, J. and Kendrick, C. (1982) *Siblings: Love, Envy and Understanding*. London: Grant McIntyre.

Hodges, J. and Tizard, B. (1989) Social and family relationships of ex-institutional adolescents. *Journal of Child Psychology and Psychiatry* 30, 77–97.

Ispa, J. (1981) Peer support among Soviet day care toddlers. *International Journal of Behaviour Development* 4, 255–69.

Jenkins, J. and Smith, M. (1990) Factors protecting children living in disharmonious homes. *Journal of the American Academy of Child and Adolescent Psychiatry* 29, 60–9.

Klaus, M. and Kennell, J. (1982) *Maternal–Infant Bonding*, 2nd edn. St Louis: Mosby.

Koluchova, J. (1976) The further development of twins after severe and prolonged deprivation: a second report. *Journal of Child Psychology and Psychiatry* 17, 181–8.

Kotelchuk, M. (1976) The infant's relationship to the father: experimental evidence. In M.E. Lamb (ed.), *The Role of the Father in Child Development*. New York: Wiley.

Lamb, M.E. (1977) Father–infant and mother–infant interaction in the first year of life. *Child Development* 48, 167–81.

Lamb, M.E., Frodi, A.M., Hevang, C.P., Frodi, M. and Steinberg, J. (1982) Mother- and father–infant interaction involving play and holding in traditional and non-traditional Swedish families. *Developmental Psychology* 18, 215–21.

Lawson, A. and Ingleby, J.D. (1974) Daily routines of preschool children. *Psychological Medicine* 4, 399–415.

McGuire, J. and Richman, N. (1986) The prevalence of behaviour problems in three types of preschool groups. *Journal of Child Psychology and Psychiatry* 27, 455–72.

Melhuish, E.C. (1990) Research on day care for young children in the United Kingdom. In E.C. Melhuish and P. Moss (eds), *Day Care for Young Children: International Perspectives*. London: Routledge.

Moskovitz, S. (1985) Longitudinal follow-up of child survivors of the holocaust. *Journal of the American Academy of Child and Adolescent Psychiatry* 22 (4), 401–7.

Pedersen, F.A., Cairn, R. and Zaslow, M. (1982) Variation in infant experience associated with alternative family roles. In L. Laosa and L. Sigel (eds), *The Family as a Learning Environment*. New York: Plenum Press.

Quinton, D. and Rutter, M. (1985) Parenting behaviour of mothers raised 'in care'. In A.R. Nichol (ed.), *Longitudinal Studies in Child Care and Child Psychiatry*. Chichester: Wiley.

Robertson, J. and Robertson, J. (1971) Young children in brief separation: a fresh look. *Psychoanalytic Study of the Child* 26, 264–315.

Rutter, M. (1979) Protective factors in children's response to stress and disadvantage. In M.W. Kent and J.E. Rolf (eds), *Primary Prevention of Psychopathology*, vol. 3: *Social Competence in Children*. Boston: University Press of New England.

Rutter, M. (1981) *Maternal Deprivation Reassessed*, 2nd edn. Harmondsworth: Penguin.

Skuse, D. (1984) Extreme deprivation in early childhood. II. *Journal of Child Psychology and Psychiatry* 25, 543–72.

Sroufe, L.A. (1984) Individual patterns of adaptation from infancy to pre-school. In M. Perlmutter (ed.), *Minnesota Symposium on Child Psychology, 16*. Hillsdale, NJ: Erlbaum.

Tizard, B. (1977) *Adoption: A Second Chance*. London: Open Books.

Tizard, B. (1986) *The Care of Young Children: Implications of Recent Research*. Thomas Coram Research Unit Working and Occasional Paper no. 1. London: Institute of Education, University of London.

Vandell, D.L. and Mueller, E.C. (1980) Peer play and friendships during the first two years. In H.C. Foot, A.J. Chapman and J.R. Smith (eds), *Friendship and Social Relations in Children*. New York: Wiley.

Weisner, T.S. and Gallimore, R. (1977) My brother's keeper: child and sibling caretaking. *Current Anthropology* 18, 169–90.

WHO Expert Committee on Mental Health (1951) *Report on the Second Session, 1951*. Geneva: World Health Organization.

Zahn-Waxler, C. and Radke-Yarrow, M. (1980) The development of altruism. In N. Eisenberg-Berg (ed.), *The Development of Pro-Social Behavior*. New York: Academic Press.

11

Motherhood and Employment: The Impact of Social and Organizational Values

Suzan Lewis

This chapter discusses the mutual exclusivity of the social constructions of motherhood and employment, and their impact on
employed women's experiences. The dominant ideologies of
motherhood and employment are based on the assumption of a
gendered division of labour. Hence the ideal mother is socially
constructed as one who does not work outside the home, or whose
paid work is restricted, while the dominant beliefs surrounding
employment are based on traditionally male values and tend to
preclude the opportunity for substantial involvement in childcare.
Cultural directives prescribe that women should become mothers
and subsequently reduce their involvement in paid work, or, more
recently, that women can fulfil all the demands of full-time
exclusive mothering and full-time paid work, without modifying
the demands of either. In contrast, the patterns of work and level
of commitment prescribed for the ideal employee are such that
they exclude those who have caring responsibilities. Early sections
of this chapter look at the development of these cultural prescriptions of motherhood and employment, their historical and social
context and the way in which ideology has been reproduced and
reinforced in research within psychology. I will then argue that
these ideologies produce dilemmas of identity for working women
with and without children and I will examine some of the life
patterns which they are thereby constrained to adopt. Illustrative
examples are drawn from a programme of research with dual-
earner couples, with and without children (Lewis and Cooper,
1987, 1988, 1989). I do not claim that findings from this research
are equally applicable to employed mothers located in different
family contexts, such as single mothers. It is, for instance, more
socially sanctioned for single mothers (who are construed as being
without a male partner to support them) to be employed, than it is
for partnered mothers (Kamerman, 1981). Nevertheless, the dominant ideologies of motherhood and employment, and subsequently,

stereotypes of employed mothers which operate within the labour force, impact on all mothers at work, regardless of their family context.

The ideal mother and the ideal worker

The experiences of motherhood, and of employment, are affected and constrained by notions of the ideal mother and ideal employee. The dominant social construction of the ideal mother conforms to what has been termed the 'motherhood mandate' (Russo, 1976). This is an unwritten, but powerful rule that all women should have children and be 'good mothers' and that this is their primary role in life. This does not preclude employment, but the 'ideal' mother does not work outside the home when her children are very young, nor does she ever allow paid work to take precedence over mothering. By definition then, employed mothers, especially those who are employed full-time or who are highly committed to their career, deviate from the socially constructed ideal. The widely held belief in the importance of a mother who is available for childcare on a full-time basis has resulted in the blaming of employed mothers for problems of child development, delinquency, marital breakdown and the breakdown of the traditional nuclear family.

The term 'working mother' (with its implications that childcare is not work) has often been used as a pejorative term, to imply neglect of maternal duties. Such ideas have entered popular consciousness to become a part of a familiar discourse which has a profound impact on mothers (Brannen and Moss, 1990; Lewis and Cooper, 1989). Political policies reinforce the notion that motherhood and employment are incompatible. For instance, the lack of adequate, affordable childcare, which excludes many mothers from the workforce, has ensured that in Britain mothers of young children who are in full-time employment are in a small minority (Martin and Roberts, 1984). Thus they appear to deviate from the norm as well as the ideal, although in fact most mothers are employed in some capacity before their children are 16.

Just as dominant ideology assigns women to the family domain, it assigns men to the public sphere of paid work. Hence the labour market is dominated by men and by patriarchal values, the ideal worker being construed as someone who works full-time and continuously from the completion of full-time education until retirement and does not allow family commitments to interfere with work (Pleck, 1977). By definition, the employed mother with at least one break from employment for childbearing, does not fit the schema of the ideal worker. Women who attempt to fulfil social expectations of motherhood by modifying the male-defined pattern of continuous, full-time employment are then blamed for their lack of commitment to work. Employed mothers are thus doubly stigmatized by social definitions which cast them as deviant both as mothers and as employees.

Recently a competing cultural directive of motherhood has emerged. This states that women, particularly if they are middle class, intelligent and educated, should not bury their heads in domesticity (Johnson and Johnson, 1980). This is reflected by images, perpetuated by the media, of the 'supermother' who excels in her career, without making any concession to motherhood, whilst doing all the things 'good mothers' are expected to do. Clearly this image is as oppressive as the ideology of the stay-at-home mother, because it implies that women can comply with the cultural prescriptions of a good mother and a good worker, without modifying the demands of either.

Historical and political context

The constructions of the good mother and the employed mother may be received wisdom, but they represent a 'knowledge' which is produced within specific historical and political conditions. Since industrialization, paid work has come to be organized around the needs of men, with the assumption that they are not involved in domestic activities. Employment and family obligations are constructed as independent rather than interdependent and employers are absolved from the need to consider workers' domestic lives and responsibilities.

Currently, however, there is increased interest in the full-time employment of mothers. This is not the consequence of egalitarian or emancipatory values, but because women are needed in the workforce. Employers and government are alarmed by the skills shortage anticipated for the 1990s as a result of the demographic downturn in the number of school-leavers. Suddenly industry is interested in childcare initiatives and flexible working hours to enable mothers of young children to remain in employment. Thus the rhetoric concerning employed mothers conveniently shifts to take account of market forces. In spite of this, the belief that the mother's place is in the home with her children remains strong. Media reports of childcare initiatives to attract more women into employment are invariably followed by numerous impassioned pleas for society to consider the well-being of children. The ambivalence of the British government is apparent from its encouragement of industry to introduce child-care facilities, whilst failing to fund state childcare, or to implement policies of parental or family leave.

The social construction of employed mothers is also produced by political and social factors. Whereas capitalist societies look to private initiatives to provide childcare if and when mothers are needed in the workforce, a very different ideology pervades socialist countries. In Eastern Europe mothers have not only been enabled, but also expected to be economically active, and childcare has been made widely available and provided by the state. Employed mothers are the norm in these countries, but they nevertheless remain the primary parent, so that the expectation that they should be in full-time employment has an overloading rather than emancipating effect (Rueschemeyer, 1981). Other states, notably the Scandinavian countries, are characterized by an ideology which constructs mothers and fathers as being equally responsible for childcare. Parents benefit from widely available, state-provided childcare as well as legislation enabling mothers or fathers to take leave from employment to care for a very young or a sick child. Here again, employed mothers are the norm. The social construction of employed mothers thus varies over time and across cultures, although mothers tend to be expected to take on the major responsibility for childcare in most countries regardless of the amount of full-time daycare available.

The employed mother as a subject of research in psychology

Employed mothers, it can be argued, are problematic precisely because they are defined as problems. Employed fathers are not considered to be, or to have problems, because the social construction of fatherhood subsumes both worker and provider role. Hence employed fathers have not until recently been the subjects of research (although unemployed fathers have been extensively studied). In contrast, employed mothers are the subject of a substantial body of literature within psychology.

Assumptions about the good mother are reflected by and reproduced in research within psychology. An influx of mothers into the workforce in the 1960s created an anxiety about the impact on children. The belief that child development could be adversely affected if mothers were employed outside the home informed research into the effects of maternal employment on children. By the 1970s there was sufficient evidence for reviewers to conclude that maternal employment *per se* had no significant impact on children, or that the impact may be positive (Hoffman, 1979). Nevertheless, the questions continued to be asked (Belsky, 1988; Gottfried and Gottfried, 1988).

Other research asked what motivates mothers to work, or investigated the impact of employment on mothers' well-being or on marriage (Burke and Weir, 1976; Welch and Booth, 1977). This implies that non-employment is the natural state of mothers and ignores that fact that exclusive mothering covers a wide range of situations and relationships (New and David, 1985). Furthermore, the assumption that mothers have primary responsibility for child-care, and that their children, their marriages and their health will suffer if they are also in paid employment, helps to explain and justify women's subordinate position in the home and in the workforce, rather than exploring the reason *why* most families adopt a patriarchal division of labour.

More recently, research has begun to focus on the quality of the employed mother's experience, her satisfaction with and commitment to motherhood and employment, and the degree of conflict she experiences between the two (Brannen and Moss, 1988, 1990; Parry, 1987; Sharpe, 1984). Often the purpose of research is to investigate the impact of a mother's experiences on her children (for example, Lerner and Golambos, 1985) rather than to focus on the mother for her own sake. Nevertheless, the emphasis on the ways in which employed mothers experience their lives opens the way to question the impact of social ideology on subjective experience and also acknowledges the heterogeneity amongst mothers who are employed.

It is a mistake to believe that there exist only two categories of mothers; those who are employed and those who are not. Such bipolar thinking, which characterizes much of the early research, overlooks the fact that mothers are located in different positions in the world of work (and in society generally). The working lives of a factory worker and a professor are qualitatively very different, whether they are female or male, parents or childless. In addition, many other factors affect a mother's experience in work and family, including marital status (Kamerman, 1981), having an employed mother as a role model (Rapoport and Rapoport, 1977), ideology (Gordon, 1990) and ethnicity (Granrose, 1988).

These differences among working women with children should not be underestimated. Nevertheless there remain commonalities. There is much evidence that mothers are less able, or willing, than men to compartmentalize different areas of their lives (Hall, 1972). They carry motherhood around with them, while men are more adept at experiencing their roles sequentially. This may be because of the common cultural and ideological context which employed mothers experience. Mothers differ, however, in the ways in which they react to and cope with beliefs about the ideal mother and the ideal worker.

Ideology, stereotypes and the experience of maternal employment

The research on which this chapter is based was with 212 dual-earner couples, including couples without children, parents of young children and couples who were expecting their first child. A total of 152 couples completed questionnaires about sources and manifestations of stress, and follow-up questionnaires were completed 18 months later by new parents and couples without children. In addition, in-depth interviews were conducted with sixty couples in order to explore further issues raised by the questionnaire study. The following discussion draws upon the accounts of employed women from this sample.

Mothers are exposed to the dominant ideology of the ideal mother through the media, through family and friends, and through professionals such as doctors and health visitors, some of whom continue to express disquiet at a new mother's decision to return to employment. In the workplace colleagues and superiors may reinforce these beliefs. Mothers reported that they were exposed to explicit pressures by people at work to conform to the traditional maternal role. Typically this took the form of pressure on pregnant women to believe that they would change their mind about returning to work once the baby was born, and criticism of new mothers who did return to employment. The expectation was clearly communicated that women should expect a rush of maternal feelings after childbirth, in the light of which occupational interests should pale into significance. Thus the seeds of guilt are sown. The assumption was that children would be healthy and non-handicapped. Particular pressure to stay at home was experienced by a mother in our sample who had a handicapped child (see also chapter 7).

The guilt and the conflict experienced by employed mothers is well documented (Brannen and Moss, 1988, 1990; Sharpe, 1984). Mothers report substantially more conflict than fathers, whose employment role is socially sanctioned, and more conflict than employed mothers without children (Lewis and Cooper, 1987). This conflict is partly the result of employed mothers' having multiple responsibilities, and the sheer difficulty of fitting in the associated demands. It is exacerbated by the patriarchal division of labour in the home, whereby most mothers, whether or not they are employed, perform most of the childcare and domestic work. The ideal of a close, exclusive mother–child relationship (as outlined in chapter 10 by Tizard) underlies much of the conflict experienced by new mothers. Brannen and Moss (1990) suggest that the 'monogamous' notion of the mother–child bond is analogous to the ideology of monogamous love between adults, and induces feelings of guilt about 'abandoning' the child to someone else's care. The discontinuity between internalized norms of motherhood and actual behaviour is a further source of conflict, producing identity dilemmas (Rapoport and Rapoport, 1977).

Conflict also stems from the different and contradictory discourses to which mothers are exposed. Mothers are not expected to be involved in careers, and yet well-educated women who choose full-time motherhood, or even part-time work are often accused of wasting educational opportunities (Johnson and Johnson, 1980). Similarly, mothers who are perceived as needing the money are expected to engage in paid work, rather than full-time motherhood (Kamerman, 1981), and saying that one is going back to work for the money is a socially acceptable justification (Brannen and Moss, 1988). However, mothers who are not perceived as needing the money are accused of selfishness in pursuing a career at the 'expense' of motherhood. There is also a clear expectation that mothers' income is, and should be, of secondary importance. This myth is maintained even when mothers' contribution to household finance is substantial, by the underestimations of women's contribution. For example, childcare is considered to be mothers' primary responsibility, and so daycare expenses are often considered a charge on mothers' rather than family income (Brannen and Moss, 1985, 1988). The conflict experienced by women who do not conform to the ideals of a non-employed mother, or one whose income is secondary is illustrated by a mother who claimed that she gained substantial satisfaction from her career as a GP and would not choose to reduce the hours she works, yet stated that:

> you are brought up as a child to think that father goes out to work and mother stays at home or works a little when she wants to. I'm a little envious of women who don't have to work, in the sense that they don't have the pressure of being the major breadwinner. (Lewis and Cooper, 1989, p. 152)

The myth of motherhood as women's occupation spills over into the workplace to inform the stereotypical view that motherhood always takes precedence over paid work, and hence that mothers lack occupational commitment and ambition. Many employers communicate to mothers that they are undesirable or unimportant employees by the lack of helpful, family-orientated policies, such as flexitime, which might mitigate conflict, and/or by actions designed to discourage mothers from maintaining job involvement. In our study, actions aimed at preventing mothers from returning to work following maternity leave ranged from making new mothers redundant to moving women to lower level jobs because it had been assumed that they would not return and therefore a permanent replacement had been installed. Some women were explicitly informed that they were a nuisance when they announced that they were pregnant or when they took up their rights to reinstatement. There is currently a drive to entice mothers back into the workforce, to compensate for the demographic shortfall of new young workers. It is debatable whether this represents a shift in deeply ingrained attitudes. Rather it would seem that mothers are encouraged to return to, or remain in, employment because of a shortage of skilled men, and of women without family responsibilities. By implication, these are the preferred workforce for all but the lowest level jobs, which are traditionally allocated to women with dependants.

Stereotypical assumptions about employed mothers pervade organizations. It is often assumed that all mothers can be included within the undifferentiated category of unreliable, unambitious and by implication, often incompetent workers, who lack commitment to the workforce. This stereotype informs perceptions of individual women with children, even in the face of manifest commitment and competence, and often influences promotion decisions (Rosen and Jerdee, 1974). To the extent that commitment and ambition are defined in male terms the stereotypes become self-fulfilling. Most mothers are unable to, or do not wish to conform to male patterns of work. Furthermore, as with all stereotypes, confirmatory information is more likely to be processed than that which does not fit the framework. Hence mothers who take time off for childcare, request a change to part-time work after childbirth, or otherwise appear to fit the stereotype make much more of an impression on employers and colleagues than those who do not conform to this pattern. The latter tend to be perceived as individual and exceptional women rather than as evidence of heterogeneity amongst employed mothers. A mother who has career ambitions faces a dilemma; to ask for concessions for time to be spent in mothering and risk inclusion in the stereotype with all its negative connotations, or to attempt to disprove the stereotype or to distance herself from it, by retaining a male-like level of job involvement, at the cost of time for mothering. This presents a no win situation. It can be argued that the former disadvantages women by reinforcing the stereotype, while the latter disadvantages them by setting standards with which few mothers are able to comply.

The social construction of the ideal mother, together with the male model of work and organizational stereotypes of employed mothers thus create dilemmas for mothers who are employed. In so far as mothers have options about working outside the home, they have three choices: they may conform to the image of the ideal mother and forfeit any status beyond motherhood; they may take part-time work, usually with poor conditions, so as to minimize the discrepancy with the socially constructed ideal mother, therefore reinforcing stereotypes about employed mothers; or they may conform to the male model of work, often at considerable personal cost.

All these socially constrained options may involve some threats to identity. Breakwell has discussed the crucial role of self-esteem in identity formation, as well as the need for distinctiveness and for continuity of self-definition (Breakwell, 1986). In this model, identity is treated as a social product, which can only be understood in relation to its social context. Identity is threatened in social situations where a person is unable to define herself in a consistent way over time as distinctive and unique and as a valued person. Motherhood provides women with a major source of self-esteem (see chapter 3). For women who identify closely with their occupational identity, feelings of isolation, lack of autonomy and the loss of outside employment contribute to loss of self-esteem and discontinuity of self-definition (Oakley, 1974). However, nonconformity to the image of the ideal mother also threatens the self-esteem of employed mothers who may compare themselves unfavourably with non-employed mothers, who are construed as better parents, and with workers without family responsibilities, who are construed as better workers, and with the mythical super-mother. Continued employment should facilitate continuity of self-definition, but the prevalent stereotypes of employed mothers and the hostility of some employers can threaten self-image and challenge distinctiveness by assigning all women with children to a single undifferentiated category.

Responses to cultural prescriptions of motherhood

Adopting a female pattern of work

In 1987, 11 per cent of mothers of pre-school children were in full-time employment (General Household Survey, 1989), Thus, the majority of mothers of pre-school children in Britain do stay at home and hence appear to internalize and accept the dominant view of motherhood, giving credence to the belief that mothers of young children should not work outside the home, except in cases of financial necessity (Martin and Roberts, 1984). The ideology of motherhood produces what can be termed a female pattern of work. This involves periods of part-time work, often in jobs for which women are over-qualified, or breaks from employment for childcare. By their family involvement mothers reinforce the view that they are deviant employees: deviant, that is, from the male pattern of work. They are then blamed for lack of commitment and drive. Because society ultimately values paid work over childcare, a female pattern of work perpetuates female subordination. It is usual for mothers to work several years less then men or than childless women and these years may be crucial for advancement of women with careers. The gap is reflected in pay differentials (Joshi and Newell, 1989). In a study of building society employees, Ashburner (1989) demonstrates how employers capitalize on the desire of mothers to work part-time, by recruiting women with relevant experience to low-paid part-time jobs with few opportunities for promotion. The need for training is thus reduced, and a pool of cheap labour created. Ashburner argues that mothers resort to part-time low-paid work more because of their vulnerability than through choice. The need for work which can be fitted around domestic commitments, together with the reluctance of most employers to provide part-time work with better conditions and opportunities, restricts the choice of jobs for most mothers. Once ensconced in such restricted jobs it is difficult to escape, so that mothers of older as well as young children often remain in restricted, traditionally female, work. The experience of discrimination at work can also cause some mothers to take a break from employment, or reduce the hours worked, as illustrated by a scientific officer who later decided not to return to her job after maternity leave.

> I love my work, . . . it's interesting work, but to be honest I think I should have been promoted by now. If I was a man I would have been. If it seems that I'm not going to get anywhere I might consider giving up. (Lewis and Cooper, 1989, p. 110)

If a married or cohabiting mother works part-time while her partner is in full-time employment, this reinforces the view that she is the primary parent and hence the father's job is prioritized. Mothers then perform most of the domestic and childcare chores. A woman's reduced earnings reinforces her second-class status at home. The lesser participation of fathers in childcare and domestic work tends to be justified by the fact that the man brings home income into the household and conversely, husbands of high-earning wives participate more than other men in the home (Feree, 1987). The internalization of the ideology of motherhood, leading to a discontinuous pattern of work, thus perpetuates the vicious circle of inequality. Many of the mothers I interviewed were well aware of the costs of part-time work but felt that this was an acceptable compromise, and indeed, the only choice available to permit them to retain some links with the world of work without deviating too far from their notion of a good mother. Jane, a physician, was under no illusions:

> I know that it's disastrous for my career [to work part-time], and I know that it gives Phil an excuse to leave most of the hard work at home to me, but it's the only way I can manage, right now.

For Anne, a clerical worker, part-time work was a solution to conflict between pressure to stay at home and financial needs:

> I really ought to work full-time because we could do with the money, but I feel I ought to be at home with the baby, and this way I get to spend more time with her and I guess it's not such a big difference, after tax.

The male model of work is also inadequate for fathers as it denies them the opportunity to be involved in childcare. Whilst women who request concessions for childcare are viewed as normal mothers (if unreliable workers), fathers who ask for similar concession tend to be construed as deviating from the male work role, and their individual job commitment is called into question (Lamb et al., 1983; Lewis and Cooper, 1989). Consequently fathers are more reluctant to ask for time for childcare, and may be less likely to be granted leave for this reason (Rosen and Jerdee, 1974). This again perpetuates the vicious circle of the gender division of labour at home and in the workforce.

Choosing full-time work: guilt and coping
Increasingly mothers are challenging the ideology of exclusive mothering. A growing minority is now attempting to juggle a full-time job or career with family responsibilities. This means conforming to the rigid male pattern of work, often in addition to

substantial domestic involvement. These mothers may therefore experience considerable overload, although many do not admit to this, because they fear appearing to be inadequate in terms of housework, mothering or employment (Yogev, 1982). Added to this is the guilt which many women experience about leaving their children whether for part-time or full-time work. Mothers who have less traditionally gendered divisions of labour at home and who are able to buy in alternative goods and services are less likely to feel guilty on this account (Beutell and Greenhaus, 1982), but women are seldom able to reject completely the notion of the ideal (non-employed) mother. It has been suggested that even mothers who articulate egalitarian beliefs at a conscious level experience some feelings of guilt and conflict at an unconscious level, due to the influence of internalized norms (Gilbert et al., 1981). Mothers therefore tend to be very sensitive to any suggestion that they might be doing the wrong thing, especially if, as so often happens, this comes from children themselves, who quickly absorb the idea that mothers do not have the same rights as fathers to go out to work (Sharpe, 1984).

It would be wrong to give the impression that the experience of being an employed mother is purely negative. On the contrary, all the evidence points to the many benefits of employment. It is true that multiple responsibilities can produce conflict, but they also provide the opportunity for satisfaction, such as the opportunities for creativity, or to work with others (Crosby, 1984). Paid work can fulfil important social and psychological needs, as well as financial ones. So strong are the prescriptions of motherhood, however, that many of our interviewees who acknowledged the satisfaction which they derived from their work, also admitted to feeling somewhat guilty about this very satisfaction.

Women cope with conflict and guilt about combining motherhood and employment by what has been termed 'role expansion', 'personal role redefinition' or 'structural role redefinition' (Hall, 1972). 'Role expansion' involves making extra efforts to fulfil all the socially prescribed demands of motherhood and employment. Typically mothers who work long hours try to compensate for the quantity of time spent away from home by expending endless hours of what has been termed 'quality time' with children, by taking them on outings, reading to them or playing games when they are at home (Hoffman, 1979). Because compensation is motivated by guilt it tends to become overcompensation (Hoffman, 1979). This may alleviate guilt, but it exacerbates overload. The notion of quality time with a happy and fulfilled (employed) mother is one way in which mothers negotiate their own meanings of motherhood, emphasizing the benefits to the child. Brannen and Moss (1990) argue that this contributes towards a new discourse surrounding motherhood, but they emphasize that such themes are, at best, emergent and modest. These discourses recognize the possibility of compensating for full-time mothering, but retain full-time motherhood as the standard against which all else is judged.

Personal and structural role redefinition are more active coping strategies, involving some questioning of the demands imposed by social definitions of motherhood and of the ideal worker; such strategies tend to be most successful in reducing guilt and conflict (Hall, 1972). 'Personal role redefinition' occurs when a mother attempts to change her own self-expectations without necessarily trying to alter other people's expectations or behaviour. For instance, a mother might decide to make more time for herself by declining to take work home at night, or by deciding that she does not have to spend every moment of her time at home with her child, but she may not feel it necessary to justify this to other people. For instance, Mary, a teacher, explained:

> I used to bring home marking and stuff every night, but I decided it was ridiculous. If I can't get everything done at school, people will have to wait longer, that's all. I need time with my family, and I shouldn't have to work in the evenings.

'Structural role redefinition' involves an active attempt to change other people's expectations, including renegotiation of domestic responsibilities with a partner. Modification of employers' expectations may also, if successful, produce structural role redefinition. Mary used this strategy at a later stage by talking to her headteacher and getting her to agree that it was not necessary for work to be done at home in the evenings, thus modifying an expectation which had affected all the staff in this school. Employed mothers often use these strategies effectively by negotiating part-time work. The construction of the ideal employee as one who works full-time, demonstrates career commitment by an unbroken pattern of work and leaves behind home interests and problems during working hours, does not fit the constraints which most mothers experience. Many women are, however, reluctant to redefine expectations surrounding motherhood (Harrison and Minor, 1976). Certain occupations allow more flexibility and control over time than others, and hence provide more opportunities for renegotiation and restructuring of work (Brett and Yogev, 1989).

Mothers who have career ambitions are often acutely aware of the stereotype of the working mother and the detrimental effect it would have on their careers if they were included within this framework. 'Role expansion' strategies are therefore used to ensure that the organization experiences the least possible disruption as a consequence of their motherhood (Lewis and Cooper, 1989). This involves attempts to excel at work and at home. It was apparent from our interviews that mothers who are adamant that they did not want special treatment often adopted this strategy. They did so at a cost: they were continually torn between their needs as mothers and their career, both of which were central to their identity. Others began by attempting to demonstrate that motherhood need not interfere with their commitment to male patterns of work but later reassessed their priorities and reorganized their workloads to take account of personal lives. By being open and honest about the constraints of motherhood, women may help to bring about important structural changes. One father in our study, whose wife had taken the minimum maternity leave to minimize the impact on her career, and who employed a full-time nanny, illustrated how organizational change can occur in response to specific circumstances, rather than being implemented systematically and leading to long-term structural change. He revealed that he had not really confronted issues concerning employed mothers until he interviewed a woman for a senior position in his own firm. This woman stated that she had a young child, intended to have another, to take maximum maternity leave and to leave work at 5 o'clock each day, although the informal norm was for senior staff to work to 6 or 7 p.m. Because she was very clearly the best candidate for the job, he was forced to question his own attitudes and she was recruited. It is questionable, however, whether many mothers are in a position to make such clear and successful demands.

Identifying with male values
Not all mothers who conform as closely as possible to a male career pattern experience this as a sacrifice. The need to prove that motherhood need not interfere with job commitment leads some women to identify with the male organizational culture, and hence to criticize mothers who do not, or cannot conform.

The paucity of role models of successful women with children creates a situation whereby many mothers who are ambitious select male role models. They identify with powerful men, taking on their values, including the negative stereotype of mothers who reduce their job involvement. Like the men on whom they model themselves, these women devote themselves to their career, sometimes redefining their relationship with the children so that it resembles that of the traditional father (Rothman, 1989). Mothers who use the strategy of attempting to be 'honorary men' endeavour to distance themselves from the stereotypes of employed mothers, not in relation to mothers as a group, but as individuals (see also chapter 5). That is, they often express the stereotypical attitude to mothers as unreliable workers, but exclude themselves from this category. By proving that they are in no way 'handicapped' by having children, it becomes possible to castigate those mothers who do not redefine the meaning of motherhood in this way. Relatively privileged women often disregard the different ways in which less privileged women are socially positioned and, like many men, underestimate the difficulties experienced by mothers in less favourable situations. This is illustrated by a senior civil servant and mother of two, married to a teacher and employing a full-time nanny.

> I am very critical of women in my department who take days off whenever one of their children is ill. I firmly believe that a woman has no right to take on a job unless she can make proper arrangements for childcare. It gives other women a bad name.

It is evident from this woman's final comment, that this apparent anti-woman stance also masks a fear that her own precarious position is threatened by mothers who reinforce the stereotype.

It has been suggested that women adopting 'male' behaviour and an anti-woman stance may be suffering from a 'false consciousness' (Marshall, 1987; Spender, 1985) and define their reality from a male perspective (Brittan and Maynard, 1984). However, Condor (1986) argues that we should also recognize the possibility that women actively construct their own realities. Using conceptual and linguistic resources of male rhetoric, mothers who adopt male values, including the negative stereotypes of 'other' working mothers, may actively construct their realities in a way which enables them to succeed in male-dominated structures whilst minimizing threats to their identity. By accepting rather than struggling against the stereotype and excluding themselves as 'exceptions' they can apply traditional beliefs to other mothers and retain their own credibility. In order to defend against the continual threat of inclusion within the stereotype, however, it is necessary for them to reconstruct their gender, to become 'more masculine than the men'. There is then a need to defend against experiences which are incongruent with the self-concept and vigorously to deny or distort the perspectives they share with other mothers.

The powerful stereotype of mothers in the workplace constrains and disempowers all women, whether or not they become mothers, because all women of childbearing age are considered potential mothers. It forces employed mothers to be included within the devalued categories of inadequate mother and inadequate employee or to seek out a different identity. Often this involves identifying with dominant male values and distancing themselves from other women, who could otherwise be a potential source of support. Hence the very women who achieve sufficient power to challenge male organizational structures can often only achieve this position by denying the need for the workplace to change to accommodate the needs of parents. Mothers are thus constrained by the ideology of the good employee to collude in the perpetuation of current male organizational cultures.

Childless women and the stereotype of the working mother

It is not only women with children who are subjected to the stereotype of the working mother. Childless women are constantly called upon to position themselves in relation to motherhood. Many of the childless women in our study were asked about their intentions *vis-à-vis* childbearing or about their husbands' jobs, at job interviews. The implication is that women are expected to become mothers, subordinating their own careers to those of their husbands, and therefore an element of caution must be exercised before employing women, especially in a job which involves training. Hence the stereotype of the working mother as an unreliable worker spreads by the association of gender to include all women of childbearing age.

Some women who internalize the view that motherhood and career are incompatible, and for whom career is central to their identity may opt for voluntary childlessness or delay childbearing. It has been argued that voluntary childlessness may be interpreted as a protest against the heavy burden which parenthood places on women, the restrictiveness of the traditional family, the lack of childcare and the unresponsiveness of employers (Bram, 1978). Women who remain childless by choice, do so for a variety of reasons, including not only the desire for an unimpeded career, but also a dislike of children and a preference for the freedom of this life style (Baum and Coupe, 1980). It can nevertheless be a difficult decision because of social pressure to reproduce. Childless women are often regarded as deviant and unfeminine rather than being respected for their demonstration of commitment to their career (Bram, 1978). Having constructed an identity as a career woman, a further problem can arise when they are confronted with successful women who also have children. Some of the childless women in our study were full of admiration for women who manage career and family, but others demonstrated resentment:

> I felt really annoyed that Jane was promoted at the same time as me. We both started here together, but she has had two lots of maternity leave. I feel there is no recognition for my commitment to the firm. I have never taken time off.

> I really do not believe that if a woman has a child, she deserves to get on at work.

Women who are critical of other women's attempts to accommodate motherhood within their working hours are enmeshed within powerful patriarchal discourses (Hollway, 1989). These determine and restrict the direction in which 'careers' in the broadest sense can be constructed. If the dominant construction of work and career which better fits men than women is accepted, then working women who deviate from this pattern may pose a threat to those who struggle to fit the pattern.

Making changes

I have argued that the choice of employment patterns and identities available to mothers is not a real choice, but one which is produced and constrained by social and organizational values. Equal opportunities at work have been widely heralded in the past two decades, but legally and socially this has come to mean equal opportunities for women to be like men. 'Equality' has provided mothers with the opportunities to conform to male patterns of work, and in some cases, male patterns of parenting (Rothman, 1989). Some women, however, are questioning the social and organizational values which dictate their prescribed roles. In a study of women managers, Marshall (1987) discusses the need to reclaim what she calls 'female grounding'. This means accepting femaleness and allowing this core aspect of self to find expression, something which women managers in a man's world often find difficult. If they can develop in this way women can gain a sense of self-worth which is not contingent upon other people's, especially men's approval, but at the same time does not deny the importance of relationships with others. There is mounting evidence from the accounts of employed mothers, particularly those with an explicit feminist ideology, of attempts to do this by reconstructing careers and ambition to include domestic and occupational lives (Kagan and Lewis, 1990). The construction of a career in terms of one-dimensional structuring is criticized, while success is defined in diverse and complex ways, which includes all aspects of people's lives (Gordon, 1990). Thus women may include raising children as one of their aspirations and achievements within a life-long 'career' and modify other conditions accordingly. This argument is quite problematic, for, as Gordon (1990) points out, making a decision to stand back in occupational terms can be interpreted as simply choosing what is inevitable. However, she argues that such choices do not only involve a concern for children, but also a critique of the masculine way in which paid work is organized.

The process of reformulating a career and the conflicts involved are illustrated by a personnel officer who returned to paid work after two short maternity leaves, and then decided when her children were 4 and 2 years old to take a complete break from employment.

> It is a difficult decision to make because I know that I am doing what they all expected me to do . . . what a lot of people thought I ought to do, but for the wrong reasons. It is a real problem. As a feminist I have always insisted that mothers could work, could be ambitious, successful, and I felt that I had to prove that by doing these things myself. But I have to be clear about why I do things . . . I just don't think that going on working full-time all through my career without doing anything else is necessarily the best thing for me. I want to spend more time with the kids, for me, and I want to do other things.

In other cases it was couples rather than mothers who redefined the notion of a career to include parenting. One couple, for instance, both social workers, negotiated a job-share to enable them to share both paid work and childcare. The father took over the job on a full-time basis during maternity leave, and again later to enable the mother to take a further degree. This broader definition of career, or working life, acknowledges that women with family responsibilities do have particular needs and that self-fulfilment need not be defined in conventional male terms, for women or for men.

For effective reformulations of careers it is necessary to progress beyond personal role definition by women towards structural role redefinition, and towards changes in fathers' behaviours and in organizational expectations. There is a need for more family-orientated social policy, to encourage parents to share childcare and combine this with paid employment. There is also a need for more flexible work patterns and alternative career routes to be acceptable for all employees. This would enable shared parenting to become more possible.

There has been much discussion recently, in both the academic and popular press, of the need for organizations to implement family-orientated policies (Berry-Lound, 1990). Childcare assistance, career breaks and other schemes are widely recommended as strategies for retaining women employees in the light of the anticipated skills shortage. However, initiatives which focus only on the needs of mothers fail to challenge the assumption that parenting is exclusively a woman's issue. Nor do they challenge the male model of work. In the current context of increased competitiveness and drive for greater productivity, many organizations expect employees to demonstrate commitment by working longer hours, and hence spending less time at home. This ethos, which is of debatable value, even in terms of productivity, must be challenged. Hall (1990) recommends a three-stage approach to organizational change: raising awareness of and commitment to work/family issues among senior management, the assessment of work/family needs company-wide and finally the implementation of change. Hall's holistic approach requires management to serve as role models in legitimizing work–family boundaries by conspicuously spending time with their own families. It also involves the restructuring of career paths, such that older employees, who have taken time for childcare, are not handicapped in terms of promotion. Family-orientated personnel policies might be effective in this context, but they represent the end, not the beginning of the process of raising awareness of issues of parenting and employment. Whether or not this type of organizational development can bring about real choices of identity and life scripts for mothers and for fathers remains an empirical question.

Note

I acknowledge the editors' helpful comments on this chapter.

References

Ashburner, L. (1989) Men Managers, Women Workers. Paper presented at the Annual Conference of the British Academy of Management, Manchester.

Baum, F. and Coupe, D.R. (1980) Some characteristics of intentionally childless wives in Britain. *Journal of Biosocial Science* 12, 287–99.

Belsky, J. (1988) Infant daycare and socioemotional developments. *Journal of Child Psychology and Psychiatry* 29, 397–406.

Beutell, N. and Greenhaus, J. (1982) Interrole conflict among married women: the influence of husband and wife characteristics on conflict and coping behaviour. *Journal of Vocational Behaviour* 21, 90–110.

Berry-Lound, D. (1990) *Work and the Family*. London: Institute of Personnel Management.

Bram, S. (1978) Through the looking glass: voluntary childlessness: a critical assessment of current strategies and findings. In E. Macklin and R. Rubin (eds), *Contemporary Families and Alternative Lifestyles*. Beverly Hills, CA: Sage.

Brannen, J. and Moss, P. (1985) Dual earner households: women's contributions after the birth of the first child. In J. Brannen and G. Wilson (eds), *Give and Take in Families*. London: Allen and Unwin.

Brannen, J. and Moss, P. (1988) *New Mothers at Work*. London: Unwin Hyman.

Brannen, J. and Moss, P. (1990) *Managing Mothers: Dual Earner Households After Maternity Leave*. London: Unwin Hyman.

Breakwell, G. (1986) *Coping with Threatened Identities*. London: Methuen.

Brett, J. and Yogev, S. (1989) Restructuring Work for Family. In E.B. Goldsmith (ed.), *Work and Family Theory. Research and Application*. Beverly Hills, CA: Sage.

Brittan, A. and Maynard, M. (1984) *Sexism, Racism and Oppression*. Oxford: Basil Blackwell.

Burke, R.J. and Weir, T. (1976) Relationship of wives' employment status to husband, wife and pair satisfaction and performance. *Journal of Marriage and the Family* 30, 279–87.

Condor, S. (1986) Sex role beliefs and 'traditional' women: feminist and intergroup perspectives. In S. Wilkinson (ed.), *Feminist Social Psychology*. Milton Keynes: Open University.

Crosby, F. (1984) Job satisfaction and domestic life. In M.D. Lee and R. Kanuengo (eds), *Management of Work and Family Life*. New York: Praeger.

Feree, M.M. (1987) The struggles of Superwoman. In C. Bose, R. Feldberg and N. Sokoloff (eds), *Hidden Aspects of Women's Work*. New York: Praeger.

General Household Survey (1989) *General Household Survey 1987*. London: HMSO.

Gilbert, L.A., Holohen, C.K. and Manning, L. (1981) Coping with conflict between professional and maternal roles. *Family Relations* 30, 419–26.

Gordon, T. (1990) *Feminist Mothers*. London: Macmillan.

Gottfried, A.E. and Gottfried, A.W. (1988) *Maternal Employment and Children's Development*. New York: Plenum Press.

Granrose, C.S. (1988) Post partum work intentions among black and white college women. *Career Development Quarterly* 37 (2), 149–64.

Hall, D.T. (1972) A model of coping and role conflict. The role behaviour of college educated women. *Administrative Science Quarterly* 1, 471–86.

Hall, D.T. (1990) Promoting work/family balance. An organizational change approach. *Organizational Dynamics* 18, 5–18.

Harrison, A.O. and Minor, J.H. (1976) Interrole conflict, coping strategies and satisfaction among black working wives. *Journal of Marriage and the Family* 40, 799–805.

Hoffman, L.W. (1979) Maternal employment: 1979. *American Psychologist* 34 (10), 859–65.

Hollway, W. (1989) *Subjectivity and Method in Psychology*. London: Sage.

Johnson, C.C. and Johnson, F.A. (1980) Parenthood, marriage and careers: situational constraints and role strain. In F. Pepitone-Rockwell (ed.), *Dual Career Couples*. London: Sage.

Joshi, H. and Newell, M. (1989) *Pay Differentials and Parenthood*. University of Warwick: Institute of Employment Research.

Kagan, C. and Lewis, S. (1990) 'Where's your sense of humour?' Swimming against the tide in higher education. In E. Burman (ed.), *Feminists and Psychological Practice*. London: Sage.

Kamerman, S.B. (1981) *Parenting in an Unresponsive Society*. New York: Free Press.

Lamb, M.E., Russell, G. and Sagi, A. (1983) *Fatherhood and Family Policy*. Hillsdale, NJ: Erlbaum.

Lerner, J.V. and Golambos, N.L. (1985) Maternal role satisfaction, mother–child interaction and child temperament: a process model. *Developmental Psychology* 21, 1157–64.

Lewis, S. and Cooper, C.L. (1987) Stress in two-earner couples and stage in the life cycle. *Journal of Occupational Psychology* 60, 289–303.

Lewis, S. and Cooper, C.L. (1988) The transition to parenthood in dual earner couples. *Psychological Medicine* 18, 477–86.

Lewis, S. and Cooper, C.L. (1989) *Career Couples*. London: Unwin Hyman.

Marshall, J. (1987) Issues of identity for women managers. In D. Clutterbuck and M. Devine (eds), *Businesswoman*. London: Macmillan.

Martin, J. and Roberts C. (1984) *Women and Employment: a Lifetime Perspective*. London: HMSO.

New, C. and David, M. (1985) *For the Children's Sake: Making Childcare More than Women's Business*. Harmondsworth: Penguin.

Oakley, A. (1974) *Housewife*. Harmondsworth: Penguin.

Parry, G. (1987) Sex role beliefs. Work and attitudes and mental health in employed and non-employed mothers. *British Journal of Social Psychology* 26, 47–58.

Pleck, J.H. (1977) The work–family role system. *Social Problems* 24, 417–27.

Rapoport, R. and Rapoport, R.N. (1977) *Dual-career Families Re-examined*. London: Harper and Row.

Rosen, B. and Jerdee, T. (1974) Influence of sex-role stereotypes on personnel decisions. *Journal of Applied Psychology* 59, 9–14.

Rothman, B.K. (1989) Women as fathers: motherhood and childcare under a modified patriarchy. *Gender and Society* 3 (1), 89–104.

Rueschemeyer, M. (1981) *Professional Work and Marriage. An East–West Comparison*. London: Macmillan.

Russo, N. (1976) The motherhood mandate. *Journal of Social Issues* 32, 143–54.

Sharpe, S. (1984) *Double Identity: the Lives of Working Mothers*. Harmondsworth: Penguin.

Spender, D. (1985) *For the Record: the Making and Meaning of Feminist Knowledge*. London: Women's Press.

Welch, S. and Booth, A. (1977) Employment and health among married women with children. *Sex Roles* 3, 385–99.

Yogev, S. (1982) Are professional women overworked? Objective versus subjective perceptions of workloads. *Journal of Occupational Psychology* 55 (3), 165–70.

Afterword: Issues Related to Motherhood

Anne Woollett and Ann Phoenix

Here we draw together some of the themes developed in the book and consider their implications for ways of conceptualizing motherhood. In doing so we identify gaps in current literature and research on motherhood.

A major theme explored in earlier chapters concerns the ways in which psychology has addressed motherhood. In psychology mothers are seen as essential providers of crucial environmental experiences for their children. This is associated with the 'professionalization' of motherhood and pressures on mothers to perform well. Professionalization is common to many areas of Western life: a glimpse at the magazines on a newsagent's shelves indicates the vast array of 'how to do it' publications, giving advice on everything from decorating and cookery to car maintenance. Mothers respond to (and encourage) expectations that as 'good' mothers their major function is to maximize their children's development and therefore attempt to carry out the tasks of mothering with high degrees of professionalism and expertise by seeking out information about their children's development from a variety of sources, including childcare manuals.

Models of mothering current in developmental psychology reflect and encourage assumptions that mothers are 'responsible' for the ways in which their children develop and behave. The vast number of studies that examine mothers' behaviour in relation to their children reflects widespread recognition of the importance of mothering in Western societies. However, in spite of the number of studies expressly concerned with linking mothers' behaviour and children's development, assumptions about the responsibility of mothers for their children's development have received only limited support (Schaffer, 1986; Urwin, 1985).

By virtue of the assumption that mothers have major (if not exclusive) responsibility for their children's development and behaviour, psychological writing and childcare manuals (implicitly or explicitly) blame mothers when children demonstrate behavioural or other problems. This 'mother-blaming' is reflected in some feminist analyses of the experience of being mothered which hold mothers responsible for the miseries endured by children in childhood, for any lack of acceptance or disapproval women recall their mothers expressing towards them as well as for many adult miseries. There is, therefore, a consensus that when children have problems or behave in ways considered by society as inappropriate or antisocial, it is mothers, rather than fathers, schools and others who are blamed as if mothers constituted children's sole environment/environmental influence. Mothers are thus in a 'no win' situation, as Newson and Newson (1976) suggest:

> Parents are in fact chronically on the defensive over their parental role because the responsibility laid upon them is not only limitless but also supremely personal. Our children are a walking testament for the sort of people we are – doubly so, since they advertise both their heredity and their environment – and this is fine so long as they are feeling in a social and civilised mood and ready to do us credit. (Newson and Newson, 1976, p. 438)

Although largely ignored in developmental psychology, women's activities and experiences as mothers are given some attention in social psychology. Here a number of psychologists point to the ways in which motherhood is socially constructed and its importance for the establishment of women's adult identity (see chapter 3). There are a limited number of positive positions and identities available to women, and marriage and motherhood constitute major ones. Women who do not become mothers are negatively evaluated as both women and as adults. Being an adult woman is generally equated with being a mother, an approach which has important consequences for how women view themselves and how they are viewed by others, such as employers (see chapter 11). It also reinforces the idea that motherhood is expected to be a crucial and central aspect of women's development and a necessary developmental stage which supplants other identities and other aspects of development for women (Antonis, 1981; Boulton, 1983; Busfield, 1987). Feminist and social psychological writings also point to the dual, and hence often conflicting, nature of motherhood as experience and development which is mainly lived out in a private, domestic sphere, but which is evaluated within the public domain (chapter 1).

Women's experiences as mothers, their insider perspectives, are rarely examined. As a result little is known about how women experience motherhood, how their experiences differ and the factors that account for differences in experience. The experience of motherhood may involve many of the aspects outlined here both singly and in combination. A mother, for example, may have to combine her experience of mothering a disabled child with that of caring for two or more children and perhaps, at the same time, with divorce, being a single mother and with employment outside the home. It is difficult to deal meaningfully with all such issues at once in research studies, but understandings of the complexities of motherhood require that researchers appreciate these complexities and recognize that they occur in women of all 'races', social classes, marital statuses and sexualities. Psychologists can potentially make powerful contributions in all these areas by recognizing that motherhood is complex and multifaceted.

We have tried to indicate some of the different approaches towards motherhood. Because there is little dialogue between different traditions and theoretical perspectives there are few attempts to use ideas about women's (and especially mothers') identities to explain their relationships with their children. Nor are the ways in which mothers' experiences of children and of childcare tap into ideas about themselves usually explored. The contributors to this book have attempted to redress these omissions. Thus, for example, there are chapters by researchers working with mothers who have more than one child, mothers of girls as well as boys and mothers bringing up children who, because they are deaf, are considered disabled (chapters 7, 8 and 9). These researchers have often collected the original data for other, more narrowly developmental purposes and for this book have turned these data around and redefined their focus to discuss the implications of their findings and of this kind of research for mothers. They examine the ways in which mothers' experiences of motherhood are influenced by their circumstances and how mothers deal with any experiences of disjunction and conflict between their own experiences as mothers and 'normal motherhood' as portrayed in psychological accounts, including those in childrearing manuals. The issues that emerge from these chapters are ones that need to be taken seriously within developmental and social psychology if progress is to be made in theorizing and understanding mothering and motherhood and the ways in which motherhood has an impact on women's development.

The New Man/new father?

This book has deliberately focused on mothers, as the people crucial for their children's development; on motherhood as an important part of many women's lives and as an ideology which affects all women, those without children as well as mothers. Previous chapters have pointed to the ways in which developmental and social psychology have largely ignored mothers and mother-hood. However, it could be argued that making mothers our central focus is misplaced at a time when the emergence of the 'New Man' signals and warrants a shift from an emphasis on motherhood and mothering to one on parenthood and parenting. Since the 1970s there has been considerable interest in fathers' involvement with children and their influence on children's development and this is now a substantive area in popular childcare literature and in psychology (Burman, 1991; White and Woollett, 1992). This interest in fathers parallels changes in portrayals of men in the media. The New Man is seen advertising a whole range of (more or less) child-friendly products as caring, tender and involved in his children. However, the reality of the New Man is questionable:

> In general the new man concept seemed nothing more than an attempt to grab the potent mother–child imagery and remake it in masculine terms, hence all those absurd photographs showing musclebound half-dressed men brandishing a baby as if it were the FA cup. Even those defending the imagery talked of the baby as a new accessory. (French, 1990, p. 8)

Certainly fathers are now more visible, at birth, pushing the buggy, in the park, and in magazines extolling the joys of father-hood. Ideology has changed. Mothers, fathers and others expect fathers to be more involved with their children than they were and many people feel that there have been changes. Studies of fathers' involvement, however, find that this is little more than an increase in fathers' interest and enjoyment of their children (Backett, 1982; Lewis and O'Brien, 1987; Oakley, 1981). Boulton (1983) argues that it is because the norm is for mothers to do everything for their children that anything fathers do gets noticed and assumes significance.

Nor is there any evidence of fundamental changes in the power relations between men and women. This can be seen in their relative employment positions. While women continue to pre-dominate in part-time and casual employment (Westwood and Bhachu, 1988), men's employment (hours and conditions) continues to ensure that women have major responsibility for children, for childcare and for communication with agencies deal-ing with children, such as doctors, hospitals and schools (New and David, 1985).

> The construction of gender difference and hierarchy is created at work as well as at home – and the effect on women (less physical and

technical capacity, lack of confidence, lower pay) may well cast a shadow on the sex-relations of domestic life. (Cockburn, 1981, p. 54)

Such inequities point to the importance of changing employment away from what can be seen as a 'male' model of work (see chapter 11) as well as changing imbalances in childcare at home. Even when men are unemployed and hence have time for childcare, there is no evidence that they are more involved (Bell and McKee, 1986).

Psychology and ideology

A recurrent issue in the book is that psychological accounts of motherhood are not as 'value-free' and 'objective' as many psychologists assume. Psychological accounts tend to focus on individual mothers and families. We have suggested that the circumstances – financial, material, ideological and social – in which mothers bring up children are crucially important for mothers and for the mothering they provide as well as for children. Psychologists are themselves part of the wider society and many are parents. Many, therefore, share dominant ideological notions about what 'normal mothers' and 'normal children' should be like. Such notions enter or impinge on their research (Burman, 1991). We have tried to show that through their choice of questions and the mothers they choose to study psychologists often perpetuate and provide scientific evidence for current Western ideologies about motherhood and state practices around families. These ideas can be seen most clearly in the accounts of motherhood put across in the childcare manuals where there is a mismatch between the discourses they draw on in discussion of mutuality and flexibility between parents in 'ideal/ normal' families and those they use to emphasize the responsibilities of mothers rather than of fathers in childcare together with their precise prescriptions for maternal behaviour (see chapter 4).

Two powerful assumptions about 'normal/ideal mothers' are, firstly, that there is an appropriate age at which to have children and, secondly, that mothers should ideally not be employed outside the home while children are young. In chapters 5 and 6 we have shown how medical and social preoccupations with the problems of older or younger mothers are not substantiated. For younger mothers (under 20), financial position, social support, housing difficulties and occupational position are more powerful influences on women's lives and the environments they provide for their children than is age of the mother. It is harder to see why older mothers experience social disapproval. Arguments in terms of biology and being 'too old' are difficult to understand when women in previous generations continued to have children until later in life. In many respects women are now healthier than ever before and we are constantly reminded that obstetric knowledge is highly advanced. The pervasive idea that children need the total care and attention of their mothers has implications for women's work responsibilities and employment (chapters 10 and 11). Mothers who are employed are likely to experience conflicts and women (whether they are mothers or not) are likely to be considered 'poor bets' in the employment career stakes because they are seen as potential childbearers.

Motherhood and younger children

The preoccupation with the exclusive mother–child relationship in developmental psychology (which perpetuates concerns about maternal employment) comes in part because studies concentrate on motherhood in the early years to the exclusion of the mothering of older children. Most studies of motherhood focus on the initial transition to motherhood and a short period afterwards when mothers are caring for young children. Once women become mothers, their identity is permanently changed, even when their children grow up and leave home. But the experience of motherhood differs according to children's age:

> Most [childcare] books only cover the years from 0 to 3. After this excessively detailed guidance comes the shamble of toddlers and playgroups, then the sign off at the school gates, occasioning in part a sigh of relief, in part an awful sense of exclusion from paradise. Powerless, we watch our children taken over by strangers, paying more attention to the values dictated by Blue Peter than those they hear from us. (Hardyment, 1990a, p. 8)

The work of mothering changes as children get older and require less physical care. Once children start school and other adults become important in their lives, mothers become progressively less influential. Relationships outside the home tend to be less carefully monitored and mothers may find themselves excluded from many of the activities and interests of older children. Children begin to reflect upon their mothers' practices and become critical of the mothering they receive. Thus children's assumptions about mothers' functions and responsibilities influence how children may come to see their mothers and the extent to which they get involved in mother-blaming (Apter, 1990). The feedback children provide as they grow up is an increasingly important part of women's experiences of motherhood (Newson and Newson, 1976). We know little about the implications of this for mothers, although it seems obvious that women's relationships with their children may change from physical care and concern for their safety to a greater emphasis on companionship. By the time they reach adolescence, many children feel close to their mothers but for some, and especially boys, their worlds may have drawn apart. Although as their children get older, mothers can only be partly responsible for the way their children 'turn out', they continue to be judged by their children's behaviour, their successes and failures.

Developmental psychologists employ theoretical models which are reliant on models of monotropic or exclusive relationships. This has implications for how mothers experience the upbringing of two children (as indicated in chapter 9) but also for how they experience motherhood as their children grow up. Older children tend to be less extensively studied (Collins, 1984) and explanations of development at this age include ideas about the value of play and friendships with other children and going to school but little account is taken of these other influences in explanations of any problems children have. Children come back into major focus again in adolescence when their development and relationships with their parents are considered to constitute social problems (Coleman and Hendry, 1990).

Feminism and motherhood

The discussion above should not be considered to imply that mothers are homogeneous in their perceptions of motherhood. All the chapters are critical of psychology's lack of consideration of variability in women's experiences as mothers and in their ideas about how to bring up their children. Feminist mothers, for example, constitute a group of mothers who have particular political perspectives which are likely to have a direct impact on how they mother their children (Gieve, 1989; Gordon, 1990; Grabrucker, 1988). Feminism presents a powerful alternative analysis of motherhood. The family is seen as a socially organized (rather than a naturally or biologically organized) unit and women's position in the family is theorized to reflect gendered relationships within the wider society. Motherhood is thus recognized as one of the major institutions which oppress women and prevent them from taking more active control over their own lives. Women's emotional commitment to their children, sometimes to male partners, and the circumstances in which they mother serve to isolate them and render them relatively powerless to oppose their oppression. Feminism has sought ways to reduce the onerous and unrelenting nature of mothers' work through arguing for the provision of nurseries, shared parenting and a greater involvement of men in childcare (Gordon, 1990; Grabrucker, 1988; Stacey, 1986).

Feminist analyses emphasize the often competing demands of men and women, mothers and children in families and the pressures on women to balance the contradictory needs and demands of different family members. Within present structures, children's needs are often met only through women's suppression of their own needs. Viewing mothers and children as separate people with separate needs in families helps to clarify that what is best for children is not necessarily what is best for mothers (chapters 1 and 2).

Some recent feminist analyses, however, seem to be theorizing motherhood in ways which are unlikely to liberate mothers from the burden of expectations and responsibilities described in this book. A number of feminists have propagated what Segal (1987) calls 'maternal revivalism' and Stacey (1986) 'conservative pro-family feminism'. These new approaches take off from the often negatively tinged accounts and analyses of women's experiences of motherhood to celebrate traditional nurturant (and hence 'female') qualities associated with motherhood. They replace a commitment to redressing gendered inequities with that of recognizing women's needs for intimacy, and seeing family and children as the most appropriate means to satisfy these needs (Ruddick, 1984, 1990). Gordon puts this in personal terms:

> However the time came when having children seemed such a potentially exciting human experience that I threw caution to the wind, and now have two children. I became convinced that equality was not what we should seek: we should aim for a society where the experience of having children could be a pleasure to all parents, male and female. (Gordon, 1990, p. 2)

This has a negative impact on women in general and mothers in particular:

> The resurgence of interest in motherhood has positive and negative implications for the feminist movement. On the positive side there is a continual need for study and research of female parenting which this interest promotes and encourages . . . On the negative side, romanticizing motherhood, employing the same terminology that is used by sexists to suggest that women are inherently life-affirming nurturers, feminist activists reinforce central tenets of male supremacist ideology. (bell hooks, 1985, p. 135)

Accounts such as that of Ruddick (1984, 1990) argue a position which in many respects is similar to that which underlies traditional approaches in psychology. Ruddick (1984), for example, says 'From early on . . . a mother is governed by a third interest:

she must shape natural (*sic*) growth in such a way that her child becomes the sort of adult she can appreciate and others can accept' (Ruddick, 1984, p. 215). This statement could come straight from childcare manuals, with their emphasis on the universality of mothering practices and on mothers having a crucial part to play in their children's social development. Although Ruddick acknowledges that mothers vary enormously, such statements do not seem to recognize inherent conflicts between mothers' (and particularly 'feminist' mothers') interests and values and those of the wider society. Nor do they acknowledge the potential for mother-blaming in assuming that mothers are the key figures in their children's lives:

> The task of producing an appreciable child gives a mother a unique opportunity to explore, create, and insist on her own values; to train her children for strength and virtue; and ultimately to develop openness and reciprocity in regard to her child's most threatening differences from her, namely, moral ones. (Ruddick, 1984, p. 220)

This approach, by stating that motherhood offers unique opportunities for adult development, equates motherhood with adult female status and thereby seeks to maintain the status quo. It also fails to recognize other means of achievement for women and relegates women without children to perpetual childishness (Salmon, 1985).

If feminism is a politics which aims to emancipate women (Wilkinson, 1986), Ruddick's approach cannot claim to be feminist because it does not engage with the ways in which differences between women, such as those explored in this book, have a direct impact on women's lives. The political functions of motherhood are also glossed over. Producing children who are not a threat to society (Hardyment, 1990b) is taken for granted in such accounts without discussion of the implicit political functions mothers have in maintaining the status quo. This approach also ignores what many feminist researchers have made clear: that motherhood is stressful (Boulton, 1983; Gordon, 1990; Oakley, 1981). Ruddick's work also fails as feminism because it does not engage with the lack of acknowledgement in current models of mothers' sexuality, aggression and negative feelings around motherhood as well as their desires for an autonomous life (Gordon, 1990).

Greening motherhood

An increasingly popular political concern is that which focuses on the environment. Environmental issues have fuelled the development of a new approach to motherhood which links motherhood with wider environmental issues (McConville, 1990; Solomon, 1990). Environmental concerns in childbearing and childrearing are not new: much family planning provision has its basis in a concern on the part of richer nations for the size of the world's population in relation to the use of the world's resources (particularly food). The unwillingness of richer nations to restrain their consumption to ensure that all children are properly fed and have a reasonable standard of living underlies much discussion around aid to the Third World. In Western societies disapproval of 'single' or 'young mothers' is often expressed in terms of the cost to nations of babies whose mothers can support them only with state assistance.

In 'green' approaches to motherhood, however, the nurturant tasks of motherhood, identified in much childcare literature, are extended to nurturance of the environment. McConville (1990) adds to the list of characteristics and concerns of 'good' mothers, the prescription to mother in a way that is environmentally friendly through behaviour such as using recycled paper and not using disposable nappies.

In First World countries, mothers are generally encouraged to be extravagant of scarce resources on their children's behalf. This can be seen in advertising which encourages a view of good mothering as continuous provision of toys, clothes, disposable nappies and activities for their children's consumption. Mothers experience considerable pressure to take their children from one activity to another in cars which damage the environment (and therefore children) and to dress them in clothes which can be kept clean only by the use of environmentally destructive detergents. When public transport is scarce or too expensive, not using a car may mean their children's activities are restricted. If the advertisers are to be believed, not having their children dressed in sparkling, optically brightened clothes may threaten women's sense of themselves as mothers because one yardstick of 'good mothering' is commonly believed to be keeping children clean and well presented. The growing popularity of 'green issues' and 'green consumerism' indicates that many people (including mothers) are, rightly, anxious about the destruction of their world environment, and are not resistant to attempts to link motherhood with wider environmental issues. However, one implication for mothers is that they can be blamed for not taking sufficient care and responsibility for the environment while the more crucial responsibilities of manufacturers and governments go unquestioned.

Commonalities between traditional and new approaches to motherhood

One reason why childcare and developmental psychology literature generally romanticize the mother–child relationship (see chapters 4 and 9) is because they ignore what mothering is like for many women in the West. In portraying the reality of motherhood, much feminist literature emphasizes the negative aspects of motherhood without focusing on the pleasures that many women experience. The two sets of literature, therefore, seem dichotomized. Yet there are important overlaps. Firstly, neither fully reflects the reality of motherhood – both the joys and privations – and coming from different directions as they do, they both (including new feminist and 'green' approaches) result in mother-blaming because mothers are ultimately held responsible for the way their children turn out. No new models for how society could or should be changed to give mothers, children (and hence fathers and others) a better deal are provided. In addition, while there are commonalities in mothers' experiences, neither set of literatures fully recognizes the differences between mothers, for example of social class, 'race', marital status, or sexuality. While it is important to avoid an essentialist, determinist view of motherhood, failure to theorize these differences helps to maintain the status quo as 'normal mothers' being white, middle class, married women and other mothers being deviant/aberrant.

Differing family circumstances

In many respects motherhood and the experience of mothering are similar for all women. However, we have also tried to point to some of the many ways in which mothers' experiences differ as well as to the implications of differing circumstances for women's identities as mothers and the meaning of motherhood for them. These differences are not ignored by psychology but its treatment of some groups of mothers as normal/usual and others as deviant reinforces current ideologies about there being a correct way and correct circumstances in which to mother and hence the notion that mothers who do not conform to these norms are deviant. In theoretical terms it means that the experiences of 'deviant mothers' remain marginal and are not incorporated into models of motherhood. In practical terms it means that models developed only with women who mother under specific circumstances are of limited applicability. We argue that models need to be capable of more extensive application. We have discussed a number of situations which need to be considered, including the impact of mothering more than one child, mothering a disabled child and combining employment with motherhood. Models of mothering also need to take into consideration ethnicity, 'race', cross-national differences, social class differences and differing family forms.

Women come to motherhood by a variety of routes and have children in a variety of circumstances. Lesbian mothers have children and bring to motherhood their different sexualities. There has been little research on lesbian mothers, although there is evidence to suggest that in divorce cases where custody is disputed, lesbian mothers are less likely than heterosexual mothers to win custody of their children (Brophy, 1985, 1987). This is not surprising given that lesbian mothers are stigmatized because they have contravened dominant ideological notions about 'normal' circumstances in which to have children. It is also assumed that being raised not merely without fathers (which is in itself considered problematic) but in a lesbian household will damage children. What evidence there is indicates that concern about the development of children brought up by mothers who are lesbian is unfounded (Golombok et al., 1983).

With increases in the rates of divorce and remarriage, mothers are increasingly bringing up children on their own and in reconstituted families. Despite the rhetoric of the 'New Man', an increasing number of fathers are now physically absent from their families. By the year 2000, it is estimated that while seven out of ten children in the UK will be brought up by both 'own' parents, many children will be brought up without fathers as a result of parental divorce (Henwood et al., 1987). After divorce, fathers may or may not stay involved with their children, and with reconstituted families fathers may find themselves involved in the care and economic maintenance of other children. The proportion of children being brought up by one parent or in reconstituted families increases when children born to women who are not legally married are included, because more single women are now having children and bringing them up on their own.

What are the implications for motherhood? In most cases where parents live separately because they are divorced, the children live with their mothers. Mothers, therefore, have to manage their own feelings, domestic and economic life as well as caring for their children (Hetherington et al., 1982). This can impose an extra burden on them, particularly since, as we have seen, it is mothers who are held responsible for how their children 'turn out'. Yet, since much psychological work ignores these social trends, we know relatively little about mothering in 'reconstituted' families at a time when such families are becoming increasingly common.

Step-mothers

Step-mothers and many adoptive mothers have no biological link with children,[1] but they may have the same responsibilities as mothers who give birth and bring up their 'own' children. Women do not generally aim to become mothers when they cohabit with a man who is already a parent. In these circumstances forming a relationship with their new partner also entails motherhood. Women do not necessarily gain social status by becoming mothers in this way (although some do because they are seen as noble because they have 'taken on' children). Step-families are created when children are of varied ages and may involve complicated sets of step-sibling relationships. Step-mothers may not have daily responsibility for, or contact with, children who have 'their own' mother living elsewhere. When children are resident with step-mothers, for the woman establishing a relationship with her new partner may be complicated by having at the same time to establish relationships with her partner's children. This may be especially true because the ideologies around motherhood are such that fathers expect to be able to hand over to their new partners major household responsibility and the day-to-day care of children (Cox, 1990). It is, therefore, not surprising that step-mothering is often a difficult status (Cox, 1990; Ferri, 1984; Smith, 1990).

Adoption

Adoption situates some mothers in a contradictory position. On the one hand they are positioned as altruistic women, prepared to take in, care for and love other women's children. On the other hand most women who adopt do so because they have not been able to have children; adoption is a way of resolving their infertility. By failing to produce their 'own' child, however, they have failed as 'real women' and this may influence their view (and that of others) of themselves as mothers and as women. This sense of failure probably accounts, in part at least, for the fact that when it was easier to adopt it was common to keep adoption secret. Mothers are now less able to keep silent about the way in which they achieved motherhood because adoption practices have changed. Since the 1970s there have been fewer babies available for adoption with the result that parents are now less likely to be able to adopt children who 'pass' for their 'own'. Most research on adoption is concerned with the impact of adoption on children's development and as a consequence there is little information about how women who become mothers in this way (and the women who give up children for adoption) experience motherhood (Haimes and Timms, 1985; White and Woollett, 1992).

Reproductive technology
Women who give birth or attempt to conceive through reproductive technologies have also not demonstrated that they are 'real women' and hence may feel themselves to be inadequate, feelings reinforced by their frequent designation as 'desperate' (Franklin, 1989). For doctors, reproductive technologies are prestigious and exciting technological fields of medicine through which they can offer women a last chance of becoming mothers. Some feminists, however, question the usefulness of these techniques for many women and demonstrate how their use can give doctors even greater control over women's lives (Stanworth, 1987). Caught in the midst of such opposing views as well as their own desires to become mothers, it is not surprising that women (both those who achieve the desired pregnancy and those who do not) find reproductive technologies stressful. The enthusiasm shown by some infertile women for these technologies, in spite of their low success rate and the stresses they generate, underlines the importance for women of having their 'own' child and the problems they experience in coming to terms with childlessness.

Final words

In this book we have drawn on a variety of experiences of motherhood, experiences of women with and without children and women who are mothering in widely differing circumstances. They demonstrate how society's constructions of children and women make motherhood a crucial goal for most women. This construction is manifested in terms of the meanings associated with motherhood, the ways in which motherhood is practised and the ideologies which surround motherhood. Women's experiences and practices vary as a function of their differing personalities and motivations and their structural positions. The studies in this book have broken important new ground by highlighting aspects of motherhood that are generally ignored in research and in the literature. They suggest some of the many questions which still need to be addressed and point to ways in which future research needs to expand its focus.

Note

1 Some adoptions occur where mothers adopt their own biological children in order to allow their partners, who are not their children's biological fathers, to have

a legal status as an adoptive father. Some adoptions are also by children's grand-parents or other relatives. These are not discussed here.

References

Antonis, B. (1981) Motherhood and mothering. In Cambridge University Women's Studies Group (eds), *Women in Society: Interdisciplinary Essays*. London: Virago.

Apter, T. (1990) *Altered Loves: Mothers and Daughters during Adolescence*. Hemel Hempstead: Harvester Wheatsheaf.

Backett, K.C. (1982) *Mothers and Fathers*. London: Macmillan.

Bell, C. and McKee, L. (1986) 'His unemployment, Her problem': the domestic and marital consequences of male unemployment. In S. Allen, A. Waton, K. Purcell and S. Wood (eds), *The Experience of Unemployment*. London: Macmillan.

bell hooks (1985) *Feminist Theory from Margin to Centre*. Boston: South End Press.

Boulton, M.G. (1983) *On Being a Mother: a Study of Women with Preschool Children*. London: Tavistock.

Brannen, J. and Wilson, G. (1987) *Give and Take in Families*. London: Allen and Unwin.

Brophy, J. (1985) Child care and the growth of power: the status of mothers in child custody disputes. In J. Brophy and C. Smart (eds), *Women and Law: Explorations in Law, Family and Sexuality*. London: Routledge.

Brophy, J. (1987) Law, State and the Family: the Politics of Child Custody. PhD thesis, Faculty of Law, Sociolegal Centre, University of Sheffield.

Burman, E. (1991) Power, gender and developmental psychology. *Feminism and Psychology* 1, 141–53.

Busfield, J. (1987) Parenting and parenthood. In G. Cohen (ed.), *Social Change and the Life Course*. London: Tavistock.

Cockburn, C. (1981) The material of male power. *Feminist Review* 9, 41–58.

Coleman, J. and Hendry, L. (1990) *The Nature of Adolescence*. London: Routledge.

Collins, W. (ed.) (1984) *Development during Middle Childhood*. Washington, DC: National Academy Press.

Cox, K. (1990) The 'Cinderella Complex' in Men with Children. Paper presented at Women and Psychology Conference, University of Birmingham, July 1990.

Ferri, E. (1984) *Step Children: a National Study*. London: NFER Nelson.

Franklin, S. (1989) Deconstructing 'desperateness': the social construction of infertility in popular representations of new reproductive technologies. In M.McNeil, I. Varcoe and S. Yearsley (eds), *The New Reproductive Technologies*. London: Macmillan.

French, S. (1990) Diary. *New Society and Statesman* 15 June, p. 8.

Gieve, K. (ed.) (1989) *Balancing Acts: on Being a Mother*. London: Virago.

Golombok, S., Spencer, A. and Rutter, M. (1983) Children in lesbian families. *Journal of Child Psychology and Psychiatry* 24, 551–72.

Gordon, T. (1990) *Feminist Mothers*. London: Macmillan.

Grabrucker, M. (1988) *There's a Good Girl: Gender Stereotyping in the First Three Years of Life*. London: Women's Press.

Haimes, E. and Timms, N. (1985) *Adoption, Identity and Social Policy: The Search for Distant Relatives*. Aldershot: Gower.

Hardyment, C. (1990a) Beyond the nursery door. *Guardian* 21 April, p. 8.

Hardyment, C. (1990b) Mum's the word no more. *Guardian* 3/4 November, p. 8.

Henwood, M., Rimmer, L. and Wicks, M. (1987) *Inside the Family: Changing Roles of Men and Women*. London: Family Policy Studies Centre, Occasional Paper no. 6.

Hetherington, E.M., Cox, M. and Cox, R. (1982) Effects of divorce on parents and children. In M. Lamb (ed.), *Non-traditional Families*. Hillsdale, NJ: Erlbaum.

Lewis, C. and O'Brien, M. (eds) (1987) *Reassessing Fatherhood: New Observations on Fathers and the Modern Family*. London: Sage.

McConville, B. (1990) *Green Parent's Guide*. London: Pandora.

New, C. and David, M. (1985) *For the Children's Sake: Making Childcare More than Women's Business*. Harmondsworth: Penguin.

Newson, J. and Newson, E. (1976) *Seven Years Old in the Home Environment*. Harmondsworth: Penguin.

Oakley, A. (1981) *From Here to Maternity: Becoming a Mother*. Harmondsworth: Penguin.

Ruddick, S. (1984) Maternal Thinking. In J. Trebilcot (ed.), *Mothering: Essays in Feminist Theory*. Totowa, NJ: Rowman and Allanheld.

Ruddick, S. (1990) *Maternal Thinking: Towards a Politics of Peace*. London: Women's Press.

Salmon, P. (1985) *Living in Time: a New Look at Personal Development*. London: Dent.

Schaffer, H.R. (1986) Child psychology: the future. *Journal of Child Psychology and Psychiatry* 27, 761–79.

Segal, L. (1987) *Is the Future Female? Troubled Thoughts on Contemporary Feminism*. London: Virago.

Solomon, J. (1990) *Green Parenting*. London: Optima.

Smith, D. (1990) *Step Mothering*. Hemel Hempstead: Harvester Wheatsheaf.

Stacey, J. (1986) Are feminists afraid to leave home? The challenge of conservative pro-family feminism. In J. Mitchell and A. Oakley (eds), *What is Feminism?* Oxford: Basil Blackwell.

Stanworth, M. (ed.) (1987) *Reproductive Technologies: Gender, Motherhood and Medicine*. Cambridge: Polity Press.

Urwin, C. (1985) Constructing motherhood: the persuasion of normal development. In C. Steedman, C. Urwin and V. Walkerdine (eds), *Language, Gender and Childhood*. London: Routledge and Kegan Paul.

Westwood, S. and Bhachu, P. (eds) (1988) *Enterprising Women: Ethnicity, Economy and Gender Relations*. London: Routledge.

White, D. and Woollett, A. (1992) *Families: a Context for Development*. Basingstoke: Falmer.

Wilkinson, S. (ed.) (1986) *Feminist Social Psychology: Developing Theory and Practice*. Milton Keynes: Open University Press.

Index